Is It True What They Say about Freemasonry?

Is It True
What They Say about
Freemasonry?

Revised Edition

Arturo de Hoyos

and

S. Brent Morris

With a Foreword and Addendum by
James T. Tresner II

M. Evans
Lanham • New York • Boulder • Toronto • Plymouth, UK

Published by M. Evans

An imprint of The Rowman & Littlefield Publishing Group, Inc.

4501 Forbes Boulevard, Suite 2000, Lanham, Maryland 20706

http://www.rlpgtrade.com

Estover Road, Plymouth PL6 7PY, United Kingdom

Distributed by National Book Network

British Library Cataloguing in Publication Information Available

Library of Congress Cataloging-in-Publication Data

DeHoyos, Art, 1959–
    Is it true what they say about freemasonry? / Arturo de Hoyos and S. Brent Morris ; with a foreword and addendum by James T. Tresner II.
        p.   cm.
    Includes bibliographical references.
    ISBN 978-1-59077-153-2 (pbk. : alk. paper) — ISBN 978-1-59077-156-3 (electronic)
    1. Freemasonry.   2. Freemasonry—United States.   3. Anti-Masonic movements.
    4. Freemasonry—Religious aspects.   I. Morris, S. Brent.   II. Title.

HS418.D44 2010
366'.1—dc22
                                                                2009043918

♾™ The paper used in this publication meets the minimum requirements of American National Standard for Information Sciences—Permanence of Paper for Printed Library Materials, ANSI/NISO Z39.48-1992.

Printed in the United States of America

Freemasons have always controlled the upper echelons of government in the leading Western countries. . . . Masonry in fact runs, "remotely controls" bourgeois society, which its ideologists and politicians are fond of praising as open, free and democratic. . . . Masonry is ideal also for secret arms trafficking so as to convert weapons of death into cash.

—Lolly Zamoisky,
Behind the Façade of the Masonic Temple

It is only logical to conclude that if Freemasonry founded the Soviet Union, it must still be the power in charge, pulling the strings from behind-the-scenes.

—Gary H. Kah,
En Route to Global Occupation

World Jewry and Masonic governments . . . pretend to blame Bolshevism by condemning its unpopular excesses, whilst in fact they are supporting it and making it last until the means are found for it to evolve into a more lasting form.

—Léon de Poncins,
The Secret Powers behind Revolution

While the international World-Jew is slowly but surely strangling us, our so-called patriots vociferate against a man and his system which have had the courage to liberate themselves from the shackles of Jewish Freemasonry. . . .

—Adolf Hitler,
Mein Kampf

Masonry appears harmless on its surface, at least to the vast majority of its members. Yet there can be no doubt that Masonry and Christianity have been locked in an irreconcilable ideological battle since the time of Jesus.

—William T. Sill,
New World Order:
The Ancient Plan of Secret Societies

Freemasonry is demonic in nature. . . . Freemasonry is one of Satan's Master deceptions. Many ministers, elders, deacons, trustees and Sunday School teachers belong to this cult.

—Jack Harris,
Freemasonry: The Invisible Cult in Our Midst

Satan can come in and wreak spiritual and physical carnage in a home when the father is a Mason! Parents who seem to be good, God-fearing people are bewildered that their child is ill, or their teen is involved with Satanism, promiscuous sex, or trying to commit suicide. . . . Parents are often astonished to learn that Masonry can be such a cancer in the home.

—William Schnoebelen,
Masonry: Beyond the Light

The supreme shrouded secret of Freemasonry has been one thats endurance has been secured due to its undocumentation, as well as concealment from many thirty-third degreer's [*sic*]; reason being that the thirty-third degree is split in two, and only certain ones make it to the portals which quickly progress downward, to the underground bases which house the Reptilians. ALL MASONIC LODGES CONTAIN SHAFTS WHICH LEAD TO E.T. [Extra Terrestrial] UNDERGROUND BASES.

—Posted by Dan Sale, March 4, 1997,
www.reptilianagenda.com/research/
r0205000a.html

Who controls the British Crown?
Who keeps the Metric System down?
We do! We do!
Who leaves Atlantis off the maps?
Who keeps the Martians under wraps?
We do! We do!

"The Stonecutters' Song," *The Simpsons*,
episode 2F09 ("Homer the Great")

Dedicated to the memory of

John Jamieson Robinson

Researcher, Author, Master Mason

Contents

Acknowledgments

The authors would like to express their thanks and appreciation to the following sources for permission to use previously published materials:

Kessinger Publishing Company has generously given permission to use extended quotations from *The Cloud of Prejudice: A Study in Anti-Masonry* by Arturo de Hoyos.

The Scottish Rite Journal, official publication of The Supreme Council, 33°, has generously given permission to reprint "Please Look a Little Closer" (*Journal*, Nov. 1996) by Dr. James T. Tresner II, Director, Masonic Leadership Institute; and "Garden of Evil?" and "Stones of Evil" (*Journal*, Oct. and Dec. 1996) by Dr. John W. Boettjer.

Heredom, the transactions of the Scottish Rite Research Society, has generously given permission to reprint "Anti-Masonic Abuse of Scottish Rite Literature" by Arturo de Hoyos.

The authors would like to acknowledge the assistance they have received from many different sources:

Mrs. Inge Baum, retired Librarian of the Supreme Council, 33°, SJ, for her always gracious assistance.

Bro. Alain Bernheim, for his correction to our statements on French Freemasonry.

The late Bro. David Blackey Board, for his detailed research and bibliography of Léo Taxil.

Bro. John W. Boettjer, for his permission to use the articles "Garden of Evil?" and "Stones of Evil."

Bro. Roger Kessinger, Kessinger Publishing Company, for permission to use extended quotations from *The Cloud of Prejudice: A Study in Anti-Masonry* by Arturo de Hoyos.

Bros. Irwin Kirby and James Prigodich, General Secretaries, Valley of Miami, A&ASR, for information on Rev. James D. Shaw's Scottish Rite membership in Florida.

Ms. Joan K. Sansbury, Librarian of the Supreme Council, 33°, SJ, for her kind assistance.

Bro. Rollin O. Simpson, Grand Secretary, Grand Lodge of Indiana, F&AM, for information on Rev. James D. Shaw's Masonic membership in Indiana.

Bro. Eric Serejski, for his assistance in translating passages from *Le Femme et L'Enfant dans le Franc-Maçonnerie Universelle*.

Bro. Arthur Schechner, Secretary, West Dade Lodge No. 388, for information on Rev. James D. Shaw's membership in Allapattah Lodge No. 271.

Bro. William G. Wolf, Grand Secretary, Grand Lodge of Florida, F&AM, for information on Rev. James D. Shaw's Masonic membership in Florida.

Bros. Sidney Baxter, John W. Boettjer, Richard Curtis, Richard E. Fletcher, Wallace McLeod, Pete Normand, James T. Tresner II, and the late Thomas E. Weir for their invaluable textual corrections and suggestions.

Foreword

It is a mixed blessing, being asked to write a foreword for this book.

On one hand, it is a high honor to be asked to contribute a few words to the work of Masons I respect so greatly. Art de Hoyos and Brent Morris are two of the very best Masonic writers Freemasonry has produced in a long time.

On the other hand, some tasks are simply distasteful, no matter how exalted the company in which they are done. (Unstopping a clogged toilet springs to mind as an example.) Dealing with the attacks of anti-Masons is a similarly distasteful task.

A sense of betrayal makes me so personally angry with some of these individuals. I came of age in a time when policemen were your friends, your father knew best, and ministers lived by high moral codes. And I still believe that, but it's getting harder.

St. Luke says, "Whoever is faithful in a very little is faithful also in much; and whoever is dishonest in a very little is dishonest also in much" (16:10). As you will see in this book, anti-Masons are often dishonest in both little and much.

That's the betrayal! I don't expect a banker to steal my money, I don't expect a physician to prescribe poison, and I don't expect a minister to lie to me. These men, some of whom are ministers, do lie. They are not innocently mistaken; they are not led into error; they are not merely confused. They lie. Bear that in mind as you read the examples of what anti-Masons do when "quoting" Masonic writers. Dishonest in little, dishonest in much.

To sell a book or a tape, claiming it reveals truth while knowing it to contain lies is cheating. Soliciting or accepting contributions in the name of truth while telling a lie is stealing. It's hard for us to believe that of men of the cloth, but when a man presents us, in writing, with repeated proof of his deceit, we ultimately must conclude that he is deceitful.

This book is not intended to be an exhaustive defense of Freemasonry. None is needed. It is intended to show, by example, just what anti-Masons are capable of doing.

There may be some readers who, in spite of the proof of the lies told by the anti-Masons examined in this book (and in spite of the fact that they can get the original sources themselves and check them out if they doubt the integrity of Brothers de Hoyos and Morris), may still continue to believe in the honor and integrity of the anti-Masons. If so, there is little that can be said to them.

But for readers who resent being lied to and resent even more the implication that they are too stupid to know the difference, this book will come as something of a revelation.

It is not that Freemasonry considers itself above criticism. It is a human institution and, like all such institutions, imperfect and open to improvement. Criticize us if you wish—most Masons do. Examine us in depth, we have nothing to hide.

But do not lie about us.

And, especially, do not lie about us and then dare to claim you are doing the work of God.

—James T. Tresner II, Master Mason

Preface

Freemasonry is a unique human institution, generating deep loyalty in its members and great misunderstandings among its detractors. It is difficult for some people to imagine that a group of men meeting behind closed doors could be doing anything good, much less encouraging each other to live lives of greater religious, family, and civic service. Yet this is what Freemasons have done since at least 1717, when the first Grand Lodge was formed in London.

Recent critics, however, have gone beyond stating their differences with the Craft to fabricating vicious lies to defame the fraternity and its members. These detractors have convinced themselves that Freemasonry is the work of the devil. Thus, they apparently justify their perversions of truth with the thought that they are doing the Lord's work: saving an unsuspecting world from Satan. No misquotation, no distortion, no lie is too great to accomplish what these detractors perceive as their holy mission. All this is done in the name of Him who said, "I am the way, the truth, and the life" (John 14:18).

Freemasonry teaches its members tolerance, even of its assailants. The normal Masonic response to detractors has been to turn the other cheek, letting them wallow in their own ignorance. The maliciousness and deceitfulness of current attacks have grown to the point, however, that some reasoned reply is needed. It is not too demanding to expect the critics of Freemasonry to state their credentials accurately or to quote Masonic authors correctly and in context. Surely, that is being faithful in very little. The hatred of some anti-Masons is so great, however, that even this little faithfulness is too much.

This book points out several common misrepresentations made about Freemasonry and shows specific examples of willful fraud. We do not attempt to answer every charge, because this is an ultimately fruitless task. Anyone willing to overlook the easily verified lies presented here can just as easily rationalize away whatever other corruption they might encounter.

We have tried to be scrupulous in citing our sources and in accurately representing the exact words and context of quotations. Despite our best efforts, it will not surprise us if inadvertent errors have crept into our text. All mistakes of quotation and citation will be acknowledged and corrected in subsequent editions of this work. Please send note of such errors to the Masonic Information Center, 8120 Fenton Street, Silver Spring, MD 20910-4785.

We hope this book will give pause to fair-minded readers who may be caught in the headlong rush to condemn Freemasonry. The evidence presented here calls into question the research abilities of many critics of Freemasonry, as well as their integrity.

—A. H. & S. B. M.

Chapter 1

Masonry and Anti-Masonry: A Look at the Problem

> Great is the power of steady misrepresentation. . . .
> —**Charles Darwin,** *The Origin of Species*

It's hard to pinpoint which arguments a particular anti-Mason will try to use, but there are popular ploys that continue to pop up regularly. Some have been around for a long time and others seem to follow sound logic, but all are flawed. Nevertheless, these ruses are just too tempting for opponents of Masonry. It's not enough for them to disagree with the fraternity, they must demonize it beyond recognition. Most of these lies have been repeated so often that it's relatively easy to find them in print somewhere. The reasoning of Masonry's detractors seems to be, "Why should I do serious research when with little effort I can find ready arguments to support my position?"

Dr. Robert A. Morey, himself a critic of Freemasonry, has a low opinion of the standards of research used by his fellow anti-Masons:

> Anti-masonic writers have generally been as unreliable as Masonic apologists. In their zeal to attack Freemasonry, they have been willing to use fantasy, fraud, and deceit. They have even created bogus documents when needed. Their writings must not be taken at face value.[1]

In this work we exhibit examples of deluded fantasy, willful fraud, and outright deceit, all used to attack Freemasonry under the good name of Christianity. As we expose these tactics, we hope readers will pause to consider what motivates some people to use them.

1

THE STRUCTURE OF AMERICAN FREEMASONRY

Freemasonry is a fraternal movement loosely embracing several organizations. Its self-defined principal tenets are "Brotherly Love, Relief, and Truth"— social friendship, the practice of charity, and ethical philosophy. Freemasons advance through several degrees or levels of membership (think of the Boy Scouts with rankings of Tenderfoot through Eagle Scout). Organized under administrative bodies, these organizations are often called orders, rites, or systems. The foundation of all Freemasonry is the *Grand Lodge* system, which oversees the three oldest and primary degrees: Entered Apprentice, Fellow Craft, and Master Mason. Although other Masonic organizations are similarly run by their own "Grand" bodies, none may operate contrary to the policies of the Grand Lodge. Because of their number and similarity of titles, the differences between Masonic groups can be confusing, even for members of the fraternity. There are too many Masonic groups to name them all, but the most popular will be briefly described.

Grand Lodge

To say that someone is a Mason means that he has passed through the Degrees of Blue Lodge or *Ancient Craft Masonry*, under the authority of a Grand Lodge. Grand Lodges normally operate exclusively within a geographic jurisdiction, usually a state. Grand Lodges attend to the administrative affairs of the fraternity and charter local lodges, which "make Masons" by conferring the three degrees. It is important to note that once someone is a Master Mason, he is as much a Mason as any other member worldwide. No matter what other Masonic organizations he may subsequently join, and whatever degree or position of prominence he may hold in any other Masonic organization, he remains subject to the authority of the Grand Lodge. Because Grand Lodges are the supreme Masonic authorities in their respective jurisdictions, they are not subject to any other Masonic organizations. Grand Lodges are generally run by officers elected by representatives from each lodge in the jurisdiction. Among other things, Grand Lodges exercise the executive administrative power to determine which organizations may be considered "Masonic" in their jurisdiction, and they reserve the right to prohibit their members from joining any organization which requires Masonic membership. All other Masonic organizations are said to be "appendant" to a Grand Lodge.

York Rite

The York Rite is a cooperation of three separate and distinct organizations, working on the state and national levels, which compliment and work with each other. Although there are minor jurisdictional variations from state to state, the York Rite may be briefly described as follows. *Capitular Masonry* is the basic or entry level, comprising the four degrees of the Royal Arch Chapter. *Cryptic Masonry* is the intermediate level, comprising the two degrees of the Council of Royal and Select Masters. *Chivalric Masonry*, or the Commandery of Knights Templar, is the last level, conferring three degrees which are exclusively open to Christians.

Scottish Rite

The Scottish Rite is today the largest and most prominent of the appendant bodies in American Freemasonry. With an impressive system of thirty-three degrees, its status is often confusing to non-Masons, and many anti-Masons misrepresent it as "superior" to the Grand Lodges' authority. There are two governing bodies for the Scottish Rite in the United States, one for the North and one for the South, a division that dates to the early 1800s. Basic membership in the Scottish Rite consists of twenty-nine degrees, ranging from the "4° Secret Master" to the "32° Master (or Prince) of the Royal Secret." Thirty-second Degree members who have distinguished themselves in the Southern Jurisdiction may be elected to receive the "Rank and Decoration of Knight Commander of the Court of Honor" (KCCH). A small percentage of 32° Masons (one to two percent) are made honorary members of the Supreme Council without voting power and given the title "33°, Inspector General Honorary." The governing officers of a Supreme Council are called "Sovereign Grand Inspectors General," or "Thirty-third Degree Active Members."

The Shrine and Other "Fun" Groups

The Ancient Arabic Order Nobles of the Mystic Shrine (Shriners) is often called the playground of Freemasonry. Its initiation ceremony is a fun skit or play, in which participants do not take themselves too seriously. The Shrine is primarily a philanthropic organization best known for its free hospitals for crippled children and the clowns and "funny cars" featured in parades. Membership was once restricted to York or Scottish Rite Masons, but the Shrine now admits all Master Masons as members. When the Shrine was organized in the early 1870s, the Arabian culture was considered an exotic diversion from Western society. Richard Burton's famed *Arabian Nights*, published in 1850, introduced Westerners to Aladdin and Ali Baba, and the founders of the Shrine viewed Eastern culture as remote and mythical. Adopting pseudo-Arabic titles for their officers, the Shrine ceremonial was a parody of Oriental adventures. As Western society becomes more familiar with Eastern culture, the Shrine continues to revise its rituals, eliminating aspects deemed insensitive to foreign cultures. There are a number of other "fun" groups in Masonry; among these are the *Grotto*, the *Royal Order of the Jesters*, the *Order of the Bath*, the *Tall Cedars of Lebanon*, and others. Some of these groups have philanthropic purposes, while others exist merely for social conviviality.

The Eastern Star and Other Allied Organizations

Membership in the Order of the Eastern Star is open to Masons and their female relatives. Its ritual exemplifies the virtues exhibited by Adah, Ruth, Esther, Martha, and Electa, the heroines of the Order. There are other groups for Masons and their families, including the *Amaranth*, the *White Shrine of Jerusalem*, and for youth, the *Order of DeMolay*, *Job's Daughters*, the *Rainbow Girls*, and more.

Other Masonic Organizations

Freemasons are great joiners and have created organizations to fill many specialized interests and hobbies. These groups range from Masonic stamp clubs, to book and motorcycle clubs. There are innumerable research organizations for those who enjoy Masonic history and, for those who enjoy ceremonial and Masonic philosophy, there are still many other groups which confer degrees.

WHO SPEAKS FOR MASONRY?

Any discussion of Masonic government must start and end with one essential fact: all Masonic authority originates in a Grand Lodge. The Masonic Service Association of North America (MSA) has no authority over Grand Lodges. No Supreme Council of the 33°, no respected author, nor any other group or person speaks for or controls Masonry; that prerogative rests solely with the Grand Lodges. Anyone doubting this need only check the cases when Grand Lodges have closed down the Scottish Rite, the Shrine, and other appendant Masonic bodies in their states or suspended or expelled their "high officials." It is a rare but powerful reminder of who is in charge.

If a Grand Lodge strays too far from accepted Masonic norms, other Grand Lodges will withdraw recognition and will even help organize a new Grand Lodge in the jurisdiction. A famous example occurred in 1877 when the Grand Orient of France (which functions as a Grand Lodge) modified its Constitution by removing from its principles "the existence of God and the immortality of the soul." This action caused the United Grand Lodge of England not to recognize as Masons anyone who had been initiated in lodges which either ignore or deny the belief in God. In 1913, a new Grand Lodge—the present French National Grand Lodge—was founded in Paris according to the Ancient Landmarks. It was immediately recognized by the United Grand Lodge of England and, in the course of time, by American Grand Lodges.

If it seems confusing that there is no single authority for Freemasonry, it may be helpful to consider that the same holds true for other groups as well. For example, who speaks for the Christian Church? Is the top Christian the Roman Catholic Pontiff, the President of the Latter-day Saints (Mormon) Church, the President of the World Council of Churches, the Archbishop of Canterbury, or someone else? Moreover, who determines who is a Christian—or a Jew or Moslem? Just as there is nothing to prevent a group of worshipers from calling itself "Baptist," "Presbyterian" or "Jewish," there is nothing to prevent a group of men (or women) from calling itself "Masonic." It is hardly fair to judge the world of regular Masonry by the statements of irregular groups who have appropriated the name "Mason," or by individual Masons writing without official sanction.

Anti-Masons love to trot out "high-ranking Masonic officials," hoping that somehow a good-sounding title (real or stolen) will obscure the shallowness of their arguments. David Barron's 2005 book, *The Question of Freemasonry and the Founding Fathers*, tries to argue that America's founding fathers were not evil because they were Freemasons, because it's only recently that the fraternity has become anti-Christian. On the first page of text, one reads:

> In fact, part of the attention focused on this subject has been the result of high-ranking Masonic officials who—following their personal conversion to Christ—renounced their Masonic membership and then wrote exposés about the untenable spiritual heresies permeating Masonic teachings.[2]

Former Masons Shaw, Harris, and McClung (not to mention the ominous "et al.") have titles that sound pretty impressive—so impressive that Barton didn't see any need to verify what they had to say. After all, it was negative, and that's what he needed! (In chapter 8 of this book we will expose the lies of Rev. Shaw, including his bogus claim to have received the 33rd Degree or to be a past "Master of all Scottish Rite Bodies.") Jack Harris was indeed Worshipful Master of his lodge, but in his book he tried to give credibility to the "Taxil Hoax" in which Albert Pike said that Masons secretly worship Lucifer. This is a malicious lie known to anyone who's ever been a Mason. (See chapter 2 of this book for more details.) As for Claude McClung being a "Royal Arch Mason 7th Degree," this means only that he took the first of three steps in the York Rite; we can find no evidence that he was ever an "official," much less a "high-ranking" one.

Or consider the case of the notorious P2 Lodge in Italy which was largely responsible for the collapse of the Italian government in 1981. Propaganda Lodge No. 2, *Propaganda Due*, or P2 as it became known, began as a legitimately chartered lodge. Within a few years, however, its Master, Licio Gelli, abused his authority by using his Masonic influence to gain favors. Gelli used illicit information to blackmail people into joining his lodge, the purpose of which was to gather more intelligence for his personal political agenda. Members of P2 then became involved in criminal activities.

As soon as the Grand Orient of Italy (the equivalent of an American Grand Lodge) became aware of the problem, its leaders tried to rectify the situation and, unfortunately, failed. Gelli would be controlled by no one. The Grand Orient then administered the ultimate Masonic punishment: revocation of the lodge's charter and expulsion of its members.

The former members of P2, however, ignored the judgment of the Grand Orient to whom they had pledged fealty and continued meeting under their old name. The "lodge" was now irregular or illegitimate, operating without authority. In 1975, a regular Mason, Francesco Siniscalchi, complained to the Public Prosecutor in Rome of P2's nefarious activities. When the scandal eventually broke, the press—and many non-Masons— did not understand the illegitimacy of P2, nor the fact that legitimate Masons tried to rectify the problem. This failure to differentiate between regular Masonry and the irregular P2 Lodge tarnished the good name of Masonry.

The ultimate tests of regularity (greatly simplified) are 1) does a Grand Lodge directly trace its origins through legitimate authority to one of the British Grand Lodges, and 2) does it maintain the recognition of most of the community of regular Grand Lodges, including England, Ireland, and Scotland? If an organization doesn't pass these tests, then it's not Masonic, despite what it may call itself.

The most common mistake about the organization of Masonry comes from assuming that Supreme Councils of the Scottish Rite control Masonry. This is not true. There is no Masonic degree higher than the Third Degree or Master Mason Degree in symbolic Masonry. While the number 33 may be greater than the number 3, a 33° Mason has no more authority or power in a lodge than a 3° Mason. Both are equally subordinate to the Master of their lodge, and all in turn are subordinate to the Grand Master of their Grand Lodge. An earlier statement bears repeating:

> No Supreme Council of the 33°, no respected author, nor any other group or person, speaks for or controls Masonry; that prerogative rests solely with the Grand Lodges.

You can be sure something is wrong if anyone says that a single person or organization speaks for or represents Masonry. Only a Grand Lodge has that power and then only within its jurisdiction. Any other assertion displays a fatally flawed understanding of the organization of Freemasonry.

THE ISSUE OF MASONIC "EXPERTS"

Thousands of authors have written about Freemasonry and several have achieved wide recognition for their general scholarship. Some Masonic authors have pursued theories that at best are without factual support and at worst are embarrassingly wrong. Because Freemasonry values free thought so highly, Grand Lodges as a rule neither endorse nor condemn ideas; that decision is left to individual Masons. Thus, it is quite possible to find otherwise highly regarded Masonic authors who have espoused ideas of Masonic origins or symbolism that are without substance—ideas that have been politely ignored and have been allowed to quietly fade away. Unless formally endorsed by action of a Grand Lodge, no writer can speak for Masonry, only for himself.

Dr. Robert A. Morey, a Christian critic of Freemasonry, noted, "Another error typically made by anti-Masons is the assumption that Freemasonry is based on the writings of a single individual. They usually pick Albert Pike as the official 'spokesman' of Freemasonry."[3] If not Albert Pike, then their choice might be Albert Mackey[4] or Manley Palmer Hall[5] or some other author espousing his personal theories about Masonry.

> Most anti-Masonic writers are far too gullible in believing the extravagant claims of overzealous, misinformed. or devious Masonic writers who have not done Freemasonry a favor by making outlandish statements which provided much fodder for the guns of the anti-Masons.
> Too many Masonic writers have arrogantly claimed that they speak for the whole Craft when they give their personal interpretation of the origin and symbols of Freemasonry.[6]

For example, Manley Hall didn't become a Mason until 1954, so his *Lost Keys of Freemasonry* (1923) and *The Secret Teachings of All Ages* (1928) actually represent the personal theories of a non-Mason. Further, Mr. Hall (who passed away in August 1990) was a self-avowed mystic, not a "leading authority" of Freemasonry. He was a promulgator of mysticism and theosophy, topics of interest to some Freemasons; but his writings have not received official sanction by any Masonic bodies. The fact that he held the Thirty-third Degree and was respected by many Masons and honored by the Supreme Council 33° is no more significant than the fact that various Baptist, Anglican, or Methodist authors have also been so honored.

Anti-Masons regularly parade the writings of Masonic authorities before their audiences and dissect their words, looking for a sentence here or a phrase there to be used in their attempts of vilification. They seek someone like a church authority who speaks dogmatically on teachings and doctrine, whose every word must be accepted by the faithful. Freemasonry has no such authorities.

The Masonic authorities used by anti-Masons have been historical authorities who speak with the expertise that comes from long study, but who do not—indeed, cannot—speak for all Masons. It is like the difference between the authoritative teachings of the Episcopal Church and an authoritative book on the strategies of playing golf.[7]

MORALS AND DOGMA

Few Masonic books have created as many controversies as Albert Pike's *Morals and Dogma*. It is a collection of thirty-two essays that provide a philosophical background for the lessons of the Scottish Rite degrees. The essays are largely concerned with the history of philosophy and with man's constant search for God. First published in 1871, the book was given to every 32° Mason in the Southern Jurisdiction for about a century; hundreds of thousands of copies have been distributed.[8]

Morals and Dogma is not available only from a "secret publishing house,"[9] it is not "the Bible of the Masons,"[10] nor is it "the most readily available and universally approved doctrinal book of Freemasonry."[11] It is not even widely distributed or read. It is used only by the Supreme Council 33°, Southern Jurisdiction, which in 1871 had far fewer than 5 percent of American Masons as members and in 2003 claims only 20 percent. The Northern Masonic Jurisdiction of the Scottish Rite has never used *Morals and Dogma* in any way.

The preface of *Morals and Dogma* gives the best understanding of how Pike and all succeeding Supreme Councils have viewed his book:

> **The teachings of these Readings are not sacramental**, so far as they go beyond the realm of Morality into those of other domains of Thought and Truth. The Ancient and Accepted Scottish Rite uses the word "Dogma" in its true sense, of doctrine, or teaching; and is not dogmatic in the odious sense of that term. **Every one is entirely free to reject and dissent from whatsoever herein may seem to him to be untrue or unsound.** It is only required of him that he shall weigh what is taught, and give it fair hearing and unprejudiced judgement. Of course, the ancient theosophic and philosophic speculations are not embodied as part of the doctrines of the Rite; but because it is of interest and profit to know what the Ancient Intellect thought upon these subjects, and because nothing so conclusively proves the radical difference between our human and the animal nature, as the capacity of the human mind to entertain such speculations in regard to itself and the Deity.[12] (emphasis added)

While on page 329 he states:

> **We teach the truth of none of the legends we recite.** They are to us but parables and allegories involving and enveloping Masonic instruction and vehicles of useful and interesting information. They represent the different phases of the human mind, its efforts and struggles to comprehend nature, God, the government of the Universe, the permitted existence of sorrow and evil. **To teach us wisdom and the folly of endeavouring to explain to ourselves that which we are not capable of understanding, we reproduce the speculations** of the Philosophers, the Kabbalists, the Mystagogues, and the Gnostics. **Every one being at liberty to apply our symbols and emblems as he thinks most consistent with truth and reason and with his own faith**, we give them such an interpretation only as may be accepted by all.

This is not the way to present the ultimate authority on any subject. Anti-Masons choose to ignore the clear intent of the book and to distort Pike's personal opinions into the absolute truth for all Masons.

One of the most frequently quoted passages by anti-Masons from *Morals and Dogma* concerns Pike's theory that symbolic lodges exist to hide the true secrets of Masonry from the masses:

> The Blue Degrees [1°–3°] are but the outer court or portico of the Temple. Part of the symbols are displayed there to the Initiate, but he is intentionally misled by false interpretations. It is not intended that he shall understand them; but it is intended that he shall imagine he understands them. Their true explication is reserved for the Adepts, the Princes of

Masonry. . . . It is well enough for the mass of those called Masons, to imagine that all is contained in the Blue Degrees.[13]

Anti-Masons would have us believe this passage is a public admission of the deceptions imposed on most Masons by the leaders of the Craft. Common sense is again thrown out the window. Why would such a damaging secret doctrine be printed in a widely available book? With hundreds of thousands of copies distributed, shouldn't some Blue Lodge Masons have caught on by now? Anyone, like Pike, is free to think he knows the "true" interpretation of Masonic symbolism, but it will remain his personal opinion. Only Grand Lodges have the authority to interpret the symbolism of the Blue Lodge, and they are not inclined to yield to any other power.

Pike was simply repeating one of the currently popular theories about the origins of the high degrees. In this instance, he was repeating a legend about the Knights Templar, as a note from the forthcoming reprint of *Morals and Dogma* explains:

> According to continental Masonic legends a group of medieval Knights Templar eluded arrest and extermination, and fled to Scotland, where they joined with operative stonemason's companies. The knights contributed to Masonic symbolism, and offered superficial interpretations until new members could be trusted to conceal their Templar origin. Thus, the "lower initiates" were told that they had descended from stonemasons, while the "Adepts, the Princes of Masonry," were informed that they were actually Knights Templar. Although the same symbols were used throughout, in the lower degrees they were explained in the context of Craft Masonry and Biblical history, while in the higher degrees they were unveiled as relating to knighthood and Templar history.

It is important to note that just because Albert Pike was a brilliant ritualist, an able administrator, and a well-respected Mason doesn't mean all of his opinions are right in light of today's knowledge. We might ask, do the mid-eighteenth-century pro-slavery writings of various denominations reflect the positions of those same denominations today?[14]

The Masonic encyclopedist, Henry Wilson Coil, offers a good summary of the influences on Albert Pike's Masonic writings.

> Fate decided that Pike should enter the Scottish Rite only four years after he became a Mason and before he had time or occasion thoroughly to study the history of all branches of the Society and, so, he began his study from the upper levels without knowing much of the foundation. He evidently did not know until his later life that the Scottish Rite degrees were a part of that

type of ritual which sprang up in France in 1737 and subsequent years but regarded it as Primitive Masonry which had come right on down from Greece, Asia Minor, and Egypt and out of the Ancient Mysteries and Magism, which there held sway. He found books which said so and he never had any doubt about that theory. He regarded Craft Masonry as then known to be puerile, though he said it had a deeper meaning which was hidden from its superficial adepts, who were taught to be satisfied with trite explanations. He even asserted that Craft Masonry had been devised so as not only to hide its true meaning but to cause its members to think that they understood it. [Albert G.] Mackey encouraged him in those notions, for he, too, had been made a Mason only four years before he began writing books on the subject, in which he adopted the more sensational theories of mystery and symbolism. But Mackey changed his views as soon as the work of the British realistic school began to be felt. Pike did not waver; his work was nearly complete and too voluminous to be done over.[15]

Chapter 2

Themes of Anti-Masonry[1]

Prejudices are what fools use for reason.

—Voltaire

The words *anti-Masonry* and *anti-Mason* have straightforward definitions: "opposition to Freemasonry" and "one opposed to Freemasonry,"[2] but like *anti-Semitism*, much more is involved than simple opposition to a group. Freemasonry has become a favorite whipping boy for those looking for a convenient "other" to blame for the world's problems, or at least those problems they believe are bedeviling the globe. The Masonic fraternity has been accused of supporting western capitalism,[3] Soviet communism,[4] world Jewry,[5] Satanism,[6] and secret underground extraterrestrial bases.[7] Where there is smoke, there is fire, so perhaps there are facts behind these charges that deserve further study.

John Wycliffe (1330–1384), the reformer and translator of the Bible into English, made perhaps the first published attack against Freemasons in 1383, some ten to twenty years before the *Regius Manuscript*, the earliest known document of the Freemasons. In his essay, "The Great Curs Expouned," Wycliffe attacked the "fre masons" on economic—not religious— grounds, for behaving like a trade union. "For they conspire together that no man of their craft shall take less on a day than they set. . . . And that none of them shall do ought but only hew stone, though he might profit his master . . . by laying on a wall. . . ."[8] In other words, Freemasons would not work for less than the set wage and as hewers of stone would not take on work of another craft, the layers. Wycliffe, however, had no religious concerns with Freemasonry.

SWEARING OATHS AND MEETING IN SECRET

The first published religious attack in English appeared some three hundred years later in 1698, nineteen years before the Premier Grand Lodge was formed in London in 1717. The leaflet contains two basic charges against the fraternity. First, the members swear oaths "against all without their following," presumably to support each other. Second, Freemasons are "meeters in secret," which is the way of "Evil-doers."

TO ALL GODLY PEOPLE,
In the Citie of
LONDON.

Having thought it needful to warn you of the Mischiefs and Evils practiced on the Sight of GOD by those called Freed Masons, I say take Care lest their Ceremonies and secret Swearings take hold of you; and be wary that none cause you to err from Godliness. For this devllish Sect of Men are Meeters in secret which swear against all without their Following. They are the Anti Christ which was to come leading Men from Fear of GOD. For how should men meet in secret Places and with secret Signs taking Care that none observe them to do the Work of GOD; are not these the Ways of Evil-doers?

Knowing how that GOD observeth privily them that sit in Darkness they shall be smitten and the Secrets of their Hearts layed bare. Mingle not among this corrupt People lest you be found so at the World's Conflagration.

Set forth as a Warning to this Christian Generation by
M. Winter, and Printed by *R. Sare* at Gray's
Inn-gate, in *Holbourn.*
1698.[9]

It is curious how such a reputation developed for an organization that from its earliest days was faithful to church and crown. The "Standard Original" of the Gothic Constitutions of the freemasons, as reconstructed by Prof. Wallace McLeod, begins with a clearly Christian invocation: "The might of the Father of Heaven, with the wisdom of the glorious Son, through the grace and goodness of the Holy Ghost, that be three persons in one Godhead, be with us at our beginning, and give us grace so to govern us here in our living that we may come to His bliss that never shall have ending. Amen." After the invocation and traditional history of Freemasonry, the Gothic Constitutions then give "charges" or instructions for the guidance of their members. The first two are that Freemasons be faithful to church and king. "The first charge is that ye shall be true men to God and the Holy Church; and that ye use no error nor heresy, by your understanding or by discreet or wise men's teaching. And also that ye shall be true liege men to the King without treason or falsehood; and that ye know no treason or treachery, but that ye amend it if ye may, or else warn the King or his council thereof."[10]

Perhaps private meetings (certainly not "secret" since Winter knew they were gathering together) and oath swearing were indeed causes for alarm. It is more likely that the Freemasons' spirit of toleration caused disquiet among nonmembers. The premier Grand Lodge was formed in London in 1717, just twenty-nine years after the Glorious Revolution of 1688 had deposed the Catholic James II in favor of the Protestant William and Mary. Tensions were still high between Catholics and Protestants, and it was a radical religious and political idea to suggest any friendship could exist between the two sides, and yet this seems to be what London Masons promoted.

PLOTTING TO SUBVERT RELIGION

In 1723 Rev. James Anderson published the *Constitutions of the Free-Masons* for the Grand Lodge. He summarized the existing regulations and introduced religious toleration in "Charge I. Concerning God and Religion":

> A *Mason* is oblig'd by his Tenure, to obey the moral Law; and if he rightly understands the Art, he will never be a stupid *Atheist*, nor an irreligious *Libertine*. But though in ancient Times Masons were charg'd in every Country to be of the Religion of that Country or Nation, whatever it was, yet 'tis now thought more expedient only to oblige them to that Religion in which all Men agree, leaving their particular Opinions to themselves; that is, to be *good Men and true*, or Men or Honour and Honesty; by whatever Denominations or Persuasions they may [be] distinguish'd; whereby Masonry becomes the *Center* of *Union*, and the Means of conciliating true Friendship among Persons that must else have remain'd at a perpetual Distance.[11]

The puzzlement with Anderson's summary charge is what exactly he meant by "that Religion in which all Men agree." While there has never been a formal pronouncement from the Grand Lodge of England, Charge I generally has been interpreted to mean that a beneficent God created the world and that He is the creator-father of all humankind, and that this is "that Religion in which all Men agree." By stopping religious discussions after this simple agreement, the Premier Grand Lodge apparently believed it could conciliate "true Friendship among Persons that must else have remain'd at a perpetual Distance." Such an idea is anathema to those who believe that individuals cannot decide for themselves what constituted religious truth.

Pope Clement XII took notice of Freemasonry and in 1738 issued the first encyclical against the fraternity, "In Eminenti." The encyclical is too long to quote in full, but excerpts give a flavor for the condemnation:

> Men of any Religion or sect, satisfied with the appearance of natural probity, are joined together . . . by a strict and unbreakable bond which obliges them, both by an oath upon the Holy Bible and by a host of grievous punishment, to an inviolable silence about all that they do in secret together. . . . All prudent and upright men have passed the same judgment on them as being depraved and perverted. For if they were not doing evil they would not have so great a hatred of the light. . . . Therefore, bearing in mind the great harm which is often caused by such Societies . . . and realizing that they do not hold by either civil or canonical sanctions and for the other just and reasonable motives known to us . . . these same societies . . . are to be condemned and prohibited. . . . under pain of excommunication . . . from which no one can obtain the benefit of absolution, other than at the hour of death, except through Ourselves or the Roman Pontiff of the time. . . . Moreover, We desire and command that . . . inquisitors for heresy . . . are to pursue and punish them with condign penalties as being the most suspect of heresy.[12]

It appears Clement XII followed the same logic of the 1698 London leaflet: Freemasons bind themselves together by a solemn obligation and they meet in private. (Lodge meetings were hardly secret since Masons met in public taverns, wore distinctive regalia, and were well known for drinking and singing after their meetings.) The tenets of Freemasonry were a threat not only to the true teaching of the Roman Catholic Church but also to the stability of governments and society.[13] There has been some suggestion that Clement was trying to influence the Hanoverian-Jacobite struggle in England and the restoration of the exiled Catholic James II. There has also been much fruitless speculation over what were "the other just and reasonable motives known to" Clement. A more practical motive for the condemnation could be the

Is It True What They Say about Freemasonry?

concern that the Masonic obligation might prevent a penitent from making a full confession.

PLOTTING TO SUBVERT GOVERNMENTS

The charges against Freemasonry became more specific in 1797 with the publication by Augustin Barruel, S.J. (1741–1820), of volumes one and two of *Mémoires pour servir à l'histoire du Jacobinisme* and by John Robison (1739–1805) of *Proofs of a Conspiracy against all the Religions and Governments of Europe, Carried on in the Secret Meetings of Free Masons, Illuminati, and Reading Societies, Collected from Good Authorities* (Edinburgh: William Creech, 1797). Volumes three and four of *Mémoires* were published in 1798. These two conspiracists advanced the theory that Freemasonry was behind the excesses of the French Revolution. According to their theories, the overthrow of the French monarchy was planned by the Illuminati, a group created by Adam Weishaupt (1748–1830) in Bavaria in 1776. The Illuminati were recruited from Bavarian Freemasons with the goal of infiltrating governments and implementing Weishaupt's ideas of a benign government free of monarchs and religions. His "fraternity within a fraternity" lasted until 1784 when Karl Theodor, Elector of Bavaria, discovered and suppressed the Illuminati. Weishaupt fled Bavaria and went into exile in Gotha.

Now there were charges of some substance against Freemasons. Rather than mere secret meetings, sworn oaths, and "other just and reasonable motives," Freemasons were infiltrating the governments of Europe and were behind the Reign of Terror. Proof was not necessary as Robison was a Mason himself, Barruel was a Jesuit, and the Pope had personally condemned the fraternity. The worry of the Illuminati and the Terror was such that George Washington was asked if he believed the Illuminati or Jacobins had infiltrated American Masonic lodges. He replied to Rev. G. W. Snyder on October 24, 1798, that he "did not believe that the Lodges of Free Masons in this Country had, as Societies, endeavoured to propagate the diabolical tenets of the first, or pernicious principles of the latter (if they are susceptible of separation)."

Papal condemnations continued after "In Eminenti," and the most sweeping was in Leo XIII's 1884 "Humanum Genus." He said mankind is "separated into two diverse and opposite parts, of which the one steadfastly contends for truth and virtue, the other of those things which are contrary to virtue and to truth. The one is the kingdom of God on earth, namely, the true Church of Jesus Christ. . . . The other is the kingdom of Satan. . . ." Leo said that Freemasonry belongs to the kingdom of Satan. He went on and condemned Freemasonry for supporting various unacceptable principles including that "power is held by the command or permission of the people, so that, when the popular will changes, rulers may lawfully be deposed" and that "each [youth] must be left at liberty to follow, when he comes of age, whatever [religion] he may prefer." Leo XIII also seemed to blame the demise of Papal civil authority on a Masonic conspiracy led by Freemason Giuseppe Garibaldi, the liberator and unifier of Italy.[14]

WORSHIPPING LUCIFER

The most malicious charge against the fraternity was the hoax created by Gabriel Antoine Jogand-Pagès (1854–1907) that Freemasons secretly worship Lucifer in the higher degrees. Jogand-Pagès is better known by his *nom de plume* of Léo Taxil. He was a French freethinker notorious for his irreligious and pornographic writings. In 1881, he published *The Secret Loves of Pius IX* and received the First Degree of Masonry. By 1882, he had worn out his welcome in his lodge and was expelled without advancing beyond 1° Entered Apprentice. Sometime after this, he concocted his grand scheme, apparently to embarrass the Roman Catholic Church and wreak a twisted vengeance on his former Masonic brothers.

Much to the shock of his freethinking friends and to the surprise of French Catholics, Taxil "converted" to Catholicism in 1885, a year after "Humanum Genus." He convinced a priest he was a murderer and did penance in a monastery. He then dropped the bombshell: shortly before joining the church, he had been a Freemason and could reveal their inner workings. Taxil knew his admission would get special attention because Freemasonry was a particular concern of Pope Leo XIII.

Taxil began writing a series of books about which he said, "My first

Is It True What They Say about Freemasonry?

books on Freemasonry consisted in a mixture of rituals, with short innocent parts inserted, apparently harmlessly interpreted. Each time an obscure passage occurred, I explained it in a way agreeable to Catholics who see Master Lucifer as the supreme grand master of Freemasons."[15]

After writing on Freemasonry for two years, he obtained an audience with Leo XIII in 1887. Following this, he revealed (actually invented) the innermost secret of Freemasonry: the New and Reformed Palladian Rite, a Lucifer-worshipping inner circle of men and women who ran Masonry. He created an evil Grand Mistress of Palladism, Sophia Walder, and her virtuous adversary, Diana Vaughan. Diana escaped from the evils of Palladism, converted to Catholicism, but now had to remain in hiding to avoid assassination by vengeful Masons. These stories captivated the Catholic hierarchy and the French public, much like a contemporary news story of a missing person.

Palladism is a monstrous deception that never existed except in Taxil's mind. Credulous anti-Masons, fueled by "Humanum Genus" and other anti-Masonic encyclicals, started writing their own books, interpreting Masonic symbols in the light of the newly revealed Palladism. Taxil incorporated and cross-referenced these books in the growing web of his hoax.

Three years after the death of Albert Pike (1809–1891), Taxil convinced Abel Clarin de la Rive that Pike had been the "Sovereign Pontiff of Universal Freemasonry" (a nonexistent position). De la Rive subsequently published in *La Femme et L'Enfant dans la Franc-Maçonnerie Universelle* that Diana Vaughan (the nonexistent heroine) had carried Pike's "announcement" to the "Supreme Confederated councils of the World" (a nonexistent organization) that the inner circle of High Degree Freemasonry, 30°–33°, worshipped Lucifer. "That which we must say to the crowd is:— We worship a God, but it is the God that one adores without superstition. To you, Sovereign Grand Inspectors General [i.e., 33° Masons], we say this, that you may repeat it to the Brethren of the 32nd, 31st and 30th degrees—the Masonic religion should be, by all of us initiates of the high degrees, maintained in the purity of the Luciferian doctrine."[16]

Taxil's interconnected and self-referential books and quotes began collapsing on themselves as more discerning readers demanded verification and proof. Finally, on April 19, 1897, in the hall of the Geographic Society in

Paris, Léo Taxil confessed all to a stunned audience, after which a riot nearly broke out. A transcription of his confession was published six days later in the Paris weekly *Le Frondeur*.[17] De la Rive expressed his disgust and recanted his writings about Diana Vaughan in the April 1897 issue of *Freemasonry Unmasked*, a magazine devoted to the destruction of Freemasonry. "We have always been careful to publish special articles concerning Palladism and Diana Vaughan. We are now giving in this issue a complete list of these articles, which can now be considered as not having existed."[18]

The manufactured Pike quote in *La Femme et L'Enfant dans la Franc-Maçonnerie Universelle* would have died in well-deserved obscurity except for Edith Starr Miller. The American wife of Lord Queenborough, she translated and published the quote in *Occult Theocrasy*, her 1933 magnum opus aimed at exposing all of the evil forces conspiring to destroy Christianity and Western society. The fabricated quote was now available to English readers without the bothersome context of Taxil's hoax and subsequent confession. It has taken on a life of its own among conspiracists on the Internet. A quick Google search of the Internet using the search terms "Pike" and "say to the crowd" produces about 16,000 hits, most breathlessly warning readers about the evils of Freemasonry. This sadly confirms the observation of Mark Twain (Samuel Clemens), "A lie can get halfway around the world before the truth can even get its boots on."

WORKING FOR THE JEWS

In 1905 the final major anti-Masonic charge, that of being part of the "Jewish conspiracy," appeared in virulent full form with the publication of *The Protocols of the Learned Elders of Zion*. This forgery, originating in Russia, has been the justification for vicious anti-Semitism and anti-Masonry. Protocol 15 says, among other lies, "We will create and multiply free Masonic lodges in all countries of the world. . . . We will put all these lodges under a central administration known only to us. . . . Between the members of these lodges will be almost all the international and national police agents."[19] The charge of a Jewish-Masonic plot resonated with anti-Semites and conspiracists, and many books with similar charges followed. Adolf Hitler wrote in his 1925 *Mein Kampf*, "In Freemasonry, which has succumbed to [the Jew] completely, he has an excellent instrument with which to fight for his aims and put them across." Léon de Poncins continued this idea in 1929 with his book's explicit title: *Freemasonry and Judaism: The Secret Powers behind Revolution*.

Hamas, the Islamic Resistance Movement, sadly has accepted uncritically the idea of a Jewish-Masonic conspiracy. Their 1988 Covenant explicitly mentions Freemasonry three times.

> That is why you find [enemies] giving these attempts constant attention through information campaigns, films, and the school curriculum, using for that purpose their lackeys who are infiltrated through Zionist organizations under various names and shapes, such as Freemasons, Rotary Clubs, espionage groups and others, which are all nothing more than cells of subversion and saboteurs. (Article 17)
>
> With their money [the enemies] formed secret societies, such as Freemasons, Rotary Clubs, the Lions and others in different parts of the world for the purpose of sabotaging societies and achieving Zionist interests. (Article 22)
>
> [The Zionist invasion] relies greatly in its infiltration and espionage operations on the secret organizations it gave rise to, such as the Freemasons, The Rotary and Lions clubs, and other sabotage groups. (Article 28)[20]

MURDERING PROSTITUTES, AND MORE

One of the first original (and creative) anti-Masonic charges in decades came from Stephen Knight whose not-so-final *Jack the Ripper: The Final Solution* appeared in 1976. His imaginative, if convoluted, theory was that Freemasons conspired with the British crown to "ritualistically murder" several prostitutes who were aware that Prince Albert Victor, Duke of Clarence, had an illegitimate child with a Catholic commoner. It was these murders that were attributed to "Jack the Ripper." While his theory was without foundation, its flash in the pan was sufficient to attract Hollywood's attention. It became the basis for two movies: *Murder by Decree* (1979) and *From Hell* (2001). While never taken seriously by historians, "Ripperologists" have soundly debunked Knight's conjecture, and the notion is languishing.[21]

It took about two hundred years to create the major elements of most anti-Masonic charges that are seen in the twenty-first century:

- meeting in secret

- swearing oaths

- plotting to subvert governments and religions

- worshipping Lucifer

- working for/with the Jews

Conspiracists, anti-Masons, and anti-Semites have never needed solid evidence to advance their claims. In fact, the absence of evidence is often used as evidence of the conspiracy. They all seem to be looking for something or someone else—perhaps their unlucky stars—on which to blame the unfortunate conditions of the world (or the failures of their churches or the problems in their lives). How else can they understand their circumstances? They are unwilling to accept personal responsibility and desperately look for some way to explain the chaos they see. Perhaps Cassius was right, "The fault, dear Brutus, is not in our stars, but in ourselves. . . ."

Chapter 3

Léo Taxil: The Hoax of "Luciferian Masonry"

> There's a sucker born every minute.
>
> —**David Hannum**

Some hoaxes are so clever that they continue to fool people for years. The best hoaxes have the right combination of fact and fiction, and often exploit the sympathies, prejudices, or weaknesses of their intended victims. For over a hundred years, Freemasonry has been the victim of a hoax, or lie, which is often delivered as the main course in anti-Masonic sermons. No other lie has captured the imagination of anti-Masons quite like Léo Taxil's hoax about Albert Pike (figure 3-1) and Lucifer. It is an urban legend that gullible anti-Masons eagerly repeat without bothering to confirm sources. "Léo Taxil" was the pen name of Gabriel Antoine Jogand-Pagès (1854–1907) (figure 3-2), a French free thinker who was notorious for his irreligious and pornographic writings. In 1881, he published *The Secret Loves of Pius IX* and received the First Degree in Masonry. By 1882, he had worn out his welcome in his lodge and was expelled without advancing beyond the I°. Sometime after this, he concocted his grand scheme to embarrass the Roman Catholic Church and wreak a twisted vengeance on his former Masonic brothers.

The plan was complicated and devious. In 1885, Taxil "converted" to Catholicism, convinced a priest he was a murderer, and did penance in a monastery. Having confessed to murder, it was easy to convince the hierarchy he could reveal, as Pope Leo XIII put it, the "Satanic guidance of the

23

Figure 3-1. Albert Pike (1809–1891), Grand Commander of the Supreme Council, 33°, SJ, 1859–1891, slandered by Léo Taxil as the author of the false "Luciferian Doctrine" of Freemasonry. Painting by Charles L. Elliott (1844). Museum of the Supreme Council, 33°, SJ.

sect [Freemasonry]." Taxil began producing books that revealed the "secrets" of Freemasonry (figure 3-3). Since he had only received the Entered Apprentice or First Degree, he soon had to plagiarize other exposés and eventually began inventing Masonic Rites and rituals to keep up with demand from his readers.

Figure 3-2. Léo Taxil (Gabriel Antoine Jogand-Pagès) (1854–1907), anti-Mason, anti-Catholic, and pornographer, who created an elaborate hoax falsely linking Freemasonry and devil worship, the purpose of which was to defame the fraternity and to embarrass the Catholic Church. From *Los Misterios de la Francmasonería* (1887). Library of the Supreme Council, 33°, SJ.

Figure 3-3. Cover of *Les Mystères de la Franc-Maçonnerie*. The cover is typical of the lurid illustrations used to attract readers to the scurrilous "revelation" of Masonic lodge activities. Library of the Supreme Council, 33°, SJ.

The culmination of his expanding hoax was the invention of "Palladism or Luciferian High-Masonry." As Taxil put it:

> [Palladism was] prettily fabricated by me from beginning to end. . . . We located the center of Palladism at Charleston in the United States, with the late General Albert Pike, Grand Master of the Scottish Rite in South Carolina, as Founder. . . . Through us, he became the first Luciferian Pope, supreme chief of all freemasons of the globe. . . .[1]

Taxil continued the fraud as long as he could. The fictitious and pure heroine, Diana Vaughan, escapee from a Palladian lodge, tried to evade the clutches of the equally imaginary but evil Sophie Walder, Grand Mistress of Palladism. Diana, he said, carried secret instructions from Albert Pike to the "23 Supreme Confederated Councils of the World," telling them they could now reveal to their high-degree members that the "Masonic religion" is the worship of Lucifer. Readers loved the increasingly lurid details, but as the fabrication grew more complicated, it threatened to collapse under the weight of unsubstantiated details. Finally, on April 19, 1897, in the hall of the

Geographic Society in Paris, Léo Taxil confessed all to a stunned audience, after which a riot nearly broke out. A transcription of his confession was published six days later in the Paris weekly *Le Frondeur*. (A bibliography of accounts of Taxil's hoax about Freemasonry and Lucifer appears at the end of this chapter. A translation of Taxil's full confession can be found in Appendix I: The Confession of Léo Taxil.)

THE CONTINUED USE OF TAXIL'S HOAX

Like a vampire in a bad horror movie, Taxil's hoax keeps coming back from the grave. Once anti-Masons have convinced themselves that Freemasonry is the work of Satan, they are tempted by the enticing fruit of Taxil's "Luciferian Conspiracy." The quotation usually starts, "On July 14, 1889, Albert Pike, Sovereign Pontiff of Universal Freemasonry, addressed to the 23 Supreme Confederated Councils of the world the following instructions. . . ." If you hear those words, that is all you need to read to know the author has fallen prey to this infamous hoax.

The hoax is so well known that it has been explained time and time again for over a century. The *New Catholic Encyclopedia*, no supporter of Freemasonry, says this about Léo Taxil:

> Taxil purported to reveal the existence of "Palladium," the most secret Masonic order, which practiced devil-worship. He recounted the story of its high priestess Diana Vaughan; and ended by publishing the *Memoires d'une ex-Palladiste* after her conversion to Catholicism: When doubts began to spread, Taxil realized the time had come to end the deceit. In a conference in Paris (April 19, 1897), he cynically admitted his hoax, whose aim, he said, was to hold up Catholicism to derision.[2]

Dr. Robert A. Morey parts company with most of his fellow anti-Masons on the issue of there being a diabolical Masonic religion.

> Of all the attacks against the Craft, none is so vicious as the charge that Masons are a secret cult of Devil worshipers or Satanists and that at some point in the higher degrees they must pass through a Luciferian initiation.[3]

It's not entirely certain when the quotation concerning Pike was fabricated nor where it was first published. However, the author of this infamous passage was Léo Taxil. In this published confession Taxil admitted to creating the bogus quote:

> We saw indeed some Masonic journals, such as *La Renaissance Symbolique*, swallow a dogmatic circular about Luciferian occultism, a circular dated July 14, 1889, written by myself in Paris, and which I disclosed as having been brought from Charleston to Europe by Miss Diana Vaughn on behalf of Albert Pike, its author.

We can trace modern appearances of this Luciferian hoax to Lady Queenborough, Edith Starr Miller, who wrote *Occult Theocrasy* in 1933. Her work is often excerpted and treated as gospel truth, usually without attribution. Such practices are known as plagiarism in other disciplines, but neither serious research nor intellectual integrity stand in the way of the headlong rush to slander Freemasonry.

Lady Queenborough found her quotation in the 1894 book by Abel Clarin de la Rive, *La Femme et L'Enfant dans la Franc-Maçonnerie Universelle* (*Woman and Child in Universal Freemasonry*). Mr. de la Rive, like Lady Queenborough, was duped by the hoax; they are guilty only of incompetent research and an eager willingness to believe the worst about Freemasonry.

After Taxil's public confession, Abel Clarin de la Rive expressed his disgust and recanted his writings about Diana Vaughan in the April 1897 issue of *Freemasonry Unmasked*, a magazine devoted to the destruction of the Craft. As much as he hated Freemasonry, de la Rive at least had the integrity to admit Taxil's hoax:

> With frightening cynicism the miserable person we shall not name here [Taxil] declared before an assembly especially convened for him that for twelve years he had prepared and carried out to the end the most extraordinary and most sacrilegious of hoaxes. We have always been careful to publish special articles concerning Palladism and Diana Vaughan. We are now giving in this issue a complete list of these articles, which can now be considered as not having existed.[4]

Other anti-Masons, however, are not as principled as de la Rive. Former Masons in particular are guilty of a vile form of premeditated false witness. By repeating the quote, they are using their status as former Masons to impute a false accuracy to the quote—a practice they could have never encountered in their Masonic experiences. This infamous band includes ex-Masons William Schnoebelen,[5] Jack Harris,[6] and Harmon R. Taylor.[7]

Some authors using Taxil, like the Reverend Pat Robertson, simply quote Lady Queenborough's translation without attribution, leaving his readers with no way to independently verify the facts. Others, like Dr. James Holly and Martin Short, have used the quotation accompanied by "weasel words" they hope will absolve them from responsibility for repeating lies. For example, this is how Dr. Holly tried to cover himself when he quoted Mr. de la Rive to defame the fraternity:

> In the late nineteenth century many anti-Masonic books were written, purporting to be written by Masons. Some have argued that this is one such book. There is no conclusive evidence either way.[8]

Employing less ambiguous terms than Dr. Holly, Martin Short admitted there were problems with the bogus quote, but he, too, felt no compunction against using it to smear Freemasonry.

> There are problems with this quotation: its meaning is not immediately clear and its authenticity is in doubt. It was first attributed to Pike in 1894 by a French authoress who detested Freemasonry, yet no original text seems to exist. Genuine or not, England's Grand Lodge dismisses it by pointing out Pike must have been eighty at the time and "may have been dotty."
> Yet the quote sounds authentic. Its pyrotechnic language and bombastic poesy recalls Pike's earlier writings, and the message is not so different from that of Morals and Dogma. If genuine, it indicates there is a Satanic—or Luciferian—strain in American Masonry. . . .[9]

Apparently, even the public confession of Taxil and the subsequent recantation by Mr. de la Rive do not seem conclusive enough for Dr. Holly, Mr. Short, and their ilk.[10]

In spite of all that's been written on the truth of the Taxil hoax, it continues to attract shallow researchers and conspiracy theorists. For example, Dr. Joye Jeffries Pugh included the bogus quote in her 2006 book Eden: The Knowledge of Good and Evil 666. She prefaced it by stating that "Albert Pike [was] an esoteric Jew who some claim was a homosexual." A little research would have shown Dr. Pugh that Pike was neither Jewish nor a homosexual. However, research is apparently unnecessary for Dr. Pugh, who claims to have prophetic abilities, which began "at 6 years of age after having an unusual and prophetic dream about the End of Time."[11]

Mr. Jack Chick showed some cleverness in his use of the bogus Albert Pike quote in the 1991 edition of his comic book, The Curse of Baphomet

That's your interpretation, Ed! We Masons **don't** believe that!

Who said that?

Albert Pike, the Grand Commander, Sovereign Pontiff of Universal Freemasonry.

Maybe **YOU** don't, Alex, but one of your leaders did. He taught that **SATAN** is the god of Masonry.

Listen to what **he** said...

"That which we must say to the **CROWD** is: we worship a god, but it is the god that one adores without superstition. To **YOU** Sovereign Grand Inspectors General, we say this, that you may repeat it to the brethren of the 32nd, 31st and 30th degrees – the **MASONIC RELIGION** should be, by all of us initiates of the **high** degrees, maintained in the purity of the **LUCIFERIAN** doctrine. If Lucifer were not god, would Adonay (Jesus)... calumniate (spread false and harmful statements about) him?... YES, **LUCIFER IS GOD...**"*

*"The Freemason" (the organ of English Freemasonry), 19th January, 1935.

Baphomet

General Albert Pike, 33˚

"That which we must say to the **CROWD** is: we worship a god, but it is the god that one adores without superstition. To **YOU** Sovereign Grand Inspectors General, we say this, that you may repeat it to the brethren of the 32nd, 31st and 30th degrees – the **MASONIC RELIGION** should be, by all of us initiates of the **high** degrees, maintained in the purity of the **LUCIFERIAN** doctrine. If Lucifer were not god, would Adonay (Jesus)... calumniate (spread false and harmful statements about) him?... YES, **LUCIFER IS GOD...**"*

*A.C. De La Rive, La Femme et l'Enfant dans la Franc-Maçonnérie Universelle (page 588).

Baphomet

General Albert Pike, 33˚

Figure 3-4. A fictitious reference to a legitimate Masonic publication demonstrates the zeal of anti-Masons in using the discredited Taxil fabrication. Following an exposure of this deception, the reference was changed but the bogus quote remains. From Jack T. Chick, *The Curse of Baphomet*.

(figure 3-4). Rather than plagiarizing Lady Queenborough, as have so many of his allies, he used a fictitious reference to a legitimate publication: "'The Freemason' (the organ of English Freemasonry), 19th January, 1935"![12] Although he has removed the nonexistent reference from current editions, the bogus quote remains. After all, Mr. Chick's readers can and did confirm that the quote never appeared in *The Freemason*, but the lie was indeed published in de la Rive's anti-Masonic book *La Femme et l'Enfant dans la Franc-Maçonnerie Universelle*.

Mr. C. Fred Kleinknecht, who was then Grand Commander of the Scottish Rite, SJ, wrote to Rev. Pat Robertson on May 12, 1992. The Albert Pike quotation in Robertson's *The New World Order* was exposed to him as a fraud, and Rev. Robertson was invited to read any of Albert Pike's writings at the House of the Temple. Mr. Kleinknecht suggested that Rev. Robertson would better serve his readers if he removed the false quotation from any future editions of his book. In his closing paragraph, Mr. Kleinknecht said to Rev. Robertson, "If we must disagree, let us base our disagreement upon truth."[13] Rev. Robertson has never answered Mr. Kleinknecht.

Before commenting further on the hoax, the complete quotation from Mr. de la Rive, a modern translation, and its partial translation by Lady Queenborough, are presented in parallel columns for easy comparison.

Léo Taxil's Fabricated Luciferian Quotation of Albert Pike

Abel Clarin de la Rive. *La Femme et L'Enfant dans la Franc-Maçonnerie Universelle.* Paris & Lyon: Delhomme & Briguet, Editeurs, 1894.

pp. 587–89

Le quatorzième jour du cinquième mois de l'an 000889 de la Vraie Lumière (Par conséquent le 14 juillet 1889, ère vulgaire) Albert Pike, Souverain-Grand-Inspecteur Général, 33° et dernier degré; Très Puissant Souverain Commandeur Grand-Maître du Suprême Conseil de Charleston, premier Suprême Conseil du Globe; Grand Maître Conservateur du Palladium sacré; Souverain Pontife de la Franc-Maçonnerie Universelle, en la trente-unième [*sic*] année de son Pontificat, adressait aux 23 Suprêmes Conseils Confédérés du monde entier ces diaboliques instructions dont nous n'extrayons que les passages relatifs à la Femme:

«A la science de Faust, le vrai Maçon joindra l'impassibilité de Job. Il piétinera la superstition dans son coeur. Il

Abel Clarin de la Rive. *Woman and Child in Universal Freemasonry.* Paris & Lyons: Delhomme & Briguet, Publishers, 1894.

[translated by Eric Serejski]

The fourteenth day of the fifth month of the 889th year of True Light (consequently July 14, 1889, of the vulgar era) Albert Pike, Sovereign Grand Inspector General, 33rd and last degree; Most Puissant Sovereign Commander Grand Master of the Supreme Council of Charleston, Premier Supreme Council of the Globe; Grand Master Preserver of the sacred Palladium; As Sovereign Pontiff of Universal Freemasonry, in the thirty-first year of his Pontificate, he addressed to the 23 Confederated Supreme Councils of the entire world these diabolic instructions from which we extract only the passages related to Woman:

"To the science of Faust, the True Mason will join the impassiveness of Job. He will trample down superstition in

Lady Queenborough, Edith Starr Miller, *Occult Theocrasy.* 2 vols. 1933. Reprint. Hawthorne, Calif: The Christian Book Club of America, 1980.

p. 233

As regards the position of women in Masonry, we think that this cannot be better explained than in the words of Albert Pike himself. In *La Femme et l'Enfant dans la Franc-Maçonnerie Universelle* page 578 [*sic*], A.C. De La Rive states that on July 14, 1889, Albert Pike, Sovereign Pontiff of Universal Freemasonry, addressed to the 23 Supreme Confederated Councils of the world the following instructions, which we quote herewith in part.

"To the science of Faust, the real Mason will join the impassibility of Job, He will eradicate superstition from his

sera sans indécision et sans caprices. Il n'acceptera le plaisir que losqu'il le voudra et ne le voudra que losqu'il le devra.

«NOUS RECOMMANDONS TRÈS-INSTAMMENT DE MULTIPLI-ER LES LOGES D'ADOPTION. ELLES SONT INDISPENABLES POUR FORMER DES MAÇONS BIEN MAITRES [sic] D'EUX-MÊMES. Le prêtre essaye de dompter sa chair en s'astreignant au célibat. . . . Le vrai Maçon, au contraire, arrive à la perfection, c'est-à-dire à se dominer, *en employant son zéle dans les Loges d'Adoption à se soumettre aux épreuves naturelles.* LE COMMERCE AVEC LA FEMME COMMUNE A [sic] TOUS SES FRÈRES LUI FAIT UNE CUIRASSE CONTRE LES PASSIONS QUI ÉGARENT LE CŒUR. Celui-là seul peut vraiment posséder la volupté de l'amour, qui a vaincu, par l'usage fréquent, l'amour de la volupté. Pouvoir, à volonté, user et s'abstenir, c'est pouvoir deux fois. La femme t'enchaîne par tes désirs, disons-nous à l'adepte; eh [sic] bien, uses des femmes souvent et sans passion; tu deviendras ainsi maître de tes désirs, et tu enchaîneras la femme. D'où il résulte que le vrai Maçon parviendra facilement à résoudre le problème de la chair. . . .»

«Evidemment il n'est pas de nécessité absolue que l'homme que vous allez diriger vers les hauts grades soit immediatement parfait et ait compris notre secret dès son entrée dans la Maçonnerie. Ce que Nous vous demandons, c'est de l'observer, avec le plus grand soin pendant son Apprentissage, d'abord, *et de faire ensuite, de la Loge d'Adoption, où il pénétrera quand il sera Compagnon,* VOTRE CRITERIUM,

his heart. He will be without indecision and without whims, he will accept pleasure only when he wants it and will want it only when he must."

"WE MOST EARNESTLY RECOMMEND INCREASING THE LODGES OF ADOPTION. THEY ARE INDISPENSABLE FOR MAKING MASONS MASTERS OF THEMSELVES. The priest tries to subdue his flesh by forcing himself to be celibate. . . . The true Mason, on the contrary, reaches perfection, which is to say control over himself, *by using his zeal in Lodges of Adoption, submitting himself to natural tests.* COMMERCE WITH A WOMAN BELONGING TO ALL HIS BROTHERS FORMS AN ARMOR AGAINST PASSIONS THAT LEAD THE HEART ASTRAY. He alone can really possess the voluptuousness of love, who vanquishes, by frequent usage, the love of voluptuousness. To be able, at will, to use and to abstain, is a twofold power. Woman enslaves you by her desires, we say to the adept; so use women often and without passion; you will thus become master of your desires, and you will enslave women. From this it results that the true Mason will easily resolve the problem of the flesh. . . ."

"Evidently it is not absolutely necessary that the man whom you will lead to the highest degrees has to be immediately perfect and has to understand our secret from his entry into Masonry. What we ask of you is first to observe him with the utmost care during his Apprenticeship, and afterwards, in the Lodge of Adoption, where he will enter when he will become a Fellow Craft, to make him, YOUR

heart and cultivate decisions of character. He will accept pleasure only when he wishes it and will wish it only when he should do so.

"We earnestly recommend the creation of Lodges of Adoption. They are indispensable to the formation of Masons who are indeed Masters of themselves. The priest tries to subdue his flesh by enforced celibacy The real Mason, on the contrary, reaches perfection, that is to say achieves self mastery, by using his zeal in the Lodges of Adoption in submitting to all natural ordeals. Commerce with women, belonging to all brethren, forms for him an armor against those passions which lead hearts astray. He alone can really possess voluptuousness. To be able, at will, to use or to abstain, is a twofold power. Woman fetters thee by thy desires, we say to the adept, well, use women often and without passion; thou wilt thus become master of thy desires, and thou wilt enchain woman. From which it must perforce result that the real Mason will succeed in easily solving the problem of the flesh. . . ."

"It is evidently not absolutely necessary that the man whom you are leading towards the high grades be immediately perfect and have understood our secret on his entrance into Masonry. That which we ask you is first to observe him with the greatest care during his apprenticeship and afterwards, when he enters the Lodge of Adoption as Companion to use that as your criterion, your

VOTRE INSTRUMENT DE CONTROLE INFAILLIBLE.»

«L'Atelier de Frères, qui ne s'annexe pas *une loge de Sœurs,* est un Atelier incomplet, destiné fatalement à ne jamais produire que des Maçons, dont la politique sera le principal souci, qui se pré-occuperont surtout des intrigues et des compétitions, qui s'agiteront dans le vide, qui avanceront tantôt de trois pas pour reculer après d'autant en un mot, qui feront du mauvais travail et dont la poli-tique sera incohérente.»

. . . .

CRITERION, YOUR INSTRUMENT OF INFALLIBLE CONTROL.

"The Lodge of the Brethren which does not annex a Lodge of Sisters is an incomplete Lodge inevitability destined to never produce anything but Masons for whom politics will be the main concern, who will mostly be engaged with intrigue and competition. who will move about in emptiness, who will walk three steps forward then three steps backward, in one word, whose work will be unsatisfactory and whose politics will be incoherent."

. . . .

instrument of infallible control.

"The Lodge of Brothers which has failed to annex a Lodge of Sisters is incom-plete and destined inevitably never to produce anything but Brethren, with whom politics are the chief con-cern, men who will be chiefly preoccupied with intrigue and rivalry, who will do bad work and whose politics will be incoherent."

pp. 220–21

The theological dogma of Albert Pike is explained in the "Instructions" issued by him, on July 14, 1889, to the 23 Supreme Councils of the world and have been recorded by A. C. De La Rive in *La Femme et l'Enfant dans la Franc-Maçonnerie Universelle* (page 588) from which book we translate the quote as follows:

"That which we must say to the crowd is:—We worship a God, but it is the God that one adores without superstition.

"To you, Sovereign Grand Inspectors General, we say this, that you may repeat it to the Brethren of the 32nd, 31st and 30th degrees—The Masonic religion should be, by all of us initiates of the high degrees, maintained in the purity of the Luciferian doctrine.

. . . .

«Ce que nous devons dire à la foule, c'est:—Nous adorons un Dieu, mais c'est le Dieu qu l'on adore sans superstition.

«A vous, Souverains Grands Inspecteurs Généraux, Nous disons, pour que vous le répétiez aux Frères des 32°, 31° et 30° degrés:—La reli-gion maçonnique doit dire, par nous tous, initiés des hauts grades, maintenue dans la pureté de la doctraine LUCIFÉRIENNE.»

. . . .

"What we must say to the crowd is:—We worship a God, but it is the God that one wor-ships without superstition."

"To you, Sovereign Grand Inspectors General, we say, so that you can repeat it to the Brethren of the 32nd, 31st and 30th degrees:—The Masonic religion must be, by all of us initiates of the high grades, maintained in the purity of the LUCIFERIAN doctrine."

. . . .

«Si Lucifer n'était point Dieu, Adonaï, (le Dieu des Chrétiens) dont tous les actes attestent la cruauté, la perfidie, la haine de l'homme, la barbarie, la répul-sion pour la science, si Lucifer n'était point Dieu, Adonaï et ses prêtres le calomnieraient-ils?

"If Lucifer were not God, Adonai (the God of the Christians) whose deeds prove his cruelty, perfidy and hatred of man, his barbarism and repulsion of science, if Lucifer were not God, would Adonai and his priests slander him?"

"If Lucifer were not God, would Adonay (the God of the Christians) whose deeds prove his cruelty, perfidy, and hatred of man, barbarism and repulsion for science, would Adonay and his priests, calumniate him?

Is It True What They Say about Freemasonry?

«Oui, Lucifer est Dieu, et malheureusement Adonaï l'est aussi. Car la loi éternelle est qu'il n'y a pas de splendeur sans ombre, pas de beauté sans laideur, pas de blanc sans noir, car l'absolu ne peut exister que comme deux; car les ténèbres sont nécessaires à la lumière pour lui servir de repoussoir, comme le piédestal est nécessaire à la statue, come le frein à la locomotive.

«En dynamique analogique et universelle, on ne s'appuie que sur ce qui résiste. Aussi l'univers est-il balancé par deux forces qui le maintiennent en équilibre: la force qui attire et celle qui repousse. Ces deux forces existent en physique, en philosophie et en religion. Et la réalité scientifique du dualisme est démontrée par les phénomènes de la polarité et par la loi universelle des sympathies et des antipathies. C'est pourquoi les disciples intelligents de Zoroastre, ainsi qu'après eux les Gnostiques, les Manichéens, les Templiers ont admis, comme seule conception métaphysique logique, le système des deux principes divins se combattant de toute éternité, et l'on ne peut croire l'un inférieur à l'autre en puissance.

Donc, la doctrine du Satinisme est une hérésie; et la vraie et pure religion philosophique, c'est la *croyance en Lucifer*, égal d'Adonaï, mais Lucifer Dieu de Lumière et Dieu du Bien, luttant pour l'humanité contre Adonaï Dieu des Ténèbres et Dieu du Mal. . . .»

"Yes, Lucifer is God, and unfortunately so is Adonai. For the eternal law is that there is no splendor without shadow, no beauty without ugliness, no white without black, because the absolute can only exist as two, because darkness is necessary to light to serve as its compliment, as the pedestal is necessary to the statue, as the brake to the locomotive.

"In analogical and universal dynamics, one can only lean on that which resists. Thus the universe is balanced by two forces which maintain its equilibrium: the force that attracts and the one that repels. These two forces exist in physics, in philosophy and in religion. And the scientific reality of the divine dualism is proved by the phenomena of polarity and by the universal law of affinities and antipathies. This is why the intelligent disciples of Zoroaster, as well as, after them, the Gnostics, the Manicheans, and the Templars have admitted as the sole logical and metaphysical conception the system of the two divine principles fighting one another in all eternity, and one cannot believe one inferior to the other in power."

Thus, the doctrine of Satanism is a heresy; and the true and pure philosophical religion is the *belief in Lucifer*, equal to Adonai, but Lucifer, God of Light and God of Good, is fighting for humanity against Adonai God of Darkness and God of Evil. . . ."

"Yes, Lucifer is God, and unfortunately Adonay is also God. For the eternal law is that there is no light without shade, no beauty without ugliness, no white without black, for the absolute can only exist as two Gods: darkness being necessary to light to serve as its foil as the pedestal is necessary to the statue, and the brake to the locomotive.

"In analogical and universal dynamics one can only lean on that which will resist. Thus the universe is balanced by two forces which maintain its equilibrium: the force of attraction and that of repulsion. These two forces exist in physics, philosophy and religion. And the scientific reality of the divine dualism is demonstrated by the phenomena of polarity and by the universal law of sympathies and antipathies. That is why the intelligent disciples of Zoroaster, as well as, after them, the Gnostics, the Manicheans and the Templars have admitted, as the only logical metaphysical conception. the system of the two divine principles fighting eternally, and one cannot believe the one inferior in power to the other.

"Thus, the doctrine of Satanism is a heresy; and the true and pure philosophic religion is the belief in Lucifer, the equal of Adonay; but Lucifer, God of Light and God of Good, is struggling for humanity against Adonay, the God of Darkness and Evil."

One must not lose sight of the fact that Pike occupied simultaneously the positions of Grand Master of the Central Directory of

Washington, that of Grand Commander of the Supreme Council of Charleston and that of Sovereign Pontiff of Universal Freemasonry.

Dans une autre partie de ses Instructions, Albert Pike disait encore:

«C'est avec le plus grand soin qu'il est nécessaire de choisir les adeptes. Dans beucoup d'orients, on les prend trop au hasard; aussi tardons-nous à atteindre le but.

«Ne conférez la Maîtrise qu'au Compagnon qui se connait lui-mème. Sur le fronton des anciens temples érigés au Dieu de la Lumière, on lisait cette inscription en deux mots: «Connaistoi.» Nous donnons le même conseil à tout homme qui veut s'approcher de la science.

«N'initiez jamais au troisième degré l'homme qui, malgré les enseignements reçus aux deux grades précédents, *est demeuré esclave des préjugés du monde profane. Il ne parviendra jamais tant qu'il ne se réformera pas. Au grade le Compagnon, vous lui ouvre: les portes des Loges d'Adoption; là, vous le jugerez bien. Vou verrez si ses préjugés tombent. S'il reste esclave de ses passions,* S'IL S'ATTACHE EXCLUSIVEMENT A UNE FEMME, ne vous préoccupez plus de lui, vous perdriez votre temps. Il ne saurait être un adepte; car le mot «*adepte*» signifie celui qui est parvenu par sa volonté et par ses uvres, *qui méprise les préjugés et qui triomphe de ses passions.*»*

In another part of his Instructions, Albert Pike also said:

"It is with the greatest care that it is necessary to choose adepts. In many orients, they are taken too much at random, which explains the delay in reaching the goal."

"Only make a Master of the Fellow Craft who knows himself. On the exterior of the ancient temples built to the God of Light, one reads this two-word inscription: 'Know thyself.' We give the same advice to each man who wants to approach the science."

"Never initiate to the third degree the man who, in spite of the learning received at the two preceding degrees, *remains enslaved to the prejudices of the profane world. He will never approach before he reforms. At the Fellow Craft degree open to him the doors of the Lodges of Adoption;* there you will well judge him. You will see if his prejudices fall. If he remains enslaved of his passions, IF HE EXCLUSIVELY BINDS HIMSELF TO A WOMAN, do not worry about him anymore, you are losing your time. He cannot be an adept; because the word "*adept*" signifies one who arrived by his will and by his deeds, one who despises *prejudices and who triumphs over his passions.*"*

*Ce fut la Sur *Diana Vaughan* qu'Albert Pike,—*afin de lui donner la plus grande marque de confiance,*—chargea d'apporter son encyclique luciférienne, à Paris, pendant l'Exposition Universelle.

*It was the Sister *Diana Vaughan* that Albert Pike,—*in order to give her the greatest mark of confidence,*—charged to carry his luciferian encyclical, to Paris, during the Universal Exposition.

Is It True What They Say about Freemasonry?

AN ANALYSIS OF THE TAXIL QUOTE

There are several problems with the quotation often used by anti-Masons, some obvious and some subtle. To start with, about 450,000 out of 1.4 million American Masons have the 32° in the Scottish Rite, including ministers, rabbis, bishops, and other devout worshipers of God.[14] It is inconceivable that there would not be mass resignations and protests if these men were taught this disgusting "Luciferian doctrine." Is it believable that the millions of Scottish Rite Masons during the last two centuries could be cowed into such total silence? Dr. Robert Morey, an opponent of Masonry, put it well, "Since most Masons in the United States are members of Christian churches and many clergymen belong to the Fraternity, the idea that they are all involved in some kind of devil cult is absurd."[15]

Also, the quotation is riddled with internal inconsistencies:

- There is not now and never has been a position of "Sovereign Pontiff of Universal Freemasonry." This office is Taxil's invention and alone demonstrates the letter is a forgery.

- There is no "Confederation of Supreme Councils." It, too, is Taxil's invention.

- Neither Albert Pike, the Mother Supreme Council,[16] nor any Grand Lodge ever recognized any lodges of adoption (Masonic lodges open to men and women).

- In the United States, virtually every Scottish Rite Mason progresses to the 32° shortly after joining.[17] It is only in Europe that members advance at a different and slower rate. Why would Albert Pike suggest special treatment for 30°, 31°, and 32° Masons when that would have included nearly every American Scottish Rite Mason?

The confirming evidence of the hoax comes in de la Rive's footnote, which neither Lady Queenborough nor any other enemy of Masonry has bothered quoting. In the footnote, de la Rive explains that Pike's "Lucifer-ian encyclical" was brought to Paris by the imaginary Diana Vaughan.

*Ce fut la Sœur *Diana Vaughan* qu'Albert Pike,—*afin de lui donner la plus grande marque de confiance,*—chargea d'apporter son ency-clique luciferienne, a Paris, pendant l'Expo-sition Universelle.	*It was Sister *Diana Vaughan* that Albert Pike,—*in order to give her the greatest mark of confidence,*—charged to carry his Luciferian encyclical, to Paris, during the Universal Exposition.

After Taxil confessed his fraud, de la Rive said, "We have always been careful to publish special articles [in *Freemasonry Unmasked*] concerning Pal-ladism and Diana Vaughan. We are now giving in this issue a complete list of these articles, which can now be considered as not having existed."[18]

The originator of the hoax confessed to his calculated deception. The pub-lisher of the "Luciferian Doctrine" disavowed its authenticity. The Roman

Figure 3-5. Cover of *Woman and Child in Universal Free-masonry*, the most frequently quoted source of the false "Luciferian Doctrine" of Albert Pike. Most of the quotes, however, have been plagiarized from Edith Starr Miller's *Occult Theocrasy*. Library of the Supreme Council, 33°, SJ.

Is It True What They Say about Freemasonry?

Catholic Church confessed that it had been duped. Yet the urban legend persists. It can be found today in hundreds of pages on the Internet, breathlessly repeated with the same urgency of someone repeating the cautionary tale about someone who tried to dry a wet dog in a microwave. David Hannum was right, there is indeed a sucker born every minute.

SOME OF THE BOOKS EXPOSING TAXIL'S "LUCIFERIAN FREEMASONRY" HOAX

A little research shows how easy it is to find explanations of the Taxil hoax. The following are just a few of the many resources which expose this lie.

Allgemeines Handbuch der Freimaurerei, 3d ed. 2 vols. (Leipzig: Max Hesse's Verlag, 1901), s.v. "Taxil, Leo."

Henry W. Coil et al. *Coil's Masonic Encyclopedia* (Richmond, Va.: Macoy Publishing & Masonic Supply Co., 1961, 1996), s.v. "Taxil, Leo."

Ernst Diestel. "La Diablerie de Leo Taxil," *Le Symbolisme*, nos. 77 & 78, Sept. & Oct. 1924, pp. 212–223, 245–249.

Michel Gaudart de Soulages and Hubert Lamant. *Dictionnaire des Francs-Maçons Français* (Paris: Editions Albatros, 1980), s.v. "Taxil."

Great Soviet Encyclopedia, 3rd ed., s.v. "Taxil, Leo."

James Hastings, ed. *Encyclopedia of Religion and Ethics*, s.v. "Satanism," by E. Sidney Hartland.

Hildebrand Gerber (H. Gruber, S.J.), *Leo Taxil's Palladismus-Roman*, 3 vols. (Berlin: Verlag der Germania, 1897), vol. 2, pp. 43–59.

Michel Jarrige. "La Franc-Maçonnerie Démasquée: D'Apres un fonds inedit de la Bibliothèque National," *Politica Hermetica*, no. 4, 1990, pp. 38–53.

Jean-Pierre Laurant. "Le Dossier Léo Taxil du fonds Jean Baylot de la Bibliothèque National," *Politica Hermetica*, no. 4, 1990, pp. 55–67.

Eugen Lennhoff and Oskar Posner. *Internationales Freimauerlexikon*, reprint, 1932 ed. (Munich: Amalthea Verlag, n.d.), s.v. "Taxil, Leo."

R. Limouzin-Lamothe. *The New Catholic Encyclopedia*, s.v. "Taxil, Leo."

Curtis D. MacDougall. *Hoaxes* (New York: MacMillan Co., 1949; reprint New York: Dover Publications, Inc., 1958), pp. 98–100.

Christopher McIntosh. *Eliphas Levi and the French Occult Revival* (New York: Samuel Weiser, Inc., 1974), pp. 210–218.

Gareth J. Medway. *Lure of the Sinister: The Unnatural History of Satanism* (NYU Press, 2001), pp. 11–17, 96–98.

Alec Mellor. *Dictionnaire de la Franc-Maçonnerie et des Franc-Maçons* (Paris: Editions Pierre Belfond, 1975), s.v. "Taxil Gabriel-Antoine (Jogand-Pagès dit Léo)," "Anti-Maçonnerie: Le XIXe siècle."

———. "A Hoaxer of Genius—Leo Taxil (1890–1897)," *Our Separated Brethren, the Freemasons*, trans. B. R. Feinson (London: G. G. Harrap & Co., 1961), pp. 149–155.

Robert A. Morey. *The Truth About Masons* (Eugene, Oreg.: Harvest House Publishers, 1993), pp. 23–25.

S. Brent Morris. "Albert Pike and Lucifer: The Lie That Will Not Die," *The Short Talk Bulletin*, vol. 71, no. 6, June 1993.

Maximilian Rudwin. *The Devil in Legend and Literature* (Chicago: Open Court Publishing Co., 1931), pp. 167–168.

Rudolf Steiner. *The Temple Legend*, trans. John M. Wood (London: Rudolf Steiner Press, 1985), pp. 283–284, 408–409.

"Taxil-Schwindel, Der," *Freimaurer: Solange die Welt besteht,* catalog of a special exhibition of the History Museum of Vienna, 18 September 1992–10 January 1993, pp. 268–370.

Arthur E. Waite. *Devil Worship in France or the Question of Lucifer* (London: George Redway, 1896; reprint ed. Boston: Red Wheel/Weiser, 2003).

————. *A New Encyclopedia of Freemasonry,* new & rev. ed. (1921; reprint ed. New York: Weathervane Books, 1970), s.v. "Palladian Freemasonry."

Wesley P. Walters. "A Curious Case of Fraud," *The Quarterly Journal,* vol. 9, no. 4 (Oct.–Dec. 1989), pp. 4, 7. (Also reprinted in Jerald and Sandra Tanner, *The Lucifer-God Doctrine* [Salt Lake City, Ut.: Utah Lighthouse Ministry, 1988]).

Eugen Weber. *Satan Franc-Maçon: La mystification de Léo Taxil* (Mesnil-sur-l'Estrée, France: Collection Archives Julliard, 1964).

Gordon Wright. "Diana Vaughan: Satanist and Saint," *Notable or Notorious?* (Cambridge, Mass.: Harvard University Press, 1991), pp. 86–147.

SOME ANTI-MASONIC BOOKS USING TAXIL'S HOAX ABOUT FREEMASONRY AND LUCIFER

These are just a few of the "researchers" who've been suckered in by Taxil's stale fraud. Scores more can be found on the Internet.

Muhammad Safwat al-Saqqa Amini and Sa'di Abu Habib. *Freemasonry* (New York: Muslim World League, 1982), p. 41.

Anonymous. *Freemasonry Antichrist Upon Us,* 3rd ed. (Boring, Oreg.: CPA Books, no date), p. 32.

Cathy Bums. *Hidden Secrets of Masonry* (Mt. Carmel, Penn.: Sharing, 1990), p. 27.

Roger Chapman. *Blood Was Cheap* (Xulon Press, 2002), pp. 107–08.

Jack T. Chick. *The Curse of Baphomet* (Chino, Calif.: Chick Publications, 1991), p. [12].

John Daniel. *Scarlet and the Beast*, 3 vols. (Tyler, Tex.: Jon Kregel, Inc., 1994), Vol. I, pp. 373, 380.

J. Edward Decker, Jr. *The Question of Freemasonry* (Issaquah, Wash.: Free the Masons Ministries, no date), pp. 12–14.

J. Edward Decker, Jr., and Dave Hunt. *The God Makers* (Eugene, Oreg.: Harvest House, 1984) p. 130.

Kole Eremos. *Satan This Is Going to Hurt!* (Xulon Press, 2009), p. 307.

Des Griffin. *Fourth Reich of the Rich* (Clackamas, Oreg.: Emissary Pub., 1976), p. 70.

Jack Harris.* *Freemasonry: The Invisible Cult in Our Midst* (Towson, Md.: Jack Harris, 1983), pp. 24–25.

Gyeorgos Ceres Hatonn. *Birthing the Phoenix Vol. III* (Las Vegas: Phoenix Source Distributors, Inc., 1998), pp. 125–25.

James L. Holly. *The Southern Baptist Convention and Freemasonry* (Beaumont, Tex.: Mission and Ministry to Men, 1992), p. 18.

John Jacobsen. *The Beginning of the End* (Xulon Press, 2009), p. 223.

Gary H. Kah. *En Route to Global Occupation* (Lafayette, La.: Huntington House Pub., 1992), pp. 114, 124.

Gordon Kameron. *Freemasonry—The Truth* (Lulu.com, 2008), p. 60.

Salem Kirban. *Satan's Angels Exposed* (Salem Kirban, 1980), p.161.

Donald G. Lett Jr. *Phoenix Rising: The Rise and Fall of the American Republic* (Phoenix Rising Pub., 2008), pp. 69–70.

Texe Marrs. *Dark Secrets of the New Age* (Westchester, Ill: Crossway Books, 1987), p. 273.

Eustace Mullins. *The Curse of Canaan* (Staunton, Va.: Revelation Books, 1986).

James Randall Noblitt and Pamela Sue Perskin. *Cult and Ritual Abuse: Its History, Anthropology, and Recent Discovery in Contemporary America* (Greenwood Publishing Group, 2000), p. 136.

Joye Jeffries Pugh. *Eden: The Knowledge of Good and Evil 666* (Tate Publishing, 2006), pp. 208–9.

Pat Robertson. *The New World Order* (Waco, Tex.: Word Publishing, 1991), p. 184.

William Schnoebelen.* *Masonry: Beyond the Light* (Chino, Calif.: Chick Publications, 1991), pp. 60–61.

Martin Short. *Inside the Brotherhood* (New York: Dorset Press, 1990), p. 94.

Harmon R. Taylor.* "Mixing Oil with Water," *The Evangelist*, June 1986, pp. 47–49.

Bill Waits. *America at the End of Days* (Xulon Press, 2006), pp. 177–78.

*Former Mason who never encountered the Taxil quote during his membership.

Chapter 4

Rev. John Ankerberg and Dr. John Weldon: The Secret Teachings of the Masonic Lodge

> Men never do evil so completely and cheerfully as when they do it from religious conviction.
>
> **—Blaise Pascal, *Pensées***

The more familiar one becomes with anti-Masons and their tactics, the more obvious it becomes that they resort to the old trick of repackaging. Advertisers know that packaging and presentation are often more important than substance itself. Any mother knows that the bright eye-catching box of a kid's breakfast cereal is a lure to distract from a healthier whole-grain product, but that doesn't matter to the child, who falls for the bright box and the free toy inside. Many anti-Masons have capitalized on this marketing ploy. Some, like Léo Taxil and Jack Chick, appeal to the uneducated and play on their emotions, fears, and prejudices. But others are craftier and more sophisticated. Parading under the guise of scholarship and piety, they are even more dangerous.

Perhaps the most impressive-looking modern American anti-Masonic book is *The Secret Teachings of the Masonic Lodge: A Christian Perspective* by Rev. John Ankerberg and Dr. John Weldon.[1] With over 300 pages in twenty chapters and 750 endnotes, the book appears to be a scholarly analysis of Freemasonry. On closer examination, however, one discovers that the authors lull their readers into a false sense of security by alleging a reliance on "authoritative" sources of information. In fact, Rev. Ankerberg and Dr. Weldon are satisfied to quote both non-Masons (such as "Djwhal Khul")[2] and anti-Masons (such as Jonathan Blanchard) while falsely claiming they are Masons. This use of false witnesses and their manipulation of text is so subtle that it is difficult, even for objective readers, to avoid being deceived.

SOURCES

Rev. Ankerberg and Dr. Weldon want their readers to believe that their work is objective. To assist this illusion, they explain that they (or their research associates) wrote to the Grand Masters of fifty American Grand Lodges: "As an official Masonic leader, which books and authors do you recommend as being authoritative on the subject of Freemasonry?"[3] (See chapter 1, "The Issue of Masonic Experts.")

Only twenty-five Grand Masters responded, each recommending several Masonic authors. Topping the list were nine names. In order, they were Henry Wilson Coil, Joseph Fort Newton, Albert G. Mackey, Carl H. Claudy, H. L. Haywood, Alphonse Cerza, Robert F. Gould, Allen E. Roberts, and finally, Albert Pike. Henry Coil led the list with the recommendation of eleven of the Grand Lodges, while Albert Pike was recommended by only four of them. In other words, forty-six Grand Masters (92 percent) had no comments on Pike. In spite of this, Ankerberg and Weldon cite Coil and Pike almost equally, about thirty times each.

Manley Palmer Hall, on the other hand, received so few recommendations that Rev. Ankerberg and Dr. Weldon omitted his standing from their list of Masonic authorities. Yet Hall is also cited some twenty-five times. Hall's books are presented as the writings of a "33d Degree Mason."[4] As noted in chapter 1, Hall wrote the books used by Rev. Ankerberg and Dr. Weldon more than twenty-five years before he became a Mason. Wouldn't honesty, therefore, require them to inform their readers that these books were written before Mr. Hall had any personal knowledge of Masonry? Of course, this would have lessened the impact of Hall's private (and controversial) interpretations of Freemasonry.

Significantly, Rev. Ankerberg and Dr. Weldon make good use of unfriendly and questionable sources: about 250 of their endnotes (33 percent) include anti-Masonic publications.

Jonathan Blanchard and the Scottish Rite

Of the many "authorities" cited by Rev. Ankerberg and Dr. Weldon, one of their most important is Jonathan Blanchard, who founded Wheaton College, "For Christ and His Kingdom," in 1860. President Blanchard, a social reformer and abolitionist, edited *Scotch Rite Masonry Illustrated* (1887), an exposé of purported Masonic rituals (figure 4-1). In the first editions of their book Rev. Ankerberg and Dr. Weldon claimed Blanchard was a "former Sovereign Grand Commander and a 33rd Degree Mason."[5] The Sovereign Grand Commander is the presiding officer of a Scottish Rite Supreme Council and the Thirty-third Degree is the highest degree of the Rite. Surely, the testimony of such a high-ranking Scottish Rite Mason is something too good to pass up. However, the truth is that *Jonathan Blanchard was never a Mason*, much less a Sovereign Grand Commander. He was an anti-Mason from his youth, as Clyde S. Kilby's biography of Blanchard makes quite clear.[6]

After Rev. Ankerberg's and Dr. Weldon's misrepresentation of Blanchard was exposed by Arturo de Hoyos in 1992,[7] they revised their book and removed the false claim. However, no notice of correction was provided for the new editions; rather, they hoped the episode would quietly fade into the background. It is sadly ironic that Rev. Ankerberg and Dr. Weldon took a life-long anti-Mason and falsely claimed he was one of the two highest-ranking Scottish Rite Masons in the country. It's easy, though, to see how shallow research could lead to this mistake. The title page of *Scotch Rite Masonry Illustrated* states that the ritual was by an unidentified "Sovereign Grand Commander, 33°," while Rev. Jonathan Blanchard wrote the historical sketch and analysis. Since *Scotch Rite Masonry Illustrated* is virulently anti-Masonic, however, Ankerberg and Weldon didn't feel the need to do any further research to satisfy their ends.

Anti-Masons seem satisfied that if something appears in print and is

44   *Is It True What They Say about Freemasonry?*

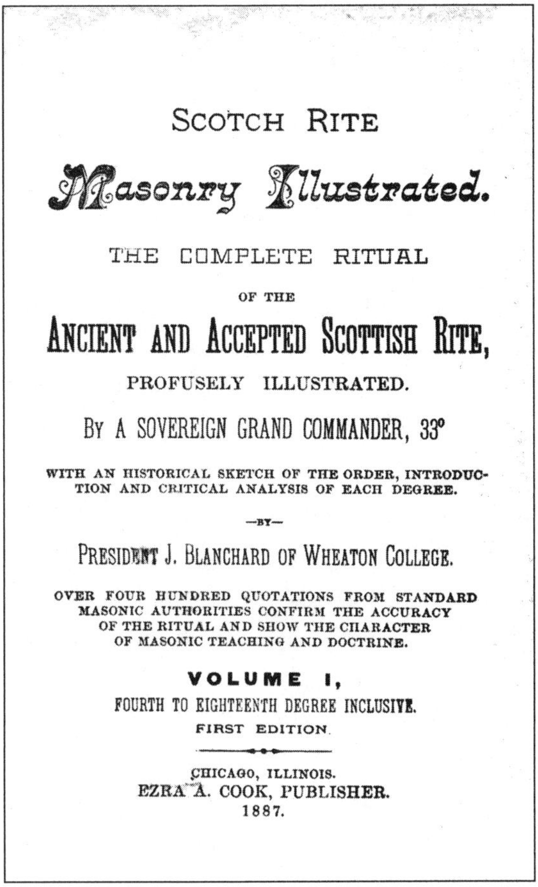
SCOTCH RITE

Masonry Illustrated.

THE COMPLETE RITUAL

OF THE

ANCIENT AND ACCEPTED SCOTTISH RITE,

PROFUSELY ILLUSTRATED.

BY A SOVEREIGN GRAND COMMANDER, 33°

WITH AN HISTORICAL SKETCH OF THE ORDER, INTRODUCTION AND CRITICAL ANALYSIS OF EACH DEGREE.

—BY—

PRESIDENT J. BLANCHARD OF WHEATON COLLEGE.

OVER FOUR HUNDRED QUOTATIONS FROM STANDARD MASONIC AUTHORITIES CONFIRM THE ACCURACY OF THE RITUAL AND SHOW THE CHARACTER OF MASONIC TEACHING AND DOCTRINE.

VOLUME I,

FOURTH TO EIGHTEENTH DEGREE INCLUSIVE.

FIRST EDITION.

CHICAGO, ILLINOIS.

EZRA A. COOK, PUBLISHER.

1887.

Figure 4-1. Title page of the first edition of *Scotch Rite Masonry Illustrated,* with historical sketch and analysis by Jonathan Blanchard. This virulently anti-Masonic book is an exposure of Cerneauism, an illegitimate pseudo-Masonic organization. Archives, Supreme Council, 33°, SJ.

negative about Freemasonry, it must be true. The rituals exposed in Blanchard's *Scotch Rite Masonry Illustrated,* for example, are usually accepted by anti-Masons as the gospel truth. This is what Rev. Ankerberg and Dr. Weldon have done. (Compare this with T. N. Sampson's initial acceptance and eventual rejection of Blanchard in chapter 9.) Blanchard's outdated book was actually an exposé of Cerneauism, an illegitimate Masonic organization founded by Joseph Cerneau and chiefly active in the 1800s.[8] Oaths of fealty and other references to the Cerneau "Supreme Council" appear repeatedly throughout Blanchard's exposé.[9] These references would have raised red flags to competent researchers, but Rev. Ankerberg and Dr. Weldon conveniently ignored or misunderstood them. Further, the article on "Scottish Rite Masonry" in *Coil's Masonic Encyclopedia*[10] (a book quoted about thirty times by

Rev. Ankerberg and Dr. Weldon) discusses the various names used by the Cerneau Supreme Councils, which the authors could have easily compared with Blanchard's book.

MASONIC "OATHS AND PENALTIES"

Even though Rev. Ankerberg and Dr. Weldon now know that *Scotch Rite Masonry Illustrated* is not the authentic ritual of the Scottish Rite, they continue to foist its text on their unwitting readers. In fact, Blanchard's text is so critical to Ankerberg's and Weldon's anti-Masonic agenda that it is referenced by them at least fifty times. For example, in a chapter in their revised edition entitled "Swearing Oaths," they reproduce eight oaths extracted from Blanchard in order to demonstrate that the Scottish Rite rituals include "physical penalties" connected with its initiation ceremonies. Because they knew Blanchard was not a Sovereign Grand Commander, they must have known the penalties were from Cerneauism and not a legitimate Supreme Council. In its early days, the Scottish Rite, like other Masonic organizations, did in fact include oaths (known as "obligations") with symbolic penalties. However, authors Ankerberg and Weldon conveniently overlook the context. Masonic rituals are symbolic dramas set in Biblical times, and the "oaths and penalties" were strong metaphors in keeping with that historical context. The *Illustrated Bible Dictionary* explains:

> OATH—a solemn statement or claim used to validate a promise. In Bible times, oaths were sometimes accompanied by protective curses to make sure the oaths were kept (1 Sam. 14:24; Gen. 24:41). . . .
>
> Sometimes people pronounced a curse upon themselves in connection with an oath they had taken. David vowed not to eat until evening with these words: "God do so to me, and more also, if I taste bread or anything else till the sun goes down." (2 Sam. 3:35). This was a strong pledge on his part that he expected to keep his promise.
>
> Oaths could be taken with symbolic gestures such as raising the hand (Gen. 14:22; Dan 12:7; Rev. 10:5–6) or touching the sex organs (Gen. 24:2; 47:29), possibly symbolizing a person's life and power. Oaths were taken very seriously (Ex. 20:7; Lev. 19:12). Lying about an oath could result in death (Ezek. 17:16–18). Jesus himself was bound by an oath (Matt. 26:63–64), as was Paul (2 Cor. 1:23; Gal. 1:20). Even God bound Himself by an oath to keep the promises He made to Abraham (Heb. 6:13–18).[11]

Ignoring all the evidence of Biblical oaths, anti-Masons will often quote Jesus' words, "swear not at all" (Matt. 5:33), without understanding their context. The Jamieson, Faussett, and Brown Bible commentary explains that the verse is not a condemnation of oaths per se, but rather that frivolous oaths are to be avoided:

> **But I say unto you, Swear not at all**—That this was meant to condemn swearing of every kind and on every occasion—as the Society of Friends and some other ultra-moralists allege—is not for a moment to be thought. For even Jehovah is said once and again to have sworn by Himself; and our Lord certainly answered upon oath to a question put to Him by the high priest; and the apostle several times, and in the most solemn language, takes God to witness that he spoke and wrote the truth; and it is inconceivable that our Lord should here have quoted the precept about not forswearing ourselves, but performing to the Lord our oaths, only to give a precept of His own directly in the teeth of it. Evidently, it is swearing in common intercourse and on frivolous occasions that is here meant.[12]

Interestingly, Jesus Christ not only used oaths, but He also used penalties. Responding to the attacks of Roman Catholic anti-Mason William J. Whalen in his book *Christianity and American Masonry*, the Reverend Dr. Lloyd Worley exposes the double standard of the anti-Masonic argument:

> Educated Freemasons everywhere say that Freemasonry uses allegory and symbol, and the parable constitutes the very fabric of our Fraternity. In other words, what the Roman Catholic Bishops are saying is that allegories, symbols or parables mean exactly what they say. But that, frankly is stupid, because allegories, symbols and parable mean more than they say. For example, will the Roman Catholic Bishops say this: "Either Jesus said what he meant, or he did not."
>
> I would hope not, because if they want to hold Jesus to the same criterion they use on the Masons, then at Mark 9:47, or Matthew 5:29, or Matthew 18:9 the Christian is bound to self mutilation if his eye (somehow) offends. And, under the same criterion, Jesus also recommends that the Christian cut off his hands and his feet if they offend (Matthew 5:30; Mark 9:43; Mark 9:45). Well, what's going on? Let me offer a slight rephrase of their Eminences' accusation: Either Jesus meant what he said, or he did not. If Jesus means what he says, the Christian is entering into a pact with his Lord by consenting to his own barbarous torture and mutilation should he break the moral code. . . . If Jesus does not mean what he says, then the Christian is agreeing to schoolboy nonsense in the Bible which borders on blasphemy!
>
> Now that doesn't sound very good, does it? And it doesn't sound very good because it is wrong. Jesus does not want his followers to mutilate themselves because it would be completely out of character with what we know of Jesus. Therefore, it is safe to think (as biblical scholars do) that Jesus' language was hyperbolic for the purpose of strongly and powerfully impressing upon his followers the importance of moral contract.

Well, friends, that is exactly what the so-called penalties of the Masonic obligations are for! They don't mean what they say, they mean much more than what they say. That is, the purpose of the so-called penalties is to cause a man which is impressed with what he is doing, to cause the man to ponder on and discuss what he has done— and all must agree that the so-called penalties have certainly achieved their desired purposes of impression and discussion.[13]

The truth of the matter is that the Scottish Rite eliminated all symbolic penalties from its obligations 150 years ago, as Ankerberg and Weldon must know:

> Albert Pike, in revising the rituals of the Southern Supreme Council of the Scottish Rite about 1855–1860, completely eradicated all such penalties from the degrees and substituted mental, moral, and symbolic condemnation, and that example was followed in the Northern Jurisdiction of the Scottish Rite about the middle of the 20th century.

The above quote is from an article on "Penalties" in *Coil's Masonic Encyclopedia*[14] (which, as we already noted, is cited repeatedly by Ankerberg and Weldon). Did they somehow misunderstand this article as well, or rather choose to ignore it because it reveals a major difference between Blanchard's exposé and the authentic rituals of the Scottish Rite?

It is difficult to believe that Rev. Ankerberg and Dr. Weldon misunderstood all the articles which contradict their claims. Rather, the evidence suggests that they are selectively picking quotes which *appear* to support their case. Thus, they quote *Coil* and other Masons only when they seem to support their case.

MISREPRESENTATION

As noted in chapter I, Freemasonry has no individual or universal authorities when it comes to the interpretation of its rituals and symbols. However, it makes sense that Rev. Ankerberg and Dr. Weldon want to talk about "authorities." They want something comparable to the *ex cathedra* and *imprimatur* of Catholicism, that is, official declarations or publications which are binding on the beliefs of its members. A rough, but useful analogy would be to contrast Catholics (who have extra-Biblical authorities, such as bishops or

Is It True What They Say about Freemasonry?

the Pope) and Baptists (who have none). Just as Baptist "authority" is limited to the individual's understanding of the Bible, *Masonic "authority" is limited to the individual Grand Lodge laws which govern the administrative affairs of the Fraternity within their private jurisdictions.* This means that the newly made Mason has as much right to interpret the symbols to his own needs as the officers of his lodge do to theirs. This freedom naturally results in diverse opinions. Because Masonic rituals vary around the world, the symbols are likewise variously interpreted. For example, in much of the United States, the trowel is symbolically used for "spreading the cement of brotherly love and affection,"[15] while in the Grand Land Lodge of Germany it is used to "figuratively wall up and cement cracks and tears in your heart against the assaults of the vices."[16]

Although Freemasonry is replete with symbolism, much of it is not interpreted in the rituals at all. Albert Pike explained:

> We teach the truth of none of the legends we recite. They are to us but parables and allegories, involving and enveloping Masonic instruction; and vehicles of useful and interesting information. They represent the different phases of the human mind, its efforts and struggles to comprehend nature, God, the government of the Universe, the permitted existence of sorrow and evil. To teach us wisdom, and the folly of endeavoring to explain to ourselves that which we are not capable if understanding, we reproduce the speculations of the Philosophers, the Kabalists, the Mystagogues and the Gnostics. **Every one being at liberty to apply our symbols and emblems as he thinks the most consistent with truth and reason and with his own faith, we give them such an interpretation only as may be accepted by all.**[17]

Ignoring this, Rev. Ankerberg and Dr. Weldon stoop to quoting the fanciful speculations of *non-Masons* while representing them as "Masonic."

Examples of this are their citations from "Djwhal Khul" (a "spirit guide" of occultist Alice Bailey),[18] theosophist Isabel Cooper Oakley,[19] and mystics Helena P. Blavatsky[20] and Corrine Heline.[21] The writings of these women have never been adopted as "authoritative" by any Grand Lodge; neither were they among the writers recommended by the twenty-five Grand Masters.

The other side of this coin demonstrates the inequity of this practice. Would Rev. Ankerberg and Dr. Weldon consider it fair for us to quote the writings or teachings of Rev. Jim Jones, David Koresh, or Christian white supremacists as representative of mainstream Christianity? If we apply the techniques that Rev. Ankerberg and Dr. Weldon use against Masonry, we begin to see how unfair their practices really are.

THE TEACHINGS OF A "LEADING CHRISTIAN"

Former Ku Klux Klan member and Louisiana political hopeful, David Duke, not only considers himself a Christian, but also considers Rev. Ankerberg and Dr. Weldon among his Christian brothers. This is demonstrated in his article "Christianity and Race" when he wrote:

> No race is so intrinsically Christian as the European, and I view all denominations that follow Christ whether they be Baptists or Catholics, Russian Orthodox or Methodist, Pentecostal or Mormons, as brothers in Christ. We may differ somewhat in our interpretation of the Scriptures, but all of us share our faith in Him.[22]

It is worth noting that many self-professed Christians consider Mr. Duke a "leading Christian" and an "authority" on the Bible and Christianity. As such, we continue to excerpt from his article, "Christianity and Race."

> Innocent children were killed simply because they were of an enemy tribe. As far as inter-racial marriage is concerned, there are unmistakable passages where God commanded, "You shall not make marriages with them;" [Deuteronomy] 7:2.
> When the Lord Thou [sic] God shall deliver them before thee; thou shalt smite them, and utterly destroy them, not show mercy unto them; Neither shalt thou make marriages with them; your daughter thou shalt not give unto his son, nor his daughter shalt thou take unto thy son. . . . For thou art a hold [sic] people unto the Lord Thy God: the Lord thy God has chosen thee to be a special people unto himself, above all people that are upon the face of the earth. (Deuteronomy 7:2–6)
> It goes on to say that if Israelites marry non-Israelites, "so will the anger of the Lord be kindled against you."
> As I read these words, I remembered my Bible study lessons of the proofs of Jesus' divinity, one being the "purity" of his line. I found that Genocide and forbidding of mixed marriages were not the only means utilized in the Bible to protect the bloodline of the Israelites. Separation or segregation is also clearly advocated.

Mr. Duke and other "Christian racial purists" use Biblical passages to oppose race mixing. Some of these "Christians" use the Bible to justify the murder of infants of mixed races. Although we cannot say how closely these

Is It True What They Say about Freemasonry?

views reflect the sentiments of Rev. Ankerberg and Dr. Weldon, they are nonetheless espoused by a self-confessed, Bible-believing Christian who considers them among his peers. On closer examination, we discover that the central religious beliefs of Mr. Duke's Christianity appear to be the same as those espoused by Rev. Ankerberg and Dr. Weldon.

If Rev. Ankerberg and Dr. Weldon protest that Mr. Duke's opinions do not represent their views of Christianity, or that merely professing Christ does not make anyone an authority on Christianity, then we similarly observe that neither the reception of the Thirty-third Degree, the appointment to a Masonic office, nor the popularity of a Masonic author makes anyone a Masonic "authority."

None of this seems to matter to Rev. Ankerberg and Dr. Weldon, however, for just as they misrepresented Jonathan Blanchard's credentials, they are satisfied to use other questionable "authorities" as long as they serve their purpose (selling their book). For example, as detailed elsewhere in this work, ex-Mason Jim Shaw was never a Past Master of a Blue Lodge, a Past Master of all Scottish Rite bodies, or a Thirty-third Degree Mason, as alleged by himself, Rev. Ankerberg, and Dr. Weldon.[23] However, as his book serves their needs, it is likewise too valuable to discard, even though it is another false witness.

ANTI-MASONIC "AUTHORITIES" OF CHOICE

It is worth noting that several of the "authorities" relied on by Rev. Ankerberg and Dr. Weldon have difficulty keeping facts straight. For example, they cite Dr. Shildes Johnson, who lists numerous "occult" groups which supposedly influenced Freemasonry. Among these groups are the Rosicrucians, the Golden Dawn, and the Illuminati. As with many of their allegations, no evidence is provided, only an accusation. Dr. Johnson's charges are particularly specious.

The modern fraternity of Freemasonry was founded in 1717, well before any of the modern Rosicrucian or occult movements. To begin with, there is much doubt whether an ancient Rosicrucian brotherhood ever existed. What is certain, however, is that modern Rosicrucian movements have no historical or lineal connection to the original phenomena.[24] Some Masonic groups have borrowed the Rosicrucian name and symbolism for their allegories,[25] but they do not assert a historical connection to the original movement any more than the Scottish Rite, Northern Masonic Jurisdiction, asserts that its 24°, "Prince of the Tabernacle," has historical ties to the Native American allegory which forms the basis of its drama.[26]

The Golden Dawn was an English occult fraternity begun in 1887, but by 1900 it fragmented due to internal strife. There are numerous groups claiming to be the Golden Dawn today; most of them are androgynous and they are all non-Masonic.[27]

The Illuminati, founded in 1776, was the brain-child of the notorious anti-cleric Adam Weishaupt. Although he infiltrated a Masonic lodge to attract members, the Elector of Bavaria outlawed the Illuminati in 1785 and its members were arrested as Weishaupt fled. His order collapsed and its secret papers were published. There are no traces of the Illuminati in Freemasonry today, nor did it influence any other than a few Masonic lodges in Bavaria over 200 years ago.[28]

Another "authority" cited by Rev. Ankerberg and Dr. Weldon is ex-Mason Jack Harris, whose book, *Freemasonry: The Invisible Cult in Our Midst*, was available with two booklets for a $20.00 "gift" to *The John Ankerberg Show* (comparison shoppers can buy Mr. Harris's paperback for as little as $1.75 on the Internet).[29] The back of Mr. Harris's book touts him as ". . . one of the most knowledgeable living authorities on the history, symbolic ritualism, and purposes of Freemasonry." Mr. Harris not only uses the bogus Léo Taxil quote, but also relies on inaccurate exposés. For example, Mr. Harris quotes an extract (without giving the source) of the Knight Templar obligation from a reprint of the anti-Masonic book, *Revised Knight Templarism Illustrated*.[30] Whatever Mr. Harris's experience in Masonry may have been, he never encountered the Taxil quote or the inaccurate Knight Templar obligation in a Masonic lodge. These are deceptions he maliciously repeats.

Even when citing authentic information, Rev. Ankerberg and Dr. Weldon abuse their sources. Thus, when quoting a paragraph from a ceremony used to install the officers of a Scottish Rite "Chapter of Rose Croix," they omit a significant part of the text (omitted text is in **bold**):

Is It True What They Say about Freemasonry?

> Teach the Knights to learn something more than the mere formulas and phrases of the ceremonial; persuade them to read the history and study the philosophy of Masonry; induce them to seek to learn the meanings of the symbols; **show them how, among the heterogeneous and incoherent mass of Masonic writings, to separate the diamonds from the worthless sands; and endeavor to improve them, by counsel and discourse, by way of conduct and conversation.**[31]

The omitted portion clearly demonstrates that Masons are cautioned concerning the existence of many worthless "Masonic" writings (just as there are nonsensical books on scientific and religious subjects). Yet Rev. Ankerberg and Dr. Weldon rely on several of the books in the "incoherent mass" to present their distorted view of Freemasonry.

One of their questionable sources is W. L. Wilmshurst, whom they label a "leading English Mason."[32] It would be interesting to know what criterion was used to arrive at this honor, because Wilmshurst's writings were challenged during his lifetime and continue to be criticized by members of the premiere Masonic research lodge (Quatuor Coronati, No. 2076, London):

> Even in the contexts of their times [J.S.M.] Ward, [A.E.] Waite, [W.L.] Wilmshurst et al. got it wrong and were reading into Freemasonry a great deal that is not present. Masonic writers of any period cannot, of course, forecast what a future generation's attitudes will be but they still have a duty to be accurate and to say when they are giving factual information and when they are speculating or giving personal interpretations. That is my complaint against such writers: their writings give the impression that they are speaking for Freemasonry and that theirs is the true interpretation—and it is not just a complaint with the benefit of hindsight but also one that their contemporaries lodged against them for so doing.[33]

Rev. Ankerberg and Dr. Weldon have a penchant (perhaps even a borderline fixation) for titles which sound authoritative to the non-Mason, and they often use irrelevant appellations when referencing the writers they quote. For example, they are quick to mention when a Masonic author holds an honorary Thirty-third Degree. If the cited author does not hold this honor, he is likely referenced by flattering appellations. For example, in addition to Wilmshurst, we find A. E. Waite and Joseph Fort Newton called "leading Masons," although no reason is indicated why they should be considered such. If "leading Mason" means a Past Master, or other officer of a lodge, then the ranks swell by tens, if not by hundreds of thousands. Authors such as Joseph Fort Newton and Harold Van Buren Voorhis were indeed prodigious writers, and they may still be popular, but they never claimed to write authoritatively for Freemasonry. R. Swinburne Clymer is called "a high Mason" (whatever that means) and Harold Van Buren Voorhis is denominated "a true Masonic giant." Our anti-Masonic authors have not bothered to keep up with the times. Clymer and Voorhis both died years before Ankerberg and Weldon wrote their book, but are referred to as if still living.[34]

After studying Rev. Ankerberg's and Dr. Weldon's "authorities" it is difficult to avoid this conclusion: a "leading Mason" or "Masonic scholar" is anyone who makes a statement useful to their purposes.

THE "MASONIC RELIGION"

There are few things which incite as much passion, or fanaticism, as religious zeal. The history of the Inquisition, the witch hunts of colonial New England, and the Iranian revolution are sad testaments to abused power and religious bigotry. Thousands suffered under the direction of religious authorities who deceived and intimidated their followers under the guise of "fighting Satan" and "saving souls."

These same watchwords are used today to marshal soldiers under the anti-Masonic banner, and Rev. Ankerberg and Dr. Weldon are willing to employ the techniques of propaganda to assist them.

> A prior general interest must exist for propaganda to be effective. Propaganda is effective not when based on *individual* prejudice, but when based on a *collective* center of interest, shared by the crowds.[35]

To assist them in this, Rev. Ankerberg and Dr. Weldon subtitled their book *A Christian Perspective*. As such, it is designed to have a broad appeal to all who profess Christianity, whether or not Rev. Ankerberg and Dr. Weldon agree with them (more sales equals more money). They have the hubris to speak for all who profess to follow Jesus Christ. Here, Ankerberg and Weldon want as many Christians as possible on their side, while elsewhere they deride the beliefs of Catholics, Mormons, and Jehovah's Witnesses, for example.[36] By drawing the lines as broadly as possible, "us" (Christians) vs. "them" (Freemasons), the uninformed Christian reader may be unwittingly biased from the outset, and the Christian Freemason is caught off guard.

A useful allegation to bias the Christian reader against Freemasonry is to claim that the fraternity is anti-Christian or, even more boldly, to claim that it is an anti-Christian religion. In fact, no Grand Lodge, no Supreme Council, and no appendant body claims to be, or functions as, a religion. Freemasonry has no unique religious doctrines, nor does it offer its own "plan of salvation." It is significant that Rev. Ankerberg and Dr. Weldon cannot produce any official documents to the contrary. Undeterred, they are content to ignore the facts and resort to innuendo and subterfuge.

Rev. Ankerberg and Dr. Weldon extract a number of passages from Pike's *Morals and Dogma* in an attempt to prove that Freemasonry is incompatible with Christianity. It is important to note that although Albert Pike described Freemasonry as "religious" he did not believe it was "a religion" in the sense that Judaism and Christianity are religions. He was explicit in this regard when he wrote: "Masonry is not a religion. He who makes of it a religious belief, falsifies and denaturalizes it." (*Morals and Dogma*, p. 161). He explained further what he meant when he wrote:

> Books, *to be of religious tendency in the Masonic sense*, need not be books of sermons, of pious exercises, or of prayers. Whatever inculcates pure, noble, and patriotic sentiments, or touches the heart with the beauty of virtue, and the excellence of an upright life, accords with *the religion of Masonry*. . . . (*Morals and Dogma*, p. 212; emphasis added)

Pike understood that this religious tendency, driven by a belief in God, motivates us to live good lives, and love our neighbors as ourselves. He stated that the "the universal, eternal, immutable religion" of Masonry could be summed up by two scriptures, which he quoted (*Morals and Dogma*, p. 219): "Pure religion and undefiled before God and the Father is this, to visit the fatherless and widows in their affliction, and to keep himself unspotted from the world" (James 1:27) and "Is not *this* the fast that I have chosen? to loose the bands of wickedness, to undo the heavy burdens, and to let the oppressed go free, and that ye break every yoke?" (Isaiah 58:6).

As a Christian, Pike was aware that faith alone, without works, is dead (see James 2:17–18). He therefore added, "The ministers of this religion are all Masons who comprehend it and are devoted to it; its sacrifices to God are good works, the sacrifices of the base and disorderly passions, the offering up of self-interest on the altar of humanity, and perpetual efforts

Rev. John Ankerberg and Dr. John Weldon   55

to attain to all the moral perfection of which man is capable" (*Morals and Dogma*, p. 219).

Although Rev. Ankerberg and Dr. Weldon, like other enemies of Freemasonry, have accused the fraternity of syncretism, Pike himself rejected this notion. He sought to acknowledge the truths, not the errors, of other people's beliefs. In his clearest statement on "the religion and Philosophy of Masonry" Pike wrote:

> That God is One, immutable, unchangeable, infinitely just and good; that Light will finally overcome Darkness,—Good conquer Evil, and Truth be victor over Error;—these, *rejecting all the wild and useless speculations of the Zend-Avesta, the Kabalah, the Gnostics, and the Schools*, are the religion and Philosophy of Masonry. (*Morals and Dogma*, p. 275, emphasis added)

JABULON, THE "MASONIC GOD"

What better way could there be to "prove" that Masonry is a religion than to reveal that Freemasons have secret modes of worship, mysterious names for God, or even their own secret god? This is just what some anti-Masons, including Rev. Ankerberg and Dr. Weldon, claim to do. The name of this god, they say, is *Jabulon*, which allegedly means "Jehovah-Baal-Osiris." Sensational as it sounds, this claim is not original. A study of their bibliography suggests that Rev. Ankerberg and Dr. Weldon based their charge on Stephen Knight's anti-Masonic book *The Brotherhood*.[37] The first anti-Mason to profit from this allegation seems to have been Walton Hannah[38] who was likely influenced by Dr. Hubert S. Box.[39]

As a "secret name for God" *Jabulon* is said to be revealed in the York Rite's Royal Arch Degree (the Seventh Degree), or the Scottish Rite's Royal Arch of Solomon Degree (the Thirteenth Degree, sometimes called Knights of the Ninth Arch).[40]

It is true that a similar word is found in some versions of these degrees (recalling that Masonic rituals vary the world over), but it is not a secret God or a secret name for God. It may be considered a poor linguistic attempt to present the name of God in three languages, such as "Dios-Dieu-Gott."

In making their claim, it is evident that Rev. Ankerberg and Dr. Weldon know little or nothing about the historical development of Masonic rituals.

Early French versions of the Royal Arch Degree relate a Masonic legend, or allegory, in which *Jabulon* was the name of an explorer, living in the time of Solomon, who discovered the ruins of an ancient temple.[41] Within the ruins, he found a gold plate upon which the name of God (Jehovah) was engraved. The context of these rituals makes it quite clear that the two names are never equated and the name of God is always spoken in reverence, just as it is in the fictional works *Ben Hur* and *The Robe*. As there are variants of this ritual, different forms of the explorer's name are also found (*Jabulum, Guibulum*, etc.). Other early sources seem to suggest, however, that it likely derived from Giblim,[42] or a misunderstanding of Hebrew letters on a Trinitarian device.[43]

The Meaning of Jabulon

Early Masons did not have the historical resources available to today's researchers. This handicap caused them to rely on their own ingenuity and they were limited in what they could write concerning the origins of this trilingual "word." However, for over a hundred years, the General Grand Royal Arch Chapter of the United States has clearly distinguished between the trilingual "word" and the name of God. In an article on the word "Bel," Masonic encyclopedist Albert Mackey tells us:

> It has, with *Jah* and *On*, been introduced into the Royal Arch as a representative of the Tetragrammaton [the Hebrew letters YHWH or JHVH, i.e., "Jehovah"], which it and the accompanying words have sometimes ignorantly been made to displace. At the session of the General Grand Chapter of the United States, in 1871, this error was corrected; and while the Tetragrammaton was declared to be the true omnific word, the other three were permitted to be retained as merely explanatory.[44]

An example of this pre-1871 misunderstanding is seen in Duncan's *Masonic Ritual and Monitor* (an outdated exposé cited by Rev. Ankerberg and Dr. Weldon some thirty times) which incorrectly declared the trilingual word to be the "Grand Omnific Royal Arch Word."[45] But Mackey's statement is clear: Jehovah is the "true omnific word" whereas *Jah, Bel*, and *On* are only explanatory. The misunderstanding appears to have arisen following (or perhaps due to) the anti-Masonic period of 1826–1842. If a statement in David Bernard's anti-Masonic exposé, *Light on Masonry* (1829), is accurate, the trilingual word (given as *Jahbuhlun*) was not used at all in some early American Royal Arch Chapters, and those that included it attached no religious explanation to it.[46] Like other exposés, however, Bernard's ritual texts cannot be fully trusted. Bernard and modern anti-Masons realized that lurid and sensational books sell readily to a gullible public. During the anti-Masonic period, William L. Stone withdrew from Freemasonry and published a book on the subject. In spite of this, he was honest enough to admit that "infamous interpolations" were added to Bernard's ritual texts. Concerning Bernard's Royal Arch exposé, Stone wrote, "The obligation has never been so given, within the range of my Masonic experience, and is not sanctioned or allowed by the Grand Chapter, having jurisdiction in the premises. Nor have I, as yet, found a Royal Arch Mason who recollects ever to have heard the obligation so given."[47]

But what did Mackey mean when he wrote that *Jah*, *Bel*, and *On* were "explanatory" of the name Jehovah? Unaware of its true origins, some early ritualists tried to explain the trilingual word using etymology. First, *Jabulon* was divided into syllables on the supposition that they were Hebrew, Chaldean, Assyrian, Egyptian, or other foreign words for God. Like Hebrew names in the Old Testament, some believed that *Jabulon* had a meaning which could be recovered. Old Testament names often had meanings which were intended to glorify God. For example, *Azaziah* means "Jehovah is strong," *Eliphaz* means "God is victorious," and *Elijah* means "Jehovah is my God." The following example explores possible roots of *Jah-Bel-On*. The current usage is discussed later.

> *Jah*—This could be a name of God used in Psalm 68:4, "Extol him that rideth upon the heavens by his name *JAH*, and rejoice before him."

> *Bel*—Rev. Ankerberg and Dr. Weldon accuse Freemasonry of paganism because some Masons tried to equate this syllable with the word *Baal*. Although Baal was the name of a Phoenician deity, it is also a Hebrew word meaning "lord" or "master,"[48] and when it forms part of a name, it was sometimes used to identify Jehovah. A son of

David, for example, is called both *Eliada*, "God Knows" (2 Samuel 5: 16) and *Beeliada*, "Baal knows" (I Chronicles 14:7). Another man, who was a friend of David, was named *Bealiah* (I Chronicles 12:5), meaning "Jehovah is Baal" or "Jehovah is Lord."[49] After winning a victory over the Philistines, David named the location *Baal-Perazim* (2 Samuel 5:20; I Chronicles 14: II), which means, "Lord of breaches."

> *On*—This Hebrew word means "force" or "power."[50] A more meaningful application is found in the *Septuagint*, an ancient Greek version of the Old Testament, wherein God announced Himself to Moses with the words *ego eimi ho On*, "I am the Being" (Exodus 3:14).[51] The words *ho On* mean "The Being," "The Eternal" or "The I AM." In the Greek New Testament the words *ho On* appear in Revelation 1:4, signifying "the One who is."[52]

Based on the above, possible meanings for *Jabulon* include "Jehovah, powerful Lord" or "Jehovah, the Lord, the I AM." Some English Royal Arch rituals suggested the syllables meant "Lord in Heaven, the Father of All," while some American rituals noted that the vowels in *Jah-Bel-On* added to the four letters which spell God's name in Hebrew (יהוה or YHWH), yielded the English pronunciation *Jehovah*. Early Bible translators combined the four letters with the vowels in the Hebrew word *adonai* (meaning "my Lord") to produce "Jahovah." Unable to find any sensible meaning in such speculations, other Grand Chapters eliminated the words altogether.

It is significant that Rev. Ankerberg and Dr. Weldon completely ignore the ritual text of Edmond Ronayne's *Chapter Masonry* (an exposé they cite elsewhere) in this matter and resort to allegation. The reason is simple. Ronayne fails to support their contention that *Jabulon* is a secret god. Rev. Ankerberg and Dr. Weldon are willing to quote Ronayne when he supports their agenda, but they ignore him when he contradicts their allegations.

According to Ronayne's exposé of the Royal Arch ritual, the presiding officer explains the Tetragrammaton and the trilingual word by saying:

This word is composed of four Hebrew characters, which you see inclosed within the triangle, corresponding in our language to JHVH, and cannot be pronounced without the aid of other letters, which are supplied by the key words on the three sides of the triangle, that being an emblem of Deity. The Syriac, Chaldeic [*sic*] and Egyptian words taken as one is therefore called the Grand Omnific Royal Arch Word.[53]

It thus becomes clear that however complex and misguided the early attempts were to find a meaning for this word, *Jabulon* is not a special or secret Masonic god. This claim is merely another invention of anti-Masonry.

ANKERBERG AND WELDON AT A GLANCE

At the end of their book, Rev. Ankerberg and Dr. Weldon provide a brief summation of their work which they call "Masonry at a Glance." Putting the shoe on the other foot and using Rev. Ankerberg and Dr. Weldon's techniques, the reader can draw the following conclusions:

General Information

- **Names:** John Ankerberg and John Weldon.

- **Goals:** Injure Freemasonry while attempting to maintain an appearance of piety; sell as many copies of their books as possible.

- **Theology:** Uncertain, but they have been embraced as "brothers in Christ" by David Duke, the Christian White Supremacist.

- **Practices:** Modeled on the techniques effectively used during the Inquisition and witch hunts: accuse the enemy of Satanism by using dubious witnesses. Innuendo and subterfuge acceptable.

- **Historic Antecedents:** Hitler, Mussolini, Franco, Kohmeni, and other ardent anti-Masons.

- **Spheres of Influence:** Church, radio, television, books, and pamphlets.

Is It True What They Say about Freemasonry?

- **Ethics:** Subjective, relative, amoral. Use of false witnesses, misinformation, and exaggerated "authorities" justifiable ("the end justifies the means").

- **Worldview:** Uncertain. Possibly conspiratorial and paranoid.

- **Source of Authority:** Themselves, but they try to make their followers believe they are acting as Christ's servants.

- **Key Themes:** Intolerance. Authors present themselves as a sure guide to truth.

- **Attitude to Other Religions:** Condescending. The authors make their living in part by condemning the religious beliefs of others.

- **Key Literature:** Chiefly anti-Masonic and historically inaccurate works. "Prooftexting" of authentic information is common.

False Claims

- Jonathan Blanchard's anti-Masonic exposé represents the true Scottish Rite rituals.

- Jim Shaw was a 33° Mason and Past Master of all Scottish Rite bodies.

- Manley Palmer Hall was a 33° Mason at the time he wrote the books cited by Ankerberg and Weldon.

- "Djwhal Khul" was a Mason.

- The "Masonic" writings of Isabel Cooper-Oakley and Corrine Heline are authoritative (if not, why are they cited?).

- The Scottish Rite uses penalties.

- *Jabulon* is the name of a Masonic god.

- Masonry is a religion.

- Masonry is occult.

- Masonry offers a system of salvation.

- Masonry is the one true religion.

- Masonry is intolerant of religion.

- Masonry dishonors the Bible and other religious literature.

- Masonry interferes with politics.

If Rev. Ankerberg and Dr. Weldon somehow "accidentally" made their false allegations or uttered their half-truths and lies unwittingly, they are unsafe guides. If they did this intentionally, we are reminded of the judgment in Proverbs 14:5, "A faithful witness will not lie: but a false witness will utter lies."

Chapter 5

Pastor Ron Carlson: Christian Ministries International[1]

False words are not only evil in themselves, but they infect the soul with evil.

—**Plato**

Pastor Ron Carlson is the founder and president of Christian Ministries International in Minnetonka, Minnesota.[2] With his sons Jason and Jared they constitute a ministry, which is professionally anti-Masonic in that they partially support themselves and their ministry by selling audiocassettes of his sermons which "expose" the "secrets" of Masonry. The quotations that follow come from one such cassette sermon, "Freemasonry and the Masonic Lodge," which appears to have been preached in Green Bay, Wisconsin. Early in his undated sermon, he establishes his credentials and objectivity:

> Now understand that what I am going to say tonight is not from anti-Masonic writings. I have spent two years almost full time researching Freemasonry and the Masonic lodge. What we are going to be sharing tonight is from the authoritative works of Masons themselves.[3]

In concluding his sermon, Pastor Carlson summarizes the results of his research, "Freemasonry is not of God, it's from the pit of Hell."[4]

His years of study lead us to expect a higher standard of research and documentation than from other critics. His position as a minister of the

Gospel lets us expect a love of truth and a sense of fairness. His promise to use "authoritative works of Masons" lets us expect accurate, factual statements. Sadly, these expectations are not met.

THE STRAW MAN FALLACY

Throughout his sermon, Pastor Carlson uses the tactics of the "Straw Man Fallacy"[5] to attack Freemasonry. The tactic is aptly named because it illustrates its self-inherent flaw. Imagine a person, wishing to destroy a real enemy, creating a straw man. Perhaps he even dresses it in the clothes of his enemy, or pins the enemy's photo on the straw man's face. Now imagine the straw man, placed in a boxing ring and an audience invited to watch the match. Our hero, donned in shorts and gloves, bobbing and weaving around the ring, eventually destroys his creation and then claims "victory" over the real enemy. This is essentially what Pastor Carlson does. He first creates easily refutable parodies of his enemies (famous Freemasons and the Masonic fraternity) and then destroys them. His self-created enemies do not have to be real; they only have to resemble his enemies for him to claim "victory." Perhaps you have seen this tactic used by enemies of the United States when they burn an actual straw-man effigy of Uncle Sam.

A SIN TO DIVULGE THE TRUTH

In common with many other anti-Masons, Pastor Carlson has chosen Albert Pike as one of his enemies. In the following example (and throughout his sermon), Pastor Carlson misquotes Pike's writings and then argues against the supposed offending passage.

> Let me read for you what Albert Pike says, page 545, concerning revealing any of the secrets, quote:
>
>> All the mysteries should be kept concealed, guarded by faithful silence, lest it should be inconsiderately divulged to the ears of the Profane. He sins against God who divulges to the unworthy the Mysteries confided to him. The danger is not merely in violating the truth, but in telling the truth.

Is It True What They Say about Freemasonry?

Albert Pike says it is a sin to divulge the truth. Now how different this is from what we read in God's word.[6]

Ironically, the truth is that Ron Carlson is not quoting Albert Pike. Here is what Pike actually wrote in *Morals and Dogma* (unacknowledged omissions by Pastor Carlson are struck out).

> ~~St. Ambrose, Archbishop of Milan, who was born in 340, and died in 393, says in his work *De Mysteriis*:~~ "All the Mystery should be kept concealed, guarded by faithful silence, lest it should be inconsiderately divulged to the ears of the Profane. . . . ~~It is not given to all to contemplate the depths of our Mysteries . . . that they may not be seen by those who ought not to behold them; nor received by those who cannot preserve them." And in another work:~~ "He sins against God, who divulges to the unworthy the Mysteries confided to him. The danger is not merely in violating the truth, but in telling truth, ~~if he allows himself to give hints of them to those from whom they ought to be concealed. . . . Beware of casting pearls before swine! Every Mystery ought to be kept secret; and, as it were, to be covered over by silence, lest it should rashly be divulged to the ears of the Profane. Take heed that you do not incautiously reveal the Mysteries!"~~

Pike was clearly quoting St. Ambrose on what he taught regarding the Christian Mysteries. It was, we find, a Christian Father who said it was a sin to tell the truth. We here discover that the pastor himself is guilty of what he accuses Masonic authorities of doing—he lies to the unwitting.

Pastor Carlson further compounds his deception as he gleefully tells his audience that:

> Albert Pike says it is a sin to divulge the truth. Now how different this is from what we read in God's word. Jesus says, "You shall know the truth, and the truth shall set you free." Jesus said, "I am the Truth." He said, "Go unto all the world and proclaim this good news." But the Masons say, "No, it is a sin for you to reveal truth."[7]

If we analyze Pastor Carlson's statement we find:

- He claims to be quoting Albert Pike when he was in fact quoting St. Ambrose, a Christian Father.

- He claims that the supposed words of Pike represent universal Masonic teachings by stating, "But the Masons say. . . ."

- He ignores that Pike wrote in his preface, "Every one is entirely free to reject and dissent from whatsoever herein may seem to be untrue or unsound." (*Morals and Dogma*, p. iv).

If unchecked, the subtle manipulation of source material aids both the construction and destruction of the ersatz Albert Pike by allowing the pastor to build on a false premise. Significantly, Pastor Carlson spouts his glib remarks on the lack of truth in Masonry in spite of the fact that virtually every American "Monitor of the Lodge" advocates the cultivation of this virtue:

> The principal tenets of our profession are three: *Brotherly Love, Relief and Truth.* . . . Truth is a divine attribute, and the foundation of every virtue. To be good and true, is the first lesson we are taught in Masonry. On this theme we contemplate, and by its dictates endeavor to regulate our conduct. Hence, while influenced by this principle, hypocrisy and deceit are unknown among us, sincerity and plain dealing distinguish us, and the heart and tongue join in promoting each other's welfare, and rejoicing in each other's prosperity.[8]

How Carlson can make the unfair allegations he does when authorized Grand Lodge publications prove contrary is astounding. Surely, he must have encountered the above paragraph on truth often during his two years of intensive research, because it appeared in every randomly selected American Blue Lodge Monitor, or book of ceremonies, we inspected. Since the publication of Thomas Smith Webb's *The Freemason's Monitor* (1797) and Jeremy Cross's *True Masonic Chart* (1820), which were models for later publications, the paragraph has appeared in virtually all American monitors. Similarly, British publications contain this paragraph almost verbatim, beginning with William Preston's *Illustrations of Masonry* (1772) to the current "Lectures of the Three Degrees" (first lecture, sixth section). Upon checking unauthorized publications, we found it in a host of ritual exposures, English and American, spanning over a hundred years.

A BOOK OF NONSENSE?

Perhaps the most flagrant demonstration of his ability to distort the truth is Pastor Carlson's claim that Albert Pike ridiculed Christianity and the Bible. Albert Pike revered Jesus Christ "above all the other great teachers" (*Morals and Dogma*, pp. 718–721), but now, Carlson has the straw man Pike insult the Bible. (Unacknowledged omissions by Pastor Carlson are struck out while his additions are in boldface.)

Well, you want to know what Masonry thinks of Christianity? First of all, concerning the Bible. Albert Pike, page eleven, *Morals and Dogma*, says, quote:

> The Holy Bible, Square and Compass, are not only styled the Great Lights in Masonry, but they are also technically called the *Furniture* of the Lodge; ~~and, as you have seen, it is held that there is no Lodge without them. This has sometimes been made a pretext for excluding Jews from our Lodges, because they cannot regard the New Testament as a holy book.~~ The Bible is an indispensable part of the furniture of the Christian Lodge, only because it is a sacred book of the Christian Religion. The Hebrew Pentateuch in a Hebrew Lodge, [**and**] the Koran in a ~~Mohammadan one~~ [**Moslem Lodge**], belong on the Altar; and one of these, ~~and the Square and Compass, properly understood, are the Great Lights by which a Mason must walk and work.~~
>
> The obligation of the candidate is always to be taken on [**to obey**] the sacred book or books of his own religion, that he may deem it more solemn and binding. . . .

So they tell us that the Bible is considered a piece of furniture in the lodge; and that it is no more valuable than the Koran, or any other scriptures of any other religions, it's simply a piece of religious literature equal with all the others. Page seventeen we read: "The Holy Scriptures were an entirely modern addition to the Lodge."

You know, but Masons will tell me, "But we got the Bible on our altar." Albert Pike says, quote:

> The Holy Scriptures were an entirely modern addition to the Lodge, like the terrestrial and celestial globes on the columns of the portico. Thus the ancient has been denaturalized by incongruous additions.

"The Bible has no place there," he is saying.[9]

In this quotation, Pike is using the technical terminology of the Craft when he refers to the *Holy Bible*, *Square*, and *Compasses* as the *furniture* of the lodge. They are, in fact, so important that without these in place a lodge is not *furnished* and cannot open. Pike's statement declaring the Bible a "modern addition" refers to the addition of a drawing of the Bible atop the symbol of the point within a circle (see figure 5-1), as he very clearly states in *Morals and Dogma* on pages 16–17. Pike believed that the symbol of the point within a circle was previously depicted without the Bible over it, and without the Saints John on its side. He was not saying, as Pastor Carlson imputes, that the Bible does not belong upon the altar of the lodge.

Figure 5-1. The point within a circle showing the Bible and the Holy Saints John. From Albert G. Mackey, *A Manual of the Lodge* (New York: Clark and Maynard, 1866), p. 56.

Pastor Carlson now makes what we believe is his most dishonest misrepresentation of Pike:

> Page 744 he goes on to say, quote (listen to what Albert Pike, the leading authority says):
>
>> The Bible, with all the allegories it contains, expresses, in an incomplete and veiled manner only, the religious science of the Hebrews. The doctrine of Moses and the Prophets, identical at bottom with that of the ancient Egyptian Mysteries, also had its outward meaning and its veils. The Hebrew books were written only to recall to memory the traditions; and they were written in Symbols unintelligible to the Profane. The Pentateuch and the prophetic poems were merely elementary books of doctrine, morals, and literature; and the true secret and traditional philosophy was only written afterward, under veils still less transparent. Thus it was that a second Bible was born, the New Testament, unknown to, or rather uncomprehended by the Christians; a collection of monstrous absurdities.
>
> Unquote. Now you tell me how any Mason can be a Christian, when they say the New Testament is a collection of, quote, "monstrous absurdities," unquote.[10]

According to Pastor Carlson, Albert Pike deemed the New Testament a collection of "monstrous absurdities." Carlson's quotation of Pike, if accurate,

Is It True What They Say about Freemasonry?

would indeed reflect a prejudice against Christianity. Upon checking *Morals and Dogma*, however, we again discover that Pike has been misquoted. Besides putting words into Pike's mouth, Carlson misunderstood the context of Pike's remarks, which concerned not the New Testament, but the Jewish Talmudic writings. (As before, Pastor Carlson's unacknowledged omissions are struck out and his additions are boldface.)

> The Bible, with all the allegories it contains, expresses, in an incomplete and veiled manner only, the religious science of the Hebrews. The doctrine of Moses and the Prophets, identical at bottom with that of the ancient Egyptians, also had its outward meaning and its veils. The Hebrew books were written only to recall to memory the traditions, and they were written in Symbols unintelligible to the Profane. The Pentateuch and the prophetic poems were merely elementary books of doctrine, morals, ~~or liturgy~~ [**and literature**]; and the true secret and traditional philosophy was only written afterward, under veils still less transparent. Thus a second Bible was born, [**the New Testament**], unknown to, or rather uncomprehended by, the Christians; a collection they say, of monstrous absurdities; ~~a monument, the adept says, wherein is everything that the genius of philosophy and that of religion have ever formed or imagined of the sublime; a treasure surrounded by thorns; a diamond concealed in a rough dark stone~~.

Read in context, this clearly says that the Christians considered the Talmudic works absurd.[11] It is difficult to see how Pastor Carlson confused the issue and his unjustified insertion of the words "the New Testament" into Pike's text only amplified his error. As he did in the case of St. Ambrose, Archbishop of Milan, Carlson makes Pike say something he never did.

Either Carlson intentionally distorted Pike, or he could not understand his writings and, therefore, misrepresented them. Either of these options makes Carlson an unsafe guide.

Luciferian Masonry

Pastor Carlson displays his research skills and sense of fairness by foisting the Léo Taxil hoax upon his audience.

> Well, friends, it gets worse. Albert Pike, who was the Supreme Pontiff of all Freemasonry, speaking on July 14, 1889, to the twenty-three Supreme Councils of the World, said this, I quote. If you're a Mason, listen to the leading authority as to what Freemasonry teaches. Albert Pike, July 14, 1889, to the twenty-three Supreme Councils of the World said, quote:

> That what we must say to the crowd is: We worship a God, but it is a God that one adores without superstition. To you, Sovereign Grand Inspectors General, we say this, that you may repeat it to the Brethren of the 32nd, 31st and 30th degrees: The Masonic religion should be, to all of its initiates of the high degrees, maintained in the purity of the Luciferian doctrine. Yes, Lucifer is God. The true and pure philosophic religion of Freemasonry is the belief in Lucifer.

Unquote. You can read in context, it goes on and it gets worse.[12]

This allegation by Pastor Carlson shows the inadequacy of his research and his naïve credulity. After spending "two years almost full time researching Freemasonry and the Masonic lodge," he still fell for Taxil's fake quotation. The context of the quote would lead a trusting listener to think it came from *Morals and Dogma*. It doesn't, and Pastor Carlson doesn't even hint where we "can read it in context." He didn't bother confirming the quotation, nor checking his sources, nor crediting the translator. But why should he? He'd already decided that Masonry is Satanic and the Taxil quotation just confirmed what he already believed.

Chapter 2 in this book, "Léo Taxil: The Hoax of 'Luciferian Masonry,'" thoroughly details the Taxil hoax and gives some of the abundant references available to those interested in the truth. *Taxil's forgeries were exposed over one hundred years ago* and the truth regarding his fraud has been widely published. It is difficult to believe that anyone could spend "two years almost full time researching Freemasonry and the Masonic lodge" and not discover the truth of the matter. It is especially deceptive for Pastor Carlson to invite his audience to "read [the quotation] in context," without citing his source, but leading his listeners to think he was quoting from *Morals and Dogma*. And this after assuring his listeners that he would refer only to the "authoritative works of Masons themselves."

TRYING TO STOP THE DISSEMINATION?

At the end of his talk, Pastor Carlson took several questions from the audience. Most of the questions are not intelligible on our audiotape, but they can be inferred from the answers. In answering the eighth question, Pastor

Carlson asserted with authority, "You won't—you cannot—find *Morals and Dogma* in a library."[13] The answer to question thirteen further highlights Pastor Carlson's research skills and his regard for accuracy.

> [*Answer to the thirteenth question*]: *Morals and Dogma?* Yeah, it's copyrighted. Yeah, "Entered according to Act of Congress, in the year 1871 in the Office of the Library of Congress." There is also . . . ah . . . a place down in Chicago where you can . . . uh . . . buy a copy, it's the publishing house for the Masonic lodge. And I wish I had the address with me. I'd give it to you, but . . . uh . . . if they have some in stock . . . uh . . . you can get one from them. Uh . . . though the last person I told that to, when they called down there—they just told me a few months ago that they had called down there—and . . . ah . . . the publishing house told them that they are now only giving them to the Masonic lodges, for the Thirty-Second Degree Masons. You can no longer buy it from their secret publishing house. And so, evidently . . . uh . . . they've heard about us and are trying to stop the dissemination of this information.[14]

Carlson contradicts himself here within a matter of seconds. First, he claims the Masonic publisher of *Morals and Dogma* is in Chicago, and if he had the address with him, he would give it to his audience, so copies could be ordered. He then turns right around and conveniently says the last person he told that to was refused a copy for not being a 32° Mason; the publisher now becomes a "secret publishing house." To top it off, Carlson's megalomania becomes apparent as he takes credit for the publisher's alleged refusal to sell the book.

We suggest this account is fictitious. *Morals and Dogma* has never been printed or published in Chicago.[15] There is no secret publishing house for Masonry. *Morals and Dogma* was originally published in 1871 for only 32° Masons, but it is widely available today from used book dealers, libraries, and over the Internet. The Supreme Council 33°, SJ, also sells used copies when they can be obtained.

If Pastor Carlson had bothered to check the public libraries near Eden Prairie, Minnesota, the location of his headquarters, he would have discovered the easy availability of *Morals and Dogma*. In February 1993, about the time he gave his sermon, there was a loan copy in the West St. Paul libraries and loan and reference copies in the Minneapolis libraries. These copies would have been available to Pastor Carlson through the Metropolitan Library Service Agency. Elsewhere in Minnesota, the public libraries of both Duluth and Winona have loan copies. Copies are plentiful over the Internet.

In April 2009, for example, the online book marketplace abebooks.com listed over 400 copies for sale, and there were reprint editions available from five publishers.

A little more research would also have revealed dozens of copies of *Morals and Dogma* in college and university libraries around the country.[16] And for those in Pastor Carlson's congregation who may have difficulty reading, *Morals and Dogma* is available from Recording for the Blind, Princeton, New Jersey.

Chapter 6

Pastor David S. Janssen:
"A Sermon on the Rituals
of Freemasonry"

A man's ignorance is as much his private property and as precious in his own eyes as his family Bible.

—Oliver Wendell Holmes,
The Young Practitioner

Pastor David S. Janssen's "A Sermon on the Rituals of Freemasonry" is an anti-Masonic sermon he delivered on September 28, 1997, at State College Christian and Missionary Alliance Church in State College, Pennsylvania.[1] The sermon was the decision of their *"entire leadership team,* or board of elders." Anti-Masons are generally content to condemn our fraternity based on their misunderstanding of the sources they haphazardly select, and Pastor Janssen is no exception. In this instance, the single source selected by Pastor Janssen was a 1914 printing of Charles T. McClenachan's *The Book of the Ancient and Accepted Scottish Rite of Freemasonry* (first edition 1867).[2] It is hardly possible to understand and fairly judge any complex topic by exposure to a single book, and in the case of Freemasonry, it is a sure way to get confused. (Imagine what impression of Christianity could result from only one book taken from the shelf in a library!) So much has been written about the fraternity from so many viewpoints that even intelligent Masons sometimes have difficulty sorting the credible from the incredible.

Throughout his sermon Pastor Janssen demonstrates his misunderstanding of both Freemasonry and its literature. He frequently implies that he has the inside scoop because of his discovery of McClenachan's book, which he calls "exceedingly rare" and "the Ritual" (it is neither).[3] (The transcript used in our first edition differed in minor points from the version posted on the Internet,[4] which the pastor apparently prefers. For this reason we will now cite exclusively from the Internet version.) Describing McClenachan's book, he says:

> This book was the first and last compilation of Scottish Rite Degrees published as a limited edition intended for assisting Masons through the Degrees of The Scottish Rite of Freemasonry. . . .
> The Ritual has been used from approximately 1885 through 1925 and perhaps up until today. It was the first and last compilation of the individual ritual degrees. McClenachan compiled the teachings of the different degrees from different books. Freemasonry published his work and went on to use it for approximately 40 years.[5]

Like the rest of the sermon, these remarks are so riddled with inaccuracies that we are obliged to examine them in some detail.

A LOOK AT SCOTTISH RITE *MONITORS*

It is, perhaps, a good idea to begin by observing that McClenachan's book was only a Scottish Rite monitor, not the ritual itself. As most Masons know, a monitor is a guide book containing some instructions, and selected brief *exoteric* (non-secret) extracts from the ceremonies, lectures, and rituals. Because monitors are intended for people familiar with the ritual, they generally do not provide the context of the selected excerpts, a fact which partially explains Pastor Janssen's misunderstanding. Pastor Janssen also appears to be ignorant of the fact that since the founding of the first Supreme Council in 1801, Scottish Rite rituals have undergone numerous refinements and revisions and differ worldwide today.[6] Even within the United States, there are significant differences between the ceremonies and rituals of the Northern Masonic Jurisdiction, the Southern Jurisdiction, and the Prince Hall Affiliation. The ceremonies sometimes differ so much that they are based on entirely different themes and have dramas set in different centuries. No matter how much they differ, however, they are all intended to teach moral lessons.

Pastor Janssen asserts that McClenachan's book was "the first and last compilation of Scottish Rite Degrees." The truth, however, is that even before the Scottish Rite was founded, excerpts of some of the ceremonies destined to become part of it were published in the United States. We know the majority of the Scottish Rite degrees came from a twenty-five degree system of Freemasonry, known as the "Order of the Royal Secret," which was founded by Etienne Morin, a Frenchman. Morin deputized several Masons to spread his rite throughout the New World (it took root in New Orleans as early as 1764). One of Morin's Masonic deputies was a Dutch Mason named Henry Andrew Francken. In 1767, Francken erected a "Lodge of Perfection" at Albany, New York, where he conferred the "Ineffable Degrees" (Fourth to Fourteenth Degrees) he received from Morin.[7] The first public description of these degrees occurred when Thomas Smith Webb published the first edition of his now-famous book, *The Freemason's Monitor* (1797).[8] The first part of Webb's *Monitor* was largely based on the work of William Preston, the renowned English Masonic ritualist,[9] but the second part of Webb's *Monitor* included "an account of the Ineffable Degrees of Masonry."

In 1801, the first Supreme Council of the 33rd Degree was organized in Charleston, South Carolina. In 1802, Webb issued a revised edition of his *Monitor* (which could now be considered the first Scottish Rite monitor), and between 1797 and 1825 almost twenty editions of Webb's *Monitor* were published.[10] Anyone familiar with the current Scottish Rite degrees in any American jurisdiction would appreciate how dramatically the rituals have changed since Webb's time.

In 1813, the Supreme Council at Charleston organized another Supreme Council in New York. From its beginning however, the latter Supreme Council was forced to contend with a rival body of dubious authority organized by a Frenchman named Joseph Cerneau.[11] Without going into detail, Cerneau's group claimed authority over the Scottish Rite degrees, even though it had never been properly chartered. Although the two bodies would contend for membership until 1867—when they eventually merged—it is important to bear in mind that the Cerneau group is considered to have been "irregular" (illegitimate) by the majority of Masonic historians.[12] Because they were both "Masonic," the ceremonies and rituals of both groups had similarities, but they were not the same.

Following an anti-Masonic period in American history (about which much has been written),[13] Freemasonry, including the Scottish Rite, began to recover, and about 1842 a small two-part Scottish Rite monitor entitled *Sublime Freemasonry* was published.[14] It included extracts from the ceremonies and rituals of the Ineffable Degrees (Fourth to Fourteenth Degrees) and the Council of Princes of Jerusalem (Fifteenth to Sixteenth Degrees). Again, a comparison of this text demonstrates revisions made between the time of this printing and Webb's *Monitor*.

Soon thereafter, both Cerneau Masons and members of the legitimate Supreme Council published numerous Scottish Rite monitors. One of the first published was by Henry C. Atwood, an enthusiastic Mason who had received the Thirty-third Degree in 1826, but who also participated in spurious branches of Masonry. He had served as Grand Master of two schismatic Grand Lodges in New York, as well as Grand Commander of two Cerneau "Supreme Councils." While serving in his first Cerneau Supreme Council, he published his book *The Master Workman*, a monitor which included a section on the Ineffable Degrees.[15] Two years later, the book was reprinted by Robert Macoy under the title *The True Masonic Guide*;[16] it continued in print for several years.

Jeremy L. Cross was a student of Thomas Smith Webb and was respected as the author/compiler of an improved monitor called *The Masonic Chart or Hieroglyphic Monitor* (1819). It included illustrations, but did not include any Scottish Rite material. Cross later joined Atwood's Cerneau group and in 1851 succeeded him as Grand Commander. The following year, Cross published *The Supplement to the Templar's Chart*, which contained instructions and extracts of the thirty Scottish Rite degrees as worked in the Cerneau Council.[17] It was reprinted for several years and appeared both as a separate publication and as the second half of his book, *The Templar's Chart*.

Masons belonging to the regular (legitimate) Scottish Rite bodies also printed monitors. Enoch T. Carson published the *Monitor of the Ancient and Accepted Rite* in 1858, which appeared as both a separate work[18] and the second half of a new edition of Webb's *Freemason's Monitor*.[19]

In considering these books, it is important to remember that Scottish Rite monitors reflected the ceremonies practiced in the year in which they were published, and were rarely updated to conform to subsequent ritual revisions. For example, the Supreme Council, Northern Masonic Jurisdiction, completed a revision of its degrees in 1860 and Will M. Cunningham prepared a monitor to accompany it. The published text appeared under the title *Manual of the Ancient and Accepted Scottish Rite* (1864).[20] Cunningham's Manual included a prefatory statement attesting to its accuracy by Killian H. Van Rensselaer, 33°, the Sovereign Grand Commander of the Supreme Council, Northern Masonic Jurisdiction. However, subsequent printings (such as the 1867 edition) failed to include any changes or modifications, even though the rituals had been revised. This problem also affected the liturgies or monitors of the Scottish Rite, Southern Jurisdiction. In 1953, its Committee on Ritual and Ceremonial forms reported, "It has also been brought to the attention of this Committee that the Liturgies published in 1877, and therefore with the approval of Albert Pike, do not agree with the present rituals."[21] Had Pastor Janssen done his homework, he would have been aware of this.

When Pastor Janssen was informed that McClenachan's monitor was outdated, and that there was no replacement, he quipped: "There has been no further compilation for good reason: Freemasonry did not want its secrets to be known." The truth of the matter is that the frequent ritual revisions in the Northern Masonic Jurisdiction make such a publication impractical. On the other hand, the Southern Jurisdiction has recently published *The Scottish Rite Ritual Monitor and Guide* (2007, 2009), which includes more material than any previous monitor.

CHARLES T. McCLENACHAN AND ALBERT PIKE

Prior to the Union of 1867, when the Cerneauists merged with the regular Supreme Council, Northern Masonic Jurisdiction, Charles T. McClenachan had been a member of three successive rival Supreme Councils. He had served as the Grand Master of Ceremonies in each of these three bodies and he would also hold the same position in the post-Union Supreme Council for nearly twenty years, from 1879 to 1896. He also served on the Supreme Council's Ritual Committee from 1868 to 1896.[22]

A study of the minutes of the rival Supreme Councils reveals that between 1864 and 1867, the "Supreme Grand Council" to which McClenachan belonged published its rituals in a five-volume set of books called *The Secret Directory*.[23] A careful survey of these rituals reveals they were largely a combination of "The Secret Directory of Manuscripts" (unpublished manuscript rituals) and Albert Pike's first revision of the rituals of the Supreme Council, SJ (the Charleston Council).

Albert Pike's influence on the Scottish Rite rituals must not be underestimated. Pike joined the Scottish Rite in 1853 and collected, as far as was within his ability, the rituals of every Masonic Rite and system. In 1855, the Supreme Council, Southern Jurisdiction, appointed him to a ritual committee, and in 1857, he published his so-called *Magnum Opus*, or first revision of the rituals, which was completed independently of other committee members.[24] Pike shared copies of his book with other prominent Masons throughout the United States, and McClenachan's Council possessed a copy. Although it was never adopted as the official ritual of the Southern Jurisdiction,[25] parts of it were used in the degrees of many jurisdictions, including *The Secret Directory*.

Pike was a keen student of philosophy and religion who believed that creating ritual drama with a quasi-historical setting would help Scottish Rite members appreciate man's attempt to discover truth and find his place in the universe. This was consistent with earlier Masonic allegories which set dramas in such places as an encampment of Knights Templar or King Solomon's Temple. Thus, dramas for one degree might be set in medieval times while another degree's might be during Old Testament times.

The purpose of Masonic allegory is not to teach historical or sectarian religious truths, but rather to teach the universal truths of ethics and virtue by presenting a lesson, usually in the form of a drama. As such, Masonic degrees might be compared with Shakespeare's plays. No sensible person would claim that Shakespeare's personal ideology was espoused by characters such as King Lear or Othello. Similarly, the words espoused by the characters in Masonic allegories ought not to be understood as "Masonic teachings" but rather as the sentiments of a character in a play. It is the play as a whole, not the specific words of one character, that teaches the lesson. This fact, lost on anti-Masons, often causes them to misunderstand the nature of fraternal ritual.

Although it neither wholly failed nor succeeded, Pike's *Magnum Opus* included far too much material for the average Mason to understand. This was due to his reliance on such sources as Godfrey Higgins's work *Anacalypsis* (1836), a massive two-volume 1,300-page "inquiry into the origin of languages, nations, and religions."[26] After twenty years of work on the rituals Pike confessed, "Undoubtedly our Rituals are very far from perfect. The task of revision was too great for the powers of a single man."[27] Aware of these shortcomings, he continued to revise the rituals for another ten years. Pike was careful to avoid teaching sectarian truths, but rather sought to teach the universal truths and ethics traditionally inculcated in Freemasonry. These practices, familiar to every Mason, include friendship, morality, brotherly love, honesty, reverence, integrity, patriotism, and the like. "To seek, therefore, to inculcate the truth of any particular creed, would be to make Masonry a realm of strife," Pike wrote.[28] Pike's Victorian writing style is sometimes difficult and confusing, even more so when removed from context. This is another reason why it is difficult for non-Masons to understand Masonic monitors.

McCLENACHAN'S BOOK

On October 20, 1864, the Supreme Council to which McClenachan belonged adopted the following resolution:

> *Whereas*, Great necessity exists for a definite, correct and authentic Manual of the degrees of the Ancient and Accepted Rite, which will materially aid those who are seeking light in this Order, and will be a guide to those who may have entered its portals, And
>
> *Whereas*, The Secret Directory, now far advanced in final establishment of all the minutiae of the Order, under the authority of the Supreme Council, should be carefully withheld from all not qualified to possess the same, and yet much of its contents freely distributed to those interested in the propagation of the Rite, therefore be it
>
> *Resolved*, That the Committee on Rituals are hereby authorized and empowered to collate, publish, and print for sale, at their own cost and expense, under the sanction and with the approval of this Supreme Council, which is hereby given, a Manual or Guide of the Ancient and Accepted Rite, which shall contain so much of the thirty degrees conferred in this Order as is not deemed secret or improper to be exposed, such as a description of the apartments, their decorations and properties, a list of officers of the various Bodies and their costumes, and such other matter as may be useful and instructive,

together with the general statutes, regulations and laws of the Lodges, Councils, Chapters, Areopagi and Consistories, the outlines, ceremonial processions, Lodges of Sorrow, side degrees, and the forms of petitions, demits, Oaths of Allegiance, dispensations, charters, diplomas, etc.[29]

In other words, the Supreme Council authorized the printing of a Scottish Rite monitor. Although it was not published until three years afterwards, McClenachan's *The Book of the Ancient and Accepted Scottish Rite* was the end product of the above resolution. We have studied the ceremonies and rituals of the various Supreme Councils, and are satisfied that McClenachan's *The Book of the Ancient and Accepted Scottish Rite* was an accurate monitor of the ritual issued in 1867. Thus the book is of historical interest to students of the evolution of Masonic ritual; any other use is haphazard at best and deceptive at worst.

The Relevance of McClenachan's Book

Now that we understand the historical context, we might ask, "What relevance does McClenachan's *The Book of the Ancient and Accepted Scottish Rite* have for us today?" The rituals of the Supreme Council, 33°, Northern Masonic Jurisdiction, have been under continuous refinement and revision, and it is noteworthy that in just three years following its publication, McClenachan's *The Book of the Ancient and Accepted Scottish Rite* was outdated. Beginning in 1870, the Supreme Council, Northern Masonic Jurisdiction, revised and adopted new rituals, and it has continued to revise them ever since. Notice of each revision is published annually in the Supreme Council's *Proceedings*, which are available for public inspection in many Masonic libraries.[30]

McClenachan's lectures, largely taken from Pike's unofficial ritual (the *Magnum Opus*), have long since been abandoned. Dramas once set in ancient times have been replaced by historic settings within the memory of those living today.[31] The old lectures and rituals of the Scottish Rite have been replaced by such varied modern settings as a Native American theme,[32] a post-Revolutionary War theme including George Washington and Benedict Arnold,[33] and even a World War II "Four Chaplains Degree."[34]

Pastor Janssen and other anti-Masons have not bothered to keep up on these facts. Rather, he assumes because McClenachan's *The Book of the Ancient and Accepted Scottish Rite* was published at least through 1914, it still reflects current practices over eighty years later. Using the pastor's logic, reprints of any book are grounds to misjudge the groups which once published or used them. For example, the notorious *Malleus Maleficarum*, or "witch-hunters' Bible" (originally published in 1487), was used throughout the Inquisition and is still in print today.[35] Does this mean that the modern Christian Church condones physical torture to extract confessions from people accused of witchcraft? And what of the Reverend Thornton Stringfellow, once pastor of a Baptist church in Virginia, who preached that slavery was a divine institution justified by the Bible? The text of his book, *Scriptural and Statistical Views in Favor of Slavery* (originally published in 1856), is available on the Internet.[36] Does this mean that the Baptist Church currently justifies slavery? Clearly, Pastor Janssen's methodology is flawed.

PASTOR JANSSEN'S TOP TEN MISUNDERSTANDINGS

Based on his misunderstanding of Masonic literature and drama, Pastor Janssen outlined ten reasons why he believes Freemasonry is incompatible with the by-laws of his Church. It is not necessary to examine every allegation, but an example or two from each of the ten groups should be sufficient to demonstrate his errors. (In the text that follows, the pastor's allegations are numbered while our comments follow.)

1. *Freemasonry Freely Uses Pagan Religions as an Inspiration for Their Ceremonies*

Pastor Janssen apparently has no problems applying double standards when they work in his favor. He has either forgotten or chooses to ignore the fact that one of the hallmarks of early Christianity was its adoption and transformation of pagan ceremonies and symbols. Using the pastor's argument, no Christian should display a Christmas tree, burn a yule log, or eat gingerbread cookies, because of their pagan origins. The use of Christmas trees resembles a practice forbidden in the Old Testament (Jeremiah 10:2–4),[37] while the latter two symbolized human sacrifice and cannibalism.[38] In fact,

Christian scholars tell us that December 25 was selected as the date for Christmas to counter a pagan festival held in honor of the god Mithras (*Sol Invictus*, "The Invincible Sun").[39] To be consistent, Pastor Janssen must also give up the observance of Easter, since the name derives from a pagan festival celebrated at the vernal equinox, in honor of the Teutonic goddess of dawn *Eastron* or *Austron*.

To carry his practice to exaggerated lengths, he must likewise avoid mentioning the days of the week, since they derive from the worship of heavenly bodies and pagan gods (Sun-day, Moon-day . . . Wodden's-day, Thor's-day, etc.). Clearly, objections to "pagan influences" in any environment can be carried to the extreme. However, if he continues to obsess over "pagan influences," perhaps he should set his own house in order first (see Matthew 7:3), and work to remove all "pagan influences" from Christian homes and churches.

The pastor is offended by a passage in McClenachan's book which reads in part: "We reproduce the speculations of the Philosophers the Kabalists, the Mystagogues, and the Gnostics." Had he paid attention to the opening of the paragraph he might have understood its context:

> *We teach the truth of none of the legends we recite. They are to us, but parables and allegories*, involving and enveloping Masonic instruction; and vehicles of useful and interesting information. They represent the different phases of the human mind, its efforts and struggles to comprehend nature, God, the government of the Universe, the permitted existence of sorrow and evil. To teach us wisdom, the folly of endeavoring to explain to ourselves, that which we are not capable of understanding, we reproduce the speculations of the Philosophers, the Kabalists, the Mystagogues and the Gnostics. Everyone being at liberty to apply our symbols and emblems as he thinks most consistent with truth and reason, and with his own faith, we give them such an interpretation only as may be accepted by all. (McClenachan, p. 313; Cf. *Morals and Dogma*, p. 329)

As a non-Mason, Pastor Janssen interprets this passage much differently than we do, as Masons. According to the pastor:

> This passage has told me that all of the symbols and the emblems of Freemasonry use the primary meaning of the symbol or emblem first. **The Scottish Rite states that it uses only the primary or first meaning of any symbol.** So when it tells you about Isis it means Isis and when it tells you about Osiris it means Osiris. When you see its symbols, the primary meaning is what you are to understand. . . . So I as an initiate in the 24th Degree am being taught to worship the Egyptian sun deity. This is idolatry plain and simple. (emphasis added)

The pastor's opinion directly contradicts the official publications of the Scottish Rite. Among other things, Pastor Janssen wants us to believe that Freemasons worship Egyptians gods. What he fails to understand is that they are used as symbols, just like characters in a play. For example, in *Morals and Dogma* Pike refers to "the legend of Osiris and Isis" (pp. 337, 483), "the legend of the contest between *Hor-ra* and *Set*" (p. 80), "the legend of the twelve labors of Hercules" (p. 448), "the legend of Ormuzd and Ahriman" (p. 425), as well as many other legends. But, as Pike clearly wrote, "*We teach the truth of none of the legends we recite. They are to us, but parables and allegories....*" For some reason Pastor Janssen, like other anti-Masons, has a hard time understanding this. Further, contrary to his remarks, Scottish Rite symbols do *not* employ the "primary or first meaning." According to the *Scottish Rite Ritual Monitor and Guide*:

> In some instances a symbol may be used in one degree only and with specific intent. In other cases a given symbol may appear in several degrees but with wholly different meanings. *The meaning of any symbol is always dependant upon its context.* Some symbols familiar to the reader may have a different or even contradictory meaning in Freemasonry than that commonly understood. Hence, the reader is cautioned not to assume, generalize, or transpose the meaning of any symbol from one degree to another. In this regard it is important to recall Pike's comments:
>
> > As there is no symbol of Masonry that has not more than one meaning—the first explanation, and even the second or third, being often itself a symbol and enigma—you will not be surprised to learn that the meaning of these degrees has often been mistaken or misrepresented. (*Liturgy, Part II*, p. 118)[40]

2. Freemasonry Teaches Universalism, That All Will Be Ultimately Saved

Pastor Janssen found a passage in McClenachan's book which he, as a non-Mason, interprets differently than Masons do. (Selecting sentences like this to support or attack a position is known as "prooftexting.") It reads, "The Masonic system regards all the human race as members of one great family—as having the same origin and same destination; all distinctions of rank, lineage, or nativity, are alike and unknown."[41] We don't believe this teaches universalism (universal salvation). It reminds us of Acts 17:26, "And hath made of one blood all nations of men for to dwell on all the face of the earth, and hath determined the times before appointed, and the bounds of their habitation." However, the ultimate interpretation is left to each Mason to decide for himself.

3. *Freemasonry Teaches the Principles of Pagan Religions as Truth*

In support of this Pastor Janssen quotes from the "argument" or rationale of the old Twenty-fifth Degree, Knight of the Brazen Serpent, which was outdated and replaced by 1880.[42] The old ritual employed an allegory which mentioned "the *fables* of Osiris and Ormuzd, and Typhon and Ahriman" (emphasis added).[43] Pastor Janssen objects to the use of "the symbols and allegories of the mysteries,"[44] but—not having read the complete ritual— he seems unaware of the Old Testament setting in which the apostasy of the Israelites is condemned. He objects to the metaphorical use of the words "purify the soul of its alloy of earthliness, that through the gate of Capricorn and the seven spheres it may at length ascend to its eternal home beyond the stars."[45] In fact, no doctrine is taught here, but rather these words belong to Horus, a character in the drama, who expresses the desire to be purified and, at death (passing the gate of Capricorn), he hopes to enter eternal rest in the heavens beyond the seven ancient planets.

Pastor Janssen displays a profound ignorance of Masonic literature. He stated:

> Even though the brazen serpent is a prototype of Christ from the Old Testament, I am not called to perpetuate the truths of the New Testament. I am called, rather, to perpetuate the truths enveloped in the ancient mysteries.

Had the pastor bothered to read a few extracts from *Morals and Dogma* he might hold a different opinion:

> Above all the other great teachers of morality and virtue, it reveres the character of the Great Master who, submissive to the will of his and our Father, died upon the Cross. All must admit, that if the world were filled with beings like him, the great ills of society would be at once relieved. For all coercion, injury, selfishness, and revenge, and all the wrongs and the greatest sufferings of life, would disappear at once. These human years would be happy; and the eternal ages would roll on in brightness and beauty; and the still, sad music of Humanity, that sounds through the world, now in the accents of grief, and now in pensive melancholy, would change to anthems,

sounding to the March of Time, and bursting out from the heart of the world.

If every man were a perfect imitator of that Great, Wise, Good Teacher, clothed with all His faith and all his virtues, how the circle of Life's ills and trials would be narrowed! The sensual passions would assail the heart in vain. Want would no longer successfully tempt men to act wrongly, nor curiosity to do rashly. Ambition, spreading before men its Kingdoms and its Thrones, and offices and honors, would cause none to swerve from their great allegiance. Injury and insult would be shamed by forgiveness. "Father," men would say, "forgive them; for they know not what they do." None would seek to be enriched at another's loss or expense. Every man would feel that the whole human race were his brothers. All sorrow and pain and anguish would be soothed by a perfect faith and an entire trust in the Infinite Goodness of God. The world around us would be new, and the Heavens above us; for here, and there, and everywhere, through all the ample glories and splendors of the universe, all men would recognize and feel the presence and the beneficent care of a loving Father.

However the Mason may believe as to creeds, and churches, and miracles, and missions from Heaven, he must admit that the Life and character of him who taught in Galilee, and fragments of whose teachings, have come down to us, are worthy of all imitation. That Life is an undenied and undeniable Gospel. Its teachings cannot be passed by and discarded. All must admit that it would be happiness to follow and perfection to imitate him. (*Morals and Dogma*, pp. 718–19)

Man is once more taught to look upward to his God. No longer to a God hid in impenetrable mystery, and infinitely remote from human sympathy, emerging only at intervals from the darkness to smite and crush humanity: but a God, good, kind, beneficent, and merciful: a Father, loving the creatures He has made, with a love immeasurable and exhaustless; Who feels for us, and sympathizes with us, and sends us pain and want and disaster only that they may serve to develop in us the virtues and excellencies that befit us to live with Him hereafter.

Jesus of Nazareth, the "Son of man," is the expounder of the new Law of Love. He calls to him the humble, the poor, the Pariahs of the world. The first sentence that he pronounces blesses the world, and announces the new gospel: "Blessed are they that mourn for they shall be comforted." He pours the oil of consolation and peace upon every crushed and bleeding heart. Every sufferer is his proselyte. He shares their sorrows, and sympathizes with all their afflictions.

He raises up the sinner and the Samaritan woman, and teaches them to hope for forgiveness. He pardons the woman taken in adultery. He selects his disciples not among the Pharisees or the Philosophers, but among the low and humble, even of the fishermen of Galilee. He heals the sick and feeds the poor. He lives among the destitute and the friendless. "Suffer little children," he said, "to come unto me; for of such is the kingdom of Heaven! Blessed are the humble-minded, for theirs is" the kingdom of Heaven; the meek, for they shall inherit the Earth; the merciful, for they shall obtain mercy; the pure in heart, for they shall see God; the peace makers, for they stall be called the children of God! First be reconciled to thy brother, and *then* come and offer thy gift at the altar! Give to him that asketh thee, and from him that would borrow of thee turn not away! Love your enemies; bless them that curse you; do good to them that hate you; and pray for them which despite fully use you and persecute you! All things whatsoever ye would that men should do to you, do ye also unto them; for this is the law and the Prophets! He that taketh not his cross, and followeth after me, is not worthy of me. A new commandment I give unto you, that ye love one another: as I have loved you, that ye also love one another: by this shall all know that ye are my disciples. Greater love hath no man than this, that a man lay down his life for his friends."

That Gospel of Love he sealed with his life. The cruelty of the Jewish Priesthood, the ignorant ferocity of the mob, and the Roman indifference to barbarian blood, nailed Him to the cross, and He expired uttering blessings upon humanity. (*Morals and Dogma*, pp. 309–10)

4. Freemasonry Teaches the Cross Is Not the Most Important Symbol of the World, but Rather the Pentagram.

This is a misapplied reference to the old Twenty-eighth Degree, Knight of the Sun, which was revised in 1880.[46] The old ritual mentions that, "All the mysteries of Magism, all the symbols of the gnosis [secret knowledge], all the figures of the occult [hidden] philosophy, all the Kabbalistic keys of prophecy, are summed up in the sign of the pentagram, the greatest and most potent of all signs."[47] The ritual does not say the pentagram is the greatest Masonic symbol or that it is greater than the Christian's cross. It merely attempts to comment on the pentagram from a comparative point of view. As noted earlier, Masonic degrees are presented in dramatic form, like a play. The context is paramount to understanding what is happening. In spite of this, however, Pastor Janssen completely misinterprets what he has read. He says:

> Freemasonry teaches that only one symbol brings the two worlds of God and humanity together and that is the pentagram. It is not the cross that gives the Mason an understanding of the two worlds, God and humanity, it is the pentagram.

It is unfortunate that the pastor sees a need to overlook other Masonic degrees in McClenachan's book, such as the Knight Commander of the Temple Degree, during which the candidate is presented with a cross:

> I present you with the pallium or mantle of the order. This cross is the sign of the Order, which we command you constantly to wear.

Is It True What They Say about Freemasonry?

Take this sign in the name of God, for the increase of faith, the defense of the Order, and the service of the poor. We place this cross upon your breast, my brother, that you may love it with all your heart; and may your right hand ever fight in its defence and for its preservation, as the symbol of knightly Masonry. (McClenachan, p. 394)

5. *Freemasonry Teaches Astrology in Its Rituals*

The passage to which Pastor Janssen objects begins, "The world, the ancients believed . . ."[48] Had Pastor Janssen paid closer attention to these five introductory words, he should have understood that the passage is describing *ancient* beliefs, not Masonic beliefs or practices. It's almost amusing that Pastor Janssen claims the Scottish Rite teaches such things because Albert Pike, who authored the offending passage, stated his opinion quite clearly.[49] In a letter written to a friend, Pike wrote:

> I think that no speculations are more barren than those in regard to the astronomical character of the symbols of Masonry, except those about the Numbers and their combinations of the Kabbalah. All that is said about Numbers in that lecture, if not mere jugglery, amounts to nothing. . . . The astronomical explanations of them, however plausible, would only show that they taught no truths, moral or religious. As to tricks played with Numbers, they only show what freaks of absurdity, if not insanity, the human intellect can indulge.[50]

6. *Freemasonry Does Not Affirm the Uniqueness of the Old and New Testaments*

Pastor Janssen seems to desire some type of special Masonic proclamation on the uniqueness of the Bible, but appears unaware that it is already called the "Great Light in Masonry" and "the rule and guide to our faith" in most American Grand Lodges.[51] However, while it is true that Freemasonry does not enter into or claim to settle religious issues for its members, it is remarkable that the pastor ignores branches of Freemasonry that are only open to Christians. For example, the Masonic Knights Templar and the Order of the Red Cross of Constantine enhance the Christian faith of their members. Pastor Janssen is bothered that the old Seventeenth Degree, Knights of the East and West (revised in 1870),[52] suggested an interdependence of the Mosaic laws and those of other cultures. A course on comparative religion shows the similarities between Hammurabi's Code and the Ten Commandments,[53] and the parallels between the Biblical Noah and the Mesopotamian hero Utnapishtim in the Gilgamesh epic.[54] These historical insights do not detract from the value of the Bible as the "inestimable gift of God to man."[55] The Bible has an honorable and unique place in Freemasonry.

7. Freemasonry States It Is Not a Religion then Affirms It Actually Is

This is one of those convoluted statements that is difficult to understand. In essence, the pastor says, "I don't care what Freemasonry says, I know better." Citing older, discarded versions of the Fourth and Twentieth Degrees, the pastor notes that "Genuine Freemasonry . . . approaches religion."[56] Similarity is not equivalence, approaching is not arriving. By analogy, the movies *Ben Hur* and *The Ten Commandments* are *religious*, but they are not *religion*. As we noted before, some of the Masonic ritual dramas are religious in character and theatrical setting, but they do not teach sectarian dogmas, nor do they make Freemasonry a religion.

8. Freemasonry Uses the Kabbalah as a Base of Teaching

Although there were references to the Kabbalah (a form of Jewish mysticism) in some early Scottish Rite degrees (and still are in some jurisdictions), they are presented in a context consistent with the setting of the drama. They portray one group's attempt to discover truth. Just as there are many types of "Christianity" there are many types of "Kabbalah." In fact, there was even a type of "Christian Kabbalah" which was used to convert Jews.[57] Not having studied the full rituals, Pastor Janssen cannot appreciate the context of the discussion. Like other anti-Masons, the pastor selectively "cherry picks" statements for his own misuse by removing them from context. He ignores the fact that Pike clearly wrote that Masonry rejected the "wild and useless speculations of . . . the Kabalah" and other traditions:

> And these doctrines, the wheat sifted from the chaff, the Truth separated from Error, Masonry has garnered up in her heart of hearts, and through

Is It True What They Say about Freemasonry?

the fires of persecution, and the storms of calamity, has brought them and delivered them unto us. That God is One, immutable, unchangeable, infinitely just and good; that Light will finally overcome Darkness,—Good conquer Evil, and Truth be victor over Error;—these, *rejecting all the wild and useless speculations of the Zend-Avesta, the Kabalah, the Gnostics, and the Schools*, are the religion and Philosophy of Masonry. (*Morals and Dogma*, p. 275)

9. Freemasonry Believes It Alone Is the Guardian of Spiritual Truths Given at the Dawn of Humanity

This refers to a statement in the old Eighth Degree, Intendant of the Buildings (abandoned in 1871),[58] in which it was stated that Freemasonry preserved "divine truth, given by God to the first men. . . ."[59] The context of the degree makes it clear they are the moral truths of integrity, virtue, and charity. Symbolic Masonry does encourage their practice and indeed maintains they will improve mankind.

10. Freemasonry Contains Material Shared in Common with Spiritist Groups

This contention is similar to the first one in this list, but it is followed by an argument that the symbolism of Freemasonry is not clearly defined. Among other things, Pastor Janssen alleges the double-headed eagle, used in the 31°, 32°, and 33°, originated with seventeenth-century alchemy. A little research would have shown a simpler origin of the double-headed eagle:

> [I]t has never been exclusively a Masonic symbol, for it dates to the formation of the holy Roman Empire under Charlemagne. He took the German eagle with its head turned right and the Roman eagle with its head facing left and merged them, so together the eagle looked upon both east and west. The imperial houses of Hapsburg and Romanov used this emblem, too.[60]

The symbol was later adopted by the Masonic "Emperors of the East and West," which was an ancestor of the Scottish Rite.[61] The other examples likewise have simple explanations, but further detail would become tedious.

Much of the pastor's misunderstanding results from the fact that he superficially read a monitor which was intended for someone familiar with the rituals as they were used from 1867 to 1870. Freemasonry does explain its symbols to its members, but the pastor has no way of knowing this. Although we do not confuse the symbol with the concept symbolized, this seems to be another problem with Pastor Janssen.

CONCLUSION

Charles T. McClenachan died in 1896, and his wife published later editions of his book, no doubt considering it a tribute to her husband's many years of hard work in Freemasonry. Earlier we asked, "What relevance does Mc-Clenachan's *The Book of the Ancient and Accepted Scottish Rite* have for us today?" It has been wisely observed that in order to appreciate our future we must remember our past. The value of McClenachan's book lies in its utility to the student of the evolution of ritual. It includes some fascinating passages which give us a glimpse into an earlier type of Freemasonry, at a time when unfamiliar allegories and tales of knighthood and intrigue were used to teach ethics and the lessons of tolerance.

Pastor Janssen, like many other non-Masons, fails to appreciate the context of extracts he reads in Masonic writings; he is ignorant of our full literature. The 1864 Resolution which authorized the printing of the "Manual or Guide" specifically required that it only "shall contain so much of the Thirty Degrees conferred in this Order as is not deemed secret or improper to be exposed."

This is because non-Masons do not have a right to read the full rituals. Not having studied the full rituals, Pastor Janssen assumes too much—far more than is warranted—and cannot recognize what he is reading or who is speaking the parts. His condemnation of Masonry is as illogical as a condemnation of Shakespeare based on Othello's murder of Desdemona, or a condemnation of Christianity based on the Inquisition, or Bible quotations removed from context.

Freemasonry does not teach the dogmatic or doctrinal truths of any one religion, nor does it teach the absurdities Pastor Janssen espouses. It teaches truths upon which all honest men agree. Its love of humanity is seen in the many philanthropies—amounting to more than $2 million per day in 1995[62]—which are open to people of all races and faiths. It encourages men of good will to celebrate their commonalities and to unite in helping their fellows.

If Pastor Janssen and other anti-Masons choose to condemn us, we invite them to do so on a basis of truth.

> Even so every good tree bringeth forth good fruit; but a corrupt tree bringeth forth evil fruit. A good tree cannot bring forth evil fruit, neither can a corrupt tree bring forth good fruit. Wherefore by their fruits ye shall know them.
>
> **—Matthew 7:17, 18, 20**

Chapter 7

Enchanter! A Virtual Anti-Mason

A great many people think they are thinking when they are merely rearranging their prejudices.

—William James

The Internet may have been the most exciting invention of the twentieth century. It has enabled an amazing increase in communication and information transfer. Researchers now think nothing of browsing the catalog of the Sorbonne before checking a reference at the British Museum—and all of this without leaving their desk. One of the first, least-structured, and most enjoyable features of the Internet was the Usenet newsgroup. Usenet news groups have been largely replaced by blogs, social networks, and other forums. One of the early popular and unmoderated newsgroups devoted to discussions of Freemasonry is alt.freemasonry. The group is loosely self-policed, but a wilder, freer forum is hard to imagine.

With this freedom, unfortunately, comes the opportunity for misuse and abuse. Internet technology allows users to mask their identities so they can anonymously post outlandish, vulgar, blasphemous, and misleading messages—all without fear of repercussion. Most Freemasons posting to newsgroups identify themselves and their lodges; many anti-Masons hide behind pseudonyms and false addresses. A visitor to alt.freemasonry can find the puerile writings of these brave participants. Over the years anti-Masons come and go, but their intent seems to be constant: save the world from the "evils" of Freemasonry and disrupt any civil discourse on the Craft. It is useless to try to address every irrational argument of these anonymous cowards; their minds are made up and closed. However, it may be instructive to look at one series of such messages.

Several postings to different newsgroups in the early 1990s ("Masonry FAQ [Frequently Asked Questions]: Blasted to Bits," "Secrets and Secrecy," and others, all written by the bravely pseudonymous Enchanter!), including alt.freemasonry, attempted to portray the Masonic fraternity as an "evil force which is permeating every corner of our society." The documents are filled with misunderstandings, misstatements, and deceptive half-truths.

THE DIFFICULTY OF DIALOGUE

Enchanter! begins by establishing an interesting logical system in which he conducts his inquisition. It enables him to accept any "evidence" that suits him, and ignore what doesn't. Non-Masons and non-33° Masons who question him are dismissed for not being "real 33° Masons."

> May I ask you [sir], what degree Mason are you? If you are less than a 33rd degree Mason, does it not make sense that I should accept the opinions of a real 33rd Mason [Albert Pike] over yours on this subject?

Then any response from a Mason is similarly dismissed because Enchanter! defines them to be unreliable.

> You obviously are a Mason, and therefore have taken vows to uphold certain secrets, even if it means telling lies.

Meaningful, civil discourse is difficult after these premises are established.[1]

THE FUNDAMENTAL MISUNDERSTANDING

The first and most fundamental misunderstanding of the document is that the Scottish Rite Supreme Councils and "real 33° Masons" somehow control Freemasonry. The author seems fixated on 33° Masons and quotes their writings religiously. As an example of the confusion, the original posting said, "Masonry is a two-faced preditor [*sic*], just as the Masonic icon of the two-headed eagle indicates." The author later acknowledged that the eagle is a symbol of the Scottish Rite and not of Freemasonry, but the basic confusion of control persists throughout.

A 33° Mason does not necessarily have more knowledge or speak more authoritatively than other Masons. One might as well assume that Eagle Scouts know more about Scouting policy and history than anyone else or that a Phi Beta Kappa graduate of a university is a more reliable source for university plans and policy than a dean. Scouting does not work this way, universities do not work this way, and Freemasonry does not work this way.

The author asks, "Is the author of the FAQ a 33° Mason?" "If not, then it would seem to me that Pike stands as a better authority on issues such as the occult sciences and Lucifer." Following this logic, Bishop John Spong of the Episcopal Church should be a better authority on issues of Christian doctrine than most other Christians. He was ordained in direct apostolic succession from Jesus Christ. In his book *Rescuing the Bible from Fundamentalism*, he has speculated that the "thorn in the flesh" of St. Paul (II Corinthians 12:7) may have been that he was a homosexual. Does this mean St. Paul was a homosexual? Does Bishop Spong speak for all Christians? Does he speak for all Episcopalians? Does this mean the members of Bishop Spong's dioceses must believe this? Anyone believing any of this understands neither Protestant Christianity nor the politics of the Episcopal Church. Enchanter! similarly misunderstands Freemasonry.

THE SOURCE OF ACCURATE INFORMATION

Every Grand Lodge in the United States publishes annual *Transactions* or *Proceedings* which detail (sometimes tediously) the motions, debates, and business conducted at their meetings. Grand Lodges print and widely distribute hundreds of copies of their proceedings. These are not secret and can be read at the Grand Lodges, in the larger Masonic libraries, or in some public and university libraries. Annual transactions are the source for accurate, official actions of any Grand Lodge. A further source of information is the annual proceedings of the Conference of Grand Masters of North America.

There are scores of Lodges devoted to studying the history of Freemasonry. The oldest such research lodge is Quatuor Coronati Lodge No. 2076 in London, founded in 1886. Its annual transactions, *Ars Quatuor Coronatorum*, are an abundance of carefully researched historical papers on Freemasonry. American Masonic research organizations with extensive publications include the American Lodge of Research (New York), the Missouri Lodge of Research, Iowa Research Lodge No. 2, the Ohio Chapter of Research (Royal Arch Masons, part of the York Rite), the Philalethes Society, and the Scottish Rite Research Society.

In short, there is a wealth of readily available information on the activities of virtually every American Masonic organization. Much of it is boring (such as debates on how lodge meeting notices should be mailed), but it is publicly available to anyone who wants to do genuine research on the actual, not imagined, activities of Freemasonry. Similarly, there are thousands of papers (some poorly and others well written) on the history, philosophy, and origins of Freemasonry, all available to anyone willing to take the effort to read them.

DEFICIENT RESEARCH

Albert Pike is the favorite whipping boy of modern anti-Masons, and Enchanter! is no exception. Pike is usually first portrayed as the central, guiding force behind Freemasonry, and then he is vilified. Pike was a circumloquacious Victorian writer whose style (to our tastes at least) was better suited for a century ago. (Certainly he never read Strunk & White!) His *Morals and Dogma of the Ancient and Accepted Scottish Rite of Freemasonry* is usually portrayed as the ultimate source of Masonic knowledge and as a sacred book for Freemasons.

In one place in *Morals and Dogma*, Pike refers to Jesus as "the mysterious founder of the Christian Church." Enchanter! quotes this passages and then uses it to launch an ad hominem attack on Pike:

> Notice how Pike avoids even writing the name of Christ, and would rather substitute a cumbersome phrase in its place.

The statement is a non sequitur; Pike's writing style has nothing to do with Masonry. More than this, the accusation is wrong; it betrays tissue-thin research. Pike had a vast vocabulary, but did not hesitate to use "Jesus," "Jesus Christ," or "Christ." Consider the following examples.

> On its face was inscribed the word Ἰχθυς [Ichthus], a fish, the initials of which represented the Greek words, Ιησους Χριστος Θεου Υιος Σωτηρ [Iesous CHristos THeou HYios Soter]; Jesus Christ, the Son of God, the Saviour. [*Morals and Dogma*, p. 547]

> The person of Jesus having disappeared, there was seen in His place a cross of Light over which a celestial voice pronounced these words: "The cross of Light is called The Word, Christ, The Gate, Joy, The Bread, The Sun, The Resurrection, Jesus, The Father, The Spirit, Life, Truth, and Grace." [*Morals and Dogma*, p. 567]

> Paul of Samosta taught that Jesus Christ was the Son of Joseph and Mary. . . . [*Morals and Dogma*, p. 564]

> According to the Church, Christ was of the same nature as God. . . . [*Morals and Dogma*, p. 565]

> None can deny that Christ taught a lofty morality. "Love one another: forgive those that despitefully use you and persecute you. . . ." [*Morals and Dogma*, p. 540]

> Jesus of Nazareth, the "Son of man," is the expounder of the new Law of Love. He called to Him the humble, the poor the Pariahs of the world. [*Morals and Dogma*, p. 309]

A SOURCE MISUNDERSTOOD

Enchanter! readily accepts and repeats negative information about Masonry without understanding the source. For example, he says:

> In *Scottish* [*sic*] *Rite Masonry Illustrated* (vol. II, p. 259) we find that the candidate, after a bizarre and somber ceremony involving coffins and skulls, hears these words voiced by the Grand Master. . . .

A quotation then follows in which the candidate is told he will have "to obey, without reserve, all that you will be commanded to do." This sounds ominous, but it has no bearing on any legitimate Masonic body, because the author has not checked his sources. The book in question is an exposure of the rituals of Cerneauism, a Masonic movement in the nineteenth century that contended against legitimate Scottish Rite Masonry in the United States. Whatever similarities may exist between Cerneau and Scottish Rite rituals are objects of curiosity and a source of Masonic research papers.

Numerous references to the Cerneau Supreme Council occur throughout *Scotch Rite Masonry Illustrated*. Confusing Cerneauism with regular Scottish Rite Masonry is like confusing the Church of Christ with the Church of Christ, Scientist. Their names are alike and their orders of worship are superficially similar, but they are fundamentally different denominations. It is shallow research to accept Blanchard's book without question. It is incompetent to confuse the Cerneau Supreme Council with regular Scottish Rite Masonry. It is irresponsible to accuse Scottish Rite Masons on the basis of an irrelevant book. (The reader will find more information on *Scotch Rite Masonry Illustrated* in the section "Jonathan Blanchard and the Scottish Rite" in chapter 3, "Rev. John Ankerberg and Dr. John Weldon: The Secret Teachings of the Masonic Lodge.")

UNSUBSTANTIATED ALLEGATIONS

Enchanter! makes several wild charges about a global conspiracy which involves Freemasonry in some vague, unspecified way. Among many other things he talks about:

> The sheer numbers of Masons involved in global reorganization. . . .
>
> The ranks of the many Christians and God-loving people who got out of Masonry because they did not like the secrets revealed at the higher levels.
>
> A small percentage of the US population are involved in freemasonry, yet in the US government (especially the secretive intelligence agencies like the FBI, CIA, NSA, etc.) there is a very high number of freemasons.
>
> This evil force which is permeating every corner of our society. . . .

If true, these allegations can be supported by objective research. There is no need to sit by idly when the public record can be checked to substantiate these claims. Any reader easily should be able to confirm Enchanter!'s statements— if only he would share his information. All we need to know is the name of the Mason, a reference to his membership, and his position.

- If Freemasonry is "permeating every corner of our society," then it should be simple to give verifiable examples.

- If so many Masons are "involved in global reorganization," then it should be simple to name a dozen of them.

- If so many "Christians and God-loving people" have left Masonry "because they did not like the secrets revealed at the higher levels," then we should be able to read scores of their witnesses of their experiences.

- If the U.S. government and its intelligence agencies have "a very high number of freemasons," then there should be no problem in giving a few hundred names.

A SECRET BOOK

The author quotes extracts from the preface of *Morals and Dogma*, and then says, "Clearly this book is or was some sort of a secret." Again, the facts show otherwise. Below is the quote from Enchanter! with the words he left out indicated by being struck out.

> The following work has been prepared by authority of the Supreme Council of the Thirty-Third Degree, ~~for the southern jurisdiction of the United States~~, by the Grand Commander. . . .
>
> ~~As the cost of the work consists entirely in the printing and binding, it will be furnished at a price as moderate as possible. No individual will receive pecuniary profit from it, except the agents for its sale~~. It has been copyrighted to prevent its republication elsewhere. . . . ~~Whatever profits may accrue from it will be devoted to purposes of charity.~~
>
> It not being intended for the world at large, ~~the author~~ [Pike] ~~has felt at liberty to make, from all accessible sources, a Compendium of the Morals and Dogma of the Rite, to re-mould sentences, change and add to words and phrases, combine them with his own, and use them as if they were his own. . . . He claims, therefore, little of the merit of authorship, and has not cared to distinguish his own from that which he has taken from other sources, being quite willing that every portion of the book, in turn, may be regarded as borrowed from some old and better writer.~~

In reading the full words of the preface, several points are clear.

- *Morals and Dogma* was never intended to serve all of Freemasonry—just the Supreme Council, 33°, SJ (it was, in fact, rejected and ignored by the Northern Masonic Jurisdiction).

- The book was copyrighted because of Pike's concern that it be sold at the lowest possible cost and that all profits go to charity.

- Because he was not writing for a general public, Pike didn't worry about citing all of his sources as he normally did.

Far from proving that *Morals and Dogma* is a secret book, the full preface shows: 1) it was produced at cost for Scottish Rite Masons; 2) no individual was to profit from its sale or resale; 3) Pike used an informal reference style because the book was intended for his Brethren only. No restrictions have ever been placed on storing, reading, or loaning the book. Consider these statistics from the 1992 *Transactions of the Supreme Council*. In 1907 (the first year membership figures are summarized in the *Transactions*), there were 33,000 Scottish Rite Masons in the Southern Jurisdiction; in 1950 there were 374,000. In those 43 years, close to one million Masons joined and received a copy of *Morals and Dogma*, with no restriction on who could read it. This seems like a singularly odd way to manage a "secret book."

SELECTIVE QUOTATIONS

Enchanter! takes several quotes from *Morals and Dogma*, after first falsely claiming it is among "the writings held sacred within the Lodges." *Morals and Dogma* was published and distributed by the Southern Jurisdiction (SJ) of the Scottish Rite in the United States. (Only a little over 30 percent of American Masons have chosen to join the Scottish Rite—about 29 percent in the SJ and 33 percent in the Northern Masonic Jurisdiction [NMJ].) *Morals and Dogma* has no role in Grand Lodges; it is not used in the NMJ, it has not been published or distributed by the Southern Jurisdiction since about 1971, and it has never, ever been considered a scriptural text by any Masonic group.

A new edition is being prepared by the Supreme Council 33°, Southern Jurisdiction, and should be published by 2011.

The first quote from *Morals and Dogma* is preceded by Enchanter!'s inflammatory introductory comment, "If you read this through, I'm sure you will agree with me: it's a perversion of the Christian teachings, riddled with magic(k) and occultism."

> Ialdabaoth, to become independent of his mother [Spirit], and to pass for the Supreme Being, made the world, and man, in his own image. . . . They [Christos and Wisdom] restored Jesus to life and gave Him an ethereal body, in which He remained eighteen months on earth, and receiving from Wisdom the perfect knowledge, communicated it to a small number of His apostles. . . . [*Morals and Dogma*, pp. 563–564]

The passage is indeed found in *Morals and Dogma*, but it is a description of the beliefs of the Ophites, a Gnostic sect condemned by Irenaeus (ca. 115–ca. 202), Bishop of Lyons, in his book *Against Heresies*. The paragraph from which this quote is taken begins, "The Ophites commenced their system with a Supreme Being, long unknown to the Human race. . . ." The Ophites believed that Ialdabaoth was the son of Sophia the Mother, and that he sealed off the heavens above him to prevent those below from discovering anything above him.[2] The chapter from which Enchanter! quotes is an overview of early religious beliefs, none of which are recommended to Freemasons. On page 564 alone, Pike provides six brief summaries of bygone beliefs.

> Tatian adopted the theory of Emanation, of Eons . . .
>
> The Elxaites adopted the Seven Spirits of the Gnostics . . .
>
> The opinion of the Doketes as to the human nature of Jesus . . .
>
> Noetus termed the Son the first Utterance of the Father . . .
>
> Paul of Samosta taught that Jesus Christ was the Son . . .
>
> Arius called the Saviour the first of creatures . . .

All of this is descriptive, with nothing more prescriptive for Scottish Rite Masons than a college course on comparative religion or mythology would be. With noteworthy inconsistency, Enchanter! fails to see that his own pseudonym could also lead to charges of "magic(k) and occultism." *Enchanter!* earlier quoted two sentences from Pike's introduction to *Morals and Dogma*. Had he posted a little more of the introduction, Pike's intent would have been clear. First and foremost, neither Pike nor the Scottish Rite have ever, or could ever, require its members to believe anything in the book. This is clear to all Masons and to anyone who reads the introduction:

> Every one is entirely free to reject and dissent from whatsoever herein may seem to him to be untrue or unsound. It is only required of him that he shall weigh what is taught, and give it fair hearing and unprejudiced judgment.

Further, Pike's motives in describing early religious ideas are clear from his introduction. Anyone bothering to read the introduction knows this.

> Of course, the ancient theosophic and philosophic speculations are not embodied as part of the *doctrines* of the Rite; but because it is of interest and profit to know what the Ancient Intellect thought upon these subjects, and because nothing so conclusively proves the radical difference between our human and the animal nature, as the capacity of the human mind to entertain such speculations in regard to itself and the Deity.

This sort of selective quotation out of context is scattered throughout *Enchanter!*'s postings.

> To prevent the light of escaping at once, the Demons forbade Adam to eat the fruit.

> Satan created and governs the visible world [*Morals and Dogma* pp. 566–67] "One of the most twisted variations of Genesis I have ever heard."

The first quote is from a paragraph that begins, "Manes, founder of the Sect of the Manicheans. . . ." The second quote follows, "With the Priscillianists there were two principles. . . ." It's not surprising that they seem "twisted variations," as they were declared heresies centuries ago. Pike is describing "ancient theosophic and philosophic speculations," just as he explained in his introduction. Just after the last quote above, Pike says, "Such were some of the ancient notions concerning the Deity; and taken in connection with what has been detailed in the preceding Degrees, this Lecture affords you a true picture of the ancient speculations" (*Morals and Dogma*, p. 568).

CONCLUSION

Enchanter! appears to have a vendetta against Freemasonry and is willing to go to great lengths to defame the organization and its members, all behind a cloak of anonymity. He removed Pike's explanatory material to *Morals and Dogma*, ignored his introduction, took his words out of context, and tried to pass them off as something from "writings held sacred within the Lodges." Enchanter! is not fair to Pike, he is not honest about Masonry, he ignores the organization and structure of the fraternity, and he insults the intelligence of his readers.

It is not clear to us whether he has done his own research or whether he has relied on some other anti-Masonic text. Thus we cannot decide if he is a naively incompetent researcher or a maliciously deliberate liar. We leave that decision to the objective reader.

Chapter 8

Ron Campbell and Charisma & Christian Life Magazine: "Unearthing the Mysteries of Freemasonry"

> But he that filches from me my good name
> Robs me of that which not enriches him
> And makes me poor indeed.
> **—William Shakespeare, *Othello*, Act III, Scene 3**

The November 1997 issue of *Charisma & Christian Life* magazine contained an article by Ron Campbell, "Unearthing the Mysteries of Freemasonry." The article was noteworthy because of the number of false statements or misunderstandings about Freemasonry, including the following:

- Masonic scholar Albert Mackey, in his *Manual of the Lodge*, taught that the legend of Hiram Abif was borrowed from the ancient mysteries of early Egypt, Mesopotamia, and Greece.

- Albert Pike . . . taught that the square and compass—along with the Bible—were "the great lights in Freemasonry." Though seeming to embrace Christianity by including the Bible in Masonic rituals, Pike actually was mixing true faith with a belief in pagan deities.

- Evangelists such as Charles Finney were openly attacked for their stand against Freemasonry.

- My heart raced as I stood there [at the House of the Temple]. . . . I shuddered as I realized how many unsuspecting men have been trapped in a deadly web of deception after visiting this eerie place.

- Most of us certainly don't understand Freemasonry's esoteric tradition, which is characterized by strange symbols such as the coffin, the all-seeing eye, the pyramid, and the compass and square.

- [T]he largest monument in our nation's capital—an obelisk— is an ancient Egyptian fertility symbol.

- George Washington—who was a practicing Mason—chose the location [of the District of Columbia], and then he commissioned another Mason, Pierre Charles L'Enfant, to design the new capital city.

- L'Enfant's plan included placing the Washington, Lincoln, and Jefferson memorials in a sinister arrangement to honor the sun god.

- [T]he US Capitol in Washington was dedicated to a pagan god in a Masonic ceremony.

- Men who join the Masonic lodge progress through "degrees of initiation" in a quest for spiritual light until they reach the highest level, the Thirty-third Degree.

- Men who join the Masonic lodge . . . view a drama depicting the symbolic death, burial, and resurrection of a hero-god, Hiram Abif.

- The compass and square, an emblem often seen in Masonic art and engraving, represents ancient pagan solar deities.

Is It True What They Say about Freemasonry?

- The Grand Chaplain then invokes the Masonic god, the Great Architect of the Universe. . . .

- Those who request a Masonic funeral are buried lying east to west.

- A symbol of the sun always appears over the throne of the worshipful master in the east.

On January 14, 1998, Dr. S. Brent Morris submitted to *Charisma* "a response to the vague, undocumented innuendo of Mr. Campbell's article."[1] Receiving no acknowledgement, he wrote again on February 18, and then again on March 31 and June 8.

September 23, 1998

Dr. Stephen Strang, Publisher
Charisma & Christian Life
600 Rinehart Road
Lake Mary, FL 32746

Dear Dr. Strang,

Have you received any of my earlier letters to you or to *Charisma*? On January 14, I submitted an article to *Charisma*, "A Calmer Look at Freemasonry." On February 18, I wrote again asking if my article had been received. On March 31, I spoke with Ms. Billie Harnden on your staff, and she suggested that I write directly to you, which I did on that day. Subsequently, Ms. Harnden returned my articles, saying you would not publish anything more on Freemasonry, but she said I should ask you about rewriting my article as a letter to the editor. . . .

I am enclosing yet another copy of my response to Mr. Ron Campbell's article in the November 1997 issue, "Unearthing the Mysteries of Freemasonry." His misstatements of facts and verifiable errors are a disservice to your readers and an insult to the hundreds of thousands of Christian Masons. The readers of *Charisma* deserve accurate, verifiable information they can confirm for themselves. I would be happy to rewrite the article as a letter, if you give me your guidelines.

Please let me know if you are unwilling to publish my response and I will stop writing you; I do not want to be a pest. So far, though, I have no indication that any of my correspondence has gotten through.

Yours in Christ,

S. BRENT MORRIS

The publisher of *Charisma* had made the editorial decision to publish nothing more on Freemasonry, regardless of the false statements in the original article. After continued correspondence and calls to *Charisma*, Dr. Morris was told by Ms. Adrienne Gaines, Assistant Editor, that a 200-word letter would be published, and this length was subsequently reduced to 100 words by Mr. J. Lee Grady, Editor, who apparently feared that Dr. Morris might promote "Christian involvement in the Masonic fraternity." On September 1, 2000, Dr. Morris wrote to Mr. Grady asking if his letter had been published and if he could purchase a copy of the magazine. To date, Dr. Morris has received no reply from *Charisma*.

The information that *Charisma* did not want its readers to read is reproduced below.

A CALMER LOOK AT FREEMASONRY

by S. Brent Morris

As a Christian and Mason I read with interest and then increasing sadness Ron Campbell's article, "Unearthing the Mysteries of Freemasonry," *Charisma*, Nov. 1997. I do not expect my fellow Christians to agree with me in all aspects of living a Christian life—we humans are like that, but I did expect more attention to the accuracy than I found in Mr. Campbell's article.

Christians disagree and have disagreed on many issues of theology—the exact nature and number of the sacraments, marriage and divorce, premillennialism and postmillennialism, to name just a few. I do not have any desire to challenge Mr. Campbell's theology, but many of his innuendoes and factual statements demand clarification and correction.

Mr. Campbell does not give a single reference in his article, so it is impossible for readers to check his statements. It appears that he has based his impression of the Masonic fraternity on the writings of eighteenth- and nineteenth-century Masonic historians whose enthusiasm for Freemasonry was greater than their understanding of history. This would be much like getting an impression of modern Christianity from the nineteenth-century writings of pro-slavery preachers.

Albert Mackey (1807–1881) and Albert Pike (1809–1891) are quoted by Mr. Campbell as if their interpretations of Masonic symbols are somehow dogmatic for Masons. The two Alberts were brilliant men, and at one time their scholarship was among the best. It has been eclipsed, however, by the birth of the "authentic school" of Masonic history. While the writings of Mackey and Pike are interesting, sometimes insightful, and often stimulating, they have no more influence over the thinking of today's Masons than nineteenth-century pro-slavery arguments have over today's Christians. In his most widely distributed book, *Morals and Dogma*, Albert Pike said, "Every one is entirely free to reject and dissent from whatsoever herein may seem to him to be untrue or unsound."[2]

Evangelists such as Charles Finney may have been openly attacked for their stand against Freemasonry, but then Freemasons were openly attacked for their membership during the anti-Masonic period (ca. 1826–1840), and lodge halls looted and burned. This demonstrates only that hotheads can be found on any side of an issue. Charles Finney (1792–1895), the great nineteenth-century preacher, opposed Freemasonry, but a quick search of the Internet will find Christians both strongly opposed to and as well as supporting Rev. Finney's theology.[3] Christians disagree on many issues, both small and large. Just as no one man can speak for Freemasonry, no one man can speak for Christianity.

Rev. Finney was also a postmillennialist, opposing the doctrines of premillennialism.[4] Must Christians abandon their God-given abilities to reason and fall into lockstep with his teachings, becoming postmillennialists and anti-Masons, just because he was a great preacher? While I admire Rev. Finney's zeal in spreading the Gospel, I most respectfully disagree with his conclusions about Freemasonry. I am joined in disagreeing with Rev. Finney by many Christian Masons today: Rev. Dr. Forrest D. Haggard, 33°, Interim General Secretary of the World Office of the Churches of Christ; former Senator Jesse Helms, 33°; Bishop Carl J. Sanders, 33°, United Methodist Church; and Senator Trent Lott, 33°.

But the question of Freemasonry should not become one of competing experts. ("I'll see your two pastors and raise you one bishop.") Rather it is a matter of personal conscience. Freemasonry is a fraternity that expects its members to enter with a mature understanding of their faith. The fraternity (like Scouting) encourages its members to participate faithfully in their religion.

> Freemasonry lacks the basic elements of religion: (a) It has no dogma or theology, no wish or means to enforce religious orthodoxy; (b) It offers no sacraments; (c) It does not claim to lead to salvation by works, by secret knowledge, or by any other means. The secrets of Freemasonry are concerned with modes of recognition, not with the means of salvation. . . . Freemasonry is far from indifferent toward religion. Without interfering in religious practice, it expects each member to follow his own faith and to place his Duty to God above all other duties.[5]

Freemasonry does offer its members the opportunity to work together in the community and to be of service to their fellow citizens. In 1995, American Freemasons gave $750 million dollars to charity—over $2 million a day.[6]

Mr. Campbell's article opens with a sense of foreboding and gloom as we read a spooky description of the House of the Temple, headquarters of the Scottish Rite Supreme Council for the Southern Jurisdiction of the United States. I'm not sure what Mr. Campbell's point is. The building is patterned after the mausoleum in Helicarnassus, which was one of the ancient Seven Wonders of the World, and hence much of its decoration is appropriate to that architectural theme. If Mr. Campbell had visited the headquarters of the Scottish Rite's Northern Masonic Jurisdiction he would have found an American colonial building. And if he had journeyed across the Potomac to the George Washington Masonic National Memorial in Alexandria, he would have found differing architectural treatments on each floor. Just beneath the observation platform of the Memorial is a small Christian Chapel with a gothic design, decorated with stained glass windows depicting the Sermon on the Mount, Christ healing the blind, the Crucifixion, and the Resurrection. The design of the Supreme Council's building in Washington is no more sinister than the colonial simplicity of St. John's Church on Lafayette Square, the Byzantine charm of Sts. Helen and Constantine Church on 16th Street, or the gothic magnificence of the Washington National Cathedral.

"Unearthing the Mysteries" declares the pyramid to be a Masonic emblem and implies the obelisk is one too, but that is not so, at least not in York and Scottish Rite Masonry as practiced in the United States. The emblems

Is It True What They Say about Freemasonry?

may be used occasionally as a decorative motif, but not as a sign of anything else. Early attempts to determine the origins of the fraternity looked to Egypt and the Middle East. This theory was popular for a while. Even Thomas Paine, the revolutionary pamphleteer, promoted this plus the idea that Celtic Druids also originated in Egypt.[7] Modern scholars do not agree on the origins of the fraternity, but they are universal is relegating the Egyptian theory to well-deserved obscurity.[8] "So far as anyone knows, Egypt neither had nor has any connection with or influence on Freemasonry, except whatever influence flowed from the imaginative writings of Masonic Egyptologists and a few charlatans such as Cagliostro with his Egyptian Rite. . . ."[9]

Many Masons, more enthusiastic than discerning, willingly accept exotic theories of their fraternity's origins. Many more anti-Masons eagerly grasp at these eighteenth- and nineteenth-century theories as some sort of evidence of occult or pagan origins. However, the most widely (though not universally) accepted theory is that the fraternity evolved from medieval cathedral-building guilds—early trade unions.[10]

The uncompleted pyramid on the obverse of the Great Seal originated with the 1778 design of a $50 colonial note by Francis Hopkinson (not a Mason), not as some mystic mark of approval by the Masons. "The misinterpretation of the seal as a Masonic emblem may have been first introduced a century later in 1884. Harvard Professor Eliot Norton wrote that the reverse was 'practically incapable of effective treatment; it can hardly, (however artistically treated by the designer), look otherwise than as a dull emblem of a Masonic fraternity.'"[11]

Pierre Charles L'Enfant is not known to have been a Mason.[12] If he was one, then Mr. Campbell should be able to give us the name of his lodge, or of a lodge whose register he signed. Perhaps Mr. Campbell can point us to a letter of someone who attended lodge with Mr. L'Enfant or of some other documentation of Mr. L'Enfant's participation in the fraternity. L'Enfant's city design has withstood the centuries well. The broad boulevards and tree-lined public spaces are beautiful. However, the Washington, Lincoln, and Jefferson Memorials were not on L'Enfant's original design. In fact, the land on which the Lincoln and Jefferson Memorials sit was recovered from swamp after L'Enfant's death.

Freemasons did lay the cornerstone of the US Capitol in 1793, but not with any dedication "to a pagan god." A transcript of the ceremony and following oration were preserved in the September 25, 1793, issue of *The Columbia Mirror and Alexandria Gazette*. Anyone can read it and decide for themselves.[13]

Mr. Campbell confuses the degree structure of Freemasonry. The most important degree—in fact the all-powerful and governing degree—is the Third Degree, that of Master Mason. The Thirty-third Degree of the Scottish Rite is not the "highest level," except of the Scottish Rite. After becoming a Master Mason, a member may join many other "appendant" or "concordant" bodies: the Royal Arch Masons (conferring four degrees); the Royal and Select Masters (conferring three degrees); the Knights Templar (conferring three degrees); the Scottish Rite (conferring thirty degrees); the Order of the Red Cross of Constantine (conferring three degrees); the Allied Masonic Degrees (conferring ten degrees); and many, many more.

The legend of Hiram Abif does not involve the resurrection of a hero-god. Hiram Abif is indeed viewed as a hero faithful to his promises even unto death, but he is no god. According to the old guild legend, his body was taken from a hasty grave and reburied in a more suitable location. Reburial is a far cry from resurrection.[14]

The square and compasses do not represent "ancient pagan solar deities"; their explanation has been simple and straightforward for centuries. The square reminds us "to square our actions by the square of virtue," while the compasses teach us "to circumscribe [our] desires and keep [our] passions within due bounds."[15] Some Masons may have thought that solar deity symbolism is appropriate, but it is not the symbolism used by any American Masonic Grand Lodge.

Albert Pike did teach that the Holy Bible, square, and compasses are the three great lights in Masonry. He was simply repeating Masonic symbolism propounded by the London Grand Lodge of Ancients about 1760. Further, he was an Episcopalian and had no belief in pagan deities.

There is no Masonic god known as "The Great Architect of the Universe"; it is simply a way of referring to the Creator. This phrase was first used by John Calvin, the protestant reformer whose teachings form the core of Presbyterianism. "Calvin repeatedly calls God 'the Architect of the Uni-

Is It True What They Say about Freemasonry?

verse,' and refers to his works in nature as 'Architecture of the Universe'; ten times in the *Institutes of the Christian Religion* alone."[16] James Anderson, a Presbyterian minister, edited the Grand Lodge constitutions in 1723 and incorporated this phrase. It has been used ever since to celebrate the creative and constructive powers of God. Following the logic of Mr. Campbell, Boy Scouts are guilty of worshiping the "Scouting god" when they offer their prayers in the name of "The Great Scoutmaster."

Many Masons are indeed buried east to west—about as many as are buried north to south. This is a new charge to me, apparently original with Mr. Campbell. If, however, Masons really must be buried east to west then this information should be well known to funeral directors and can be easily verified by a visit to any cemetery.

No "symbol of the sun always appears" over the Master's seat in the symbolic east of a lodge. There is a letter "G" which stands for "geometry"—central to the guild of cathedral builders—and "God"—central to the life of all members of the Masonic fraternity.

It is clear that Mr. Campbell and I do not agree on the question of Freemasonry, and I suspect there are issues of theology on which we also disagree. However, if we must disagree, let us base our differences on substantiated facts that readers can confirm. The readers of *Charisma* deserve nothing less than accurate, up-to-date references they can confirm for themselves. I do believe clearly, however, that Mr. Campbell and I are in complete agreement on the saving grace offered humankind by Jesus' vicarious atonement.

Chapter 9

Rev. James Dayton Shaw: The Deadly Deception

> If any think they are religious, and do not bridle their tongues
> but deceive their heart, their religion is worthless.
>
> —James 1:26

Who should be better able to reveal the secrets of the lodge than a former Mason, especially one who achieved significant recognition within the fraternity? And who could be better trusted than a Christian minister? Surely what he has to say should be the "gospel truth." These are the implicit promises that *The Deadly Deception* holds out for its readers (see figure 9-1).

The Reverend James D. Shaw and Mr. Tom McKenney coauthored this engaging book. It tells the story of Rev. Shaw, from becoming a Mason and joining the Scottish Rite to leaving the fraternity. Apparently, Rev. Shaw had a born-again Christian experience and decided that it was his duty to expose Freemasonry to save other men from being victims of its, as he described, "deadly deception." The reader should expect a higher standard of accuracy from Rev. Shaw's story for two reasons. First, because of the years he spent in Masonry, and, second, because he is a minister of the Gospel of Jesus Christ, his testimony should be free of false witness.

We begin our examination of Rev. Shaw's truthfulness by examining the cover of his book. Six claims are made there, four of which are deliberate, verifiable lies. It does not bode well for the accuracy of the contents, if the

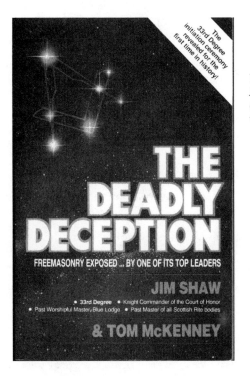

Figure 9-1. Cover of *The Deadly Deception* with six claims, four of which are deliberate and verifiable lies.

cover achieves no more than 33 percent of the truth. We review the claims individually and, through them, Rev. Shaw's devotion to truth.

SIX CLAIMS ON THE COVER OF *THE DEADLY DECEPTION*

- Freemasonry exposed . . . by one of its top leaders

- Past Worshipful Master, Blue Lodge

- Past Master of All Scottish Rite Bodies

- Knight Commander of the Court of Honor

- 33rd Degree

- The 33rd Degree initiation ceremony revealed for the first time in history!

The nature of these claims requires us to study Masonic sources, public and private, as Rev. Shaw's supporters failed to provide any primary documentation for his allegations. Anticipating criticism, however, his supporters deny the reliability of Masonic records:

> What reason have we to believe that a system based on lies and deception, with that much time, hasn't "lost" or altered the records? . . .[1]

This approach is a perplexing case of having your cake and wanting to eat it too. Rev. Shaw's supporters essentially say, "Masons and their records cannot be trusted, but don't worry. Even though we can't provide any documentation, we are trustworthy." This approach is dubious, to say the least. Rather, we prefer to rely on public documents whenever possible and let our readers verify our statements, if they so desire.

Shaw's First Claim

The full title of the book is *The Deadly Deception: Freemasonry Exposed by One of Its Top Leaders*. It is laughable to suggest that Rev. Shaw was ever a "top leader" of Freemasonry. He served the Craft decently during his membership and received some recognition for his work, but he never attained any position of prominence (at the state or national levels, for example). Rev. Shaw's co-author, Tom C. McKenney, however, was apparently embarrassed that this claim was forced on him by the publisher.

> I would like to explain to you the disputed "one of Masonry's top leaders" statement in the subtitle. That was insisted upon by the publisher; I argued against the word "top" for at least an hour on the phone, but he had his way. At any rate, it is a completely imprecise term; it could mean he was one of the top two, or one of the top two million. . . . but I'd like for you to know how it arrived in the subtitle, which I thought was much too lurid (I also argued against "exposed," but lost that one too).[2]

In order to be as fair as possible, we'll accept the claim as harmless puffery, an acceptable practice for promoting a commercial product.

The first claim is the truth.

Shaw's Second Claim

The cover claims Rev. Shaw was "Past Worshipful Master, Blue Lodge." To be elected and to serve as Master of a lodge (its presiding officer) is a great privilege and honor for any Mason. By identifying himself as a Past Master, Rev. Shaw seeks to establish himself as one who has achieved Masonic recognition through hard work. As with so many of his statements about Masonry, however, the factual record tells a different story.

Most American Masonic lodges have the following nine officers (and sometimes more):

- Master*

- Senior Warden*

- Junior Warden*

- Secretary*

- Treasurer*

- Senior Deacon

- Junior Deacon

- Senior Steward

- Junior Steward

   *Usually elected offices; others are appointed by the Master.

The Secretary and Treasurer normally are reelected for several years, while the other seven officers form the "progressive line." A Mason appointed Junior Steward at the bottom of the line will normally advance to the next office or "chair" each year, taking seven years to become Master of his lodge. Some lodges have other officers, including a Chaplain, Tyler (door keeper), Marshal, Organist, and so on.

Rev. Shaw received the First Degree in Masonry on September 11, 1945, in Evergreen Lodge No. 713 in Indianapolis, Indiana. The Second and Third

Degrees were conferred by courtesy in Biscayne Bay Lodge No. 124, Miami, Florida on May 21 and July 23, 1946. He transferred his membership to Allapattah Lodge No. 271 in Miami, Florida, on July 1, 1952, and remained a member until his resignation on October 25, 1966. Records show that he never held office in any Masonic lodge or affiliated body in Indiana.[3]

In 1964, he was appointed Junior Steward, the bottom of the line, of Allapattah Lodge; in 1965, he was appointed Junior Deacon, skipping the office of Senior Steward, and on October 25, 1966, he resigned from Masonry. The names of the principal elected officers of every Florida lodge— the Master, Senior and Junior Wardens, Secretary, and Treasurer—are published annually in the *Proceedings of the Most Worshipful Grand Lodge F&AM of Florida.* These *Proceedings* can be inspected in any of the over 300 Florida lodges or in public and Masonic libraries around the state and country. The name of James Dayton Shaw never appeared in the list of elected lodge officers. The public record reveals that he was never elected an officer in Allapattah Lodge, much less Master of the lodge.

The second claim is a lie.

APPENDIX I
REGISTRY OF PARTICULAR LODGES

LODGE	NO.	MASTER	SENIOR WARDEN	JUNIOR WARDEN	TREASURER	SECRETARY	ADDRESS SECRETARY'S	Dist. No.
John H. Pratt	261	Robt. H. Albritton	Murry Wolfson	Bertram Kaplan	Abe Cooper	Abe Horovitz	825 S. Granada Blvd., Jacksonville	16
Tamtami Trail	262	Cecil E. Drake	David J. Hoffman	Emanuel S. Beasely	Donald O. Rindy	Lewis E. Predmore	Everglades	25
Pompano	263	Leonard H. Kleve	J. D. Carlton	Oscar K. Johnson	David A. Ballou	Elmer C. Harland	2511 N.E. 20th St., Pompano Beach	27
Fellowship	265	John E. Greenslade	Howard B. Berry	Sidney Oliver Beck	Beryl Theo Morris	Walter J. Oatley	206 S. O'Brien, Tampa, 9	20
Riverside	266	Bernard H. Koosed	Arvine Geo. Ebert	Elger Price, Jr.	Frank O. Bryant, Sr.	Philip D. Myers, Sr.	1143 Pamer Ave., Jacksonville, 10	10
Orange Park	267	Johnny M. Gentry	Marvin W. Howze	Paul C. Armstrong	Anthony H. Oak	Clyde W. Holland (Lt.)	6626 Lucente Dr., Jacksonville, 10	10
Shamrock	268	Clarence J. Treadwell	Dan Treadwell	Ike C. Harmon	Leroy L. Williams	Cartte E. Webb	Cross City	6
Eureka	269	Reedy M. Crouch	Evan Trevor Owen	Herman R. Peregoy	James E. Heath	Archibal M. Black	239 S.W. 3rd Pl., Dania	27
Daytona Beach	270	Corby J. Arnett	Raymond V. Hunt	Robt. F. Strickland	Harry Hopper	Carlton M. Smith	P.O. Box 1954 Daytona Beach	15
Allapattah	271	Daniel L. Beebe	Marshall R. Dyer	Garnet R. McGlocklin	Justus P. Bailey	Harold E. Harris	3010 N.W. 36th St., Miami, 42	28
Ribault	272	Arthur C. Parsons	Columbus Webb	Herbert J. Garcia	Wm. S. Wilson	Wm. H. Weatherbee	Jax Beach	10
Belle Glade	273	Fred A. Simmons	Elglee Johnson	Wm. Jennings Norris	Frank L. Anderson	709 N.W. 16th St., Belle Glade	26
Meridian Daylight	274	John D. Shields	Sam L. Speert	Warren G. Morgan	Marion W. Clay	Joe A. Campbell	498 E. 40th St., Hialeah	29
Hibiscus	275	Jerome S. Merlin	Louis Gilliman	Mole J. L. Tendrich	Nathaniel G. Kirsch	Murray Smith	312 Washington Ave., Miami Beach	28
Bethlehem	276	James R. Watford	L. D. Register	Y. O. Register	Wm. S. Worley	Dock Barentine	Rt. 3, Bonifay	3
North Shore	277	Herbert A. Morrison, Jr.	Wm. Clennie Underwood	Albert Judson Stone	Everardus Van Wulfen	James G. Miller	P.O. Box 908, N. Miami	28
Ensley	278	Auburn L. Seale	Harold L. Beane	Daryl E. Brown	Wm. Frank Ligon, Sr.	Robt. R. Drummond, Sr.	7417 N. Palafox Hwy., Pensacola	1
Oceanway	279	Edgar H. Smith	Louis L. Broward	Robt. A. Dunaway, Sr.	Henry D. Houston	John M. Thorne, Sr.	13446 Gillespie Ave., Jacksonville	9
Unity	280	Warren B. Knight	Marvin D. Baker	Geo. R. Hart	Clarence O. Rousse	Melvin C. Wilson	5780 S.W. 4th St., Miami	29

Figure 9-2. Officers of Allapath Lodge No. 271, Free & Accepted Masons, Miami, Florida, extracted from the *1961 Proceedings of the M∴ W∴ Grand Lodge F&AM of Florida*, of which Rev. Shaw falsely claimed to be a Past Master (see *The Deadly Deception*, p. 79).

Officers of Allapatah Lodge No. 271, Free & Accepted Masons, Miami, Florida
Extracted from the *1952–67 Proceedings of the M∴ W∴ Grand Lodge F&AM of Florida*

	Master	Senior Warden	Junior Warden
1967	Edwin A. Horborouny	Raymond D. Slattery	Lester R. Grant, Jr.
1966	George B. Tate	Edwin A. Horborouny	Raymond D. Slattery
1965	David Hellings	George B. Tate	Edwin A. Horborouny
1964	Arthur W. Scott, Jr.	David K. Hellings	George B. Tate
1963	Garnet R. McGlocklin	Arthur W. Scott, Jr.	David K. Hellings
1962	Marshall R. Dyer	Garnet R. McGlocklin	Arthur W. Scott, Jr.
1961	Daniel L. Beebe	Marshall R. Dyer	Garnet R. McGlocklin
1960	Robert K. Overstreet	Daniel L. Beebe	Marshall R. Dyer
1959	Melvin C. Foster	Robert K. Overstreet	Daniel L. Beebe
1958	John R. Gillette	Melvin C. Foster	Robert K. Overstreet
1957	Charles L. McCord	John R. Gillette	Melvin C. Foster
1956	Jack M. Hams	Charles L. McCord	John R. Gillette
1955	Donald K. Curry	Jack M. Hams	Charles L. McCord
1954	Harold E. Hams	Donald K. Curry	Jack M. Harris
1953	Justus P. Bailey	Harold E. Hams	Donald K. Curry
1952	Alto V. Hanison	Justus P. Bailey	Harold E. Harris

	Treasurer	Secretary
1955–67	Justus P. Bailey	Harold E. Harris
1952–54	Joseph G. Roberts	Robert K. Overstreet

Figure 9-3. A listing of all Masters, Wardens, Secretaries, and Treasurers from 1952–67 of Allapattah Lodge No. 271, of which Rev. Shaw falsely claimed to be a Past Master (see *The Deadly Deception*, p. 79).

Shaw's Third Claim

Rev. Shaw claims to be Past Master of all Scottish Rite Bodies. Again, the record shows otherwise. In 1960 and 1961, he was appointed Captain of the Guard in the Consistory in Miami (the Consistory confers the 31° and 32° in the Scottish Rite); he held no other offices in the Consistory.

In 1961, he was appointed Prelate of the Lodge of Perfection (conferring the 4° to 14°) and served two years. He held four other appointive offices: Captain of the Host, 1963; Assistant Expert, 1964; Expert, 1965; and Master of Ceremonies, 1966, the year of his resignation.

He never advanced beyond the appointed offices in the Lodge of Perfection and was never elected to any Scottish Rite office.[4] He was not Master of even one Scottish Rite body, much less four.

The third claim is a lie.

MIAMI LODGE OF PERFECTION

Virtus Junxit, Mors
Non Separabit

Ineffable Degrees

HARRY A. GREENBERG
32°, K.C.C.H.
Venerable Master

OFFICERS 1966 - 1967

Venerable Master __Harry A. Greenberg, 32°, K.C.C.H.
Senior Warden _____Earl E. Owens, 32°, K.C.C.H.
Junior Warden _____Jack W. Fleming, 32°, K.C.C.H.
Orator _____Judge Grady L. Crawford, 32°, K.C.C.H.
Almoner _____Harley Pittman, 33°
Secretary _____Roy L. Martin, 33°
Treasurer _____James L. Mixson, 33°
Prelate ___ _____ Joseph A. Oritt, 32°
Master of Ceremonies __James D. Shaw, 32°, K.C.C.H.
Expert _____Joe A. Campbell, 32°, K.C.C.H.
Assistant Expert _____Walter I. Harms, 32°, K.C.C.H.
Captain of the Host _____Robert E. Short, 32°
Sentinels _____ Homer L. Rees, 32°, K.C.C.H.
Herman Slepian, 32°

PAST VENERABLE MASTERS

```
1917-18–SCULTHORPE, J. H. _____ 32°
1919–HILL, FRANK D. _____ 32°
1919–LEWIS, A. E. _____ 32°
†1920–BROWN, W. E. _____ 32°
*1921–ATWATER, W. M. _____ 32°, K.C.C.H.
1922–DELANEY, F. W. _____ 32°, K.C.C.H.
*1923–STRAHAN, W. J. _____ 32°, K.C.C.H.
*1924–ORR, J. B. _____ 32°, K.C.C.H.
*1925-26–WITHERILL, C. H. _____ 32°, K.C.C.H.
*1927–COFFRIN, MILO _____ 32°, K.C.C.H.
†1928–HEARN, W. N. _____ 32°
1929–HENSHAW, D. C. _____ 32°
*1930-31–SANDIFER, JOHN R., SR. _____ 32°, K.C.C.H.
1932–OPPENBORN, H. L. _____ 33°
†*1933–MARTIN, ROY L. _____ 32°
1934–LaBAW, W. B. _____ 32°
*1935–GARD, I. W. _____ 32°, K.C.C.H.
†*1936–PENDERGAST, F. G. _____ 32°
†*1937–BLAKEY, B. H. _____ 32°
*1938–RUFF, WALLACE _____ 32°, K.C.C.H.
†1939–WESTMAN, E. E. _____ 32°
*1940–RAMEY, JOHN N. _____ 32°, K.C.C.H.
1941–McCAHILL, S. S. _____ 32°
†*1942–BROWN, F. A _____ 32°
†*1943–CLINGEN, L. B. _____ 32°
†*1944–MIXSON, J. L. _____ 32°
†*1945–GOOCH, J. Y. _____ 32°
†*1946–NORFLEET, THOS. L. _____ 32°
†1947–HARRIS, W. J. _____ 32°
*1948–KIRBY, W. J. _____ 32°, K.C.C.H.
†1949–WILLIAMS, FRANK A., SR. _____ 32°
*1950–WRIGHT, H. RAYMOND _____ 32°, K.C.C.H.
†*1951–PITTMAN, HARLEY _____ 32°
†*1952–TODD, OLEN W. _____ 32°
*1953–WILLIAMS, ERNEST R. _____ 32°, K.C.C.H.
*1954–JOHNSTON, OLIN C. _____ 32°, K.C.C.H.
*1955–BOND, VERNON D. _____ 32°, K.C.C.H.
*1956–LOVERIN, JAMES H. _____ 32°, K.C.C.H.
1957–LANIER, BENJAMIN W. _____ 33°
*1958–NELSON, LESTER B. _____ 32°, K.C.C.H.
1959–CASEY, ROBERT C. _____ 32°, K.C.C.H.
1960–COX, WILLIAM J. _____ 32°, K.C.C.H.
*1961–GOLDMAN, ABRAHAM S. _____ 32°, K.C.C.H.
1962–MAGILL, CHARLES W. _____ 32°, K.C.C.H.
1963–HARRIS, HAROLD E. _____ 32°, K.C.C.H.
1964–FRIEDLAND, MELVIN A. _____ 32°, K.C.C.H.
1965–CHARLES O. WHITNEY _____ 32°, K.C.C.H.
```

†Later Invested K.C.C.H.   *Later Coronated 33°

Figure 9-4. List of 1966–1967 Officers of Miami Lodge of Perfection, Miami, Florida, showing James D. Shaw, 32°, K.C.C.H. as Master of Ceremonies (an appointed office). Below this is a list of every Past Venerable Master (the presiding officer) since 1917, the inception of Miami Lodge of Perfection. The list of Officers and Past Venerable Masters is updated and published every year. A similar list of current and past presiding officers is published for the other Scottish Rite bodies. Reunion program, Valley of Miami, Orient of Florida, May 1966.

Is It True What They Say about Freemasonry?

Shaw's Fourth Claim

Rev. Shaw was indeed invested with the Scottish Rite of Freemasonry's rank and decoration of a Knight Commander of the Court of Honour (KCCH) on December 18, 1965. (In 1965, about 1.4 percent of all Southern Jurisdiction Scottish Rite Masons were KCCHs, and about 0.6% were 33°.) The award was honorably earned and is properly claimed on the cover of his book.

The fourth claim is the truth.

DISTRICT OF COLUMBIA, 23

KENNETH MONROE ALLISON	Bethesda, Md.
CARROLL WAYNE AUSTIN	Arlington, Va.
MARTIN DALE CARLIN	Arlington, Va.
GILBERT H. DEHNEL	Hyattsville, Md.
CLAUD MAX FARRINGTON	Bethesda, Md.
ELMER WILLIAM FISHER	Beltsville, Md.
LAWRENCE WILLIAM FREUDE	Washington
MILFORD POWELL GOSLEE	Washington
GEORGE GOTTESMAN	Washington
HARLEY CLIFTON HEMINGWAY	Hyattsville, Md.
JOHN DANIEL KURTZ, III	Washington
FRANCIS BUCK LIVESEY	Chevy Chase, Md.
CHARLES STANLEY LOWELL	Chevy Chase, Md.
ERNEST GILBERT MALLETTE	Silver Spring, Md.
WILLIAM FRANCIS RABORN, JR.	Washington
WILLIAM FLORIAN ROBERTS, II	Silver Spring, Md.
HARRY BUTLER SAVAGE	Hyattsville, Md.
GEORGE CHRISTOPHER SCHLETER	Washington
JUDGE NEWELL SINGLETON	Washington
DEAN HILL STANLEY	Washington
ELMER FREDERICK STEIN	Silver Spring, Md.
ISADORE TUROFF	Washington
LIONEL ERNEST WALKER	Hyattsville, Md.

FLORIDA, 61

JAMES LEWIS ATKINSON	Key West
BRISTER D. AUSTIN	Miami
HAROLD CLINTON BECKER	Tampa
ISHMAEL WINFORD BRANT	Neptune Beach
GEORGE VERNON BROWN	Orlando
PARK HUNTER CAMPBELL	Miami
ROY FRANCIS CLARKE, SR.	Jacksonville
CARY WALTER COPPERSMITH	Tampa
ROBERT EARL COX	West Palm Beach
EVANS CRARY, JR.	Stuart
KENNETH FRANKLIN CURTIS	Orlando
CARL CLINTON DURRANCE	Tampa
HERSHEL LEROY EASTERLING	West Hollywood
GEORGE HENRY FIRKINS, JR.	Cape Kennedy
ANTHONY FLORIO	Jacksonville
HARDIN AUSTIN GOFF	Jacksonville
KENNETH CALHOUN HALL	Tampa
HENRY FRANK HANSON	Jacksonville
DEANE LOES HART, JR.	Lakeland

FRED JOHN HASLINGER	Clearwater Beach
HENRY DANIEL HEAD	Bradenton
ANSEL HOLLOWAY	Ocala
WILLIAM LLOYD HOOPER	West Palm Beach
ABE HOROVITZ	Jacksonville
LOWERY LEE JACKSON	West Palm Beach
GRADY WALTER JONES	Jacksonville
FREDERICK EMIL KELLER	Lake Park
ROBERT JACOB KENDALL	Key West
RUSSELL PAUL LEA	Jacksonville
G. SYDNEY LENFESTEY	Tampa
FREDERICK RICHARD LE VARGE, JR.	Tampa
ARVILLE CLIFFORD LOFTIS	Orlando
ARTHUR REYNOLD LUND	Clearwater
HAROLD HENSEL MARTIN	Winter Park
ERNEST EDWARD MASON	Pensacola
CHARLES ERNEST MCGEHEE	West Palm Beach
RUSSELL HUGH MCINTOSH	West Palm Beach
SETH GRAHAM MCKEEL	Lakeland
FRANK MITCHELL MCKENZIE	St. Petersburg
WILLIAM WINFORD MCKNIGHT	Jacksonville
JOSEPH EDWARD NETH	Green Cove Springs
WILLIAM HENRY NICOLS	Jacksonville
FRANK WISCONSIN NORRIS	Jacksonville
WILLIAM JACK PRUITT	Miami
ERIC ROGER PRYOR	Mary Esther
CHARLES EDWARD REED	Miami
ANDREW RAOUL REMALEY	Miami
SEYMOUR STANLEY ROSENBERG	Miami
JAMES DAYTON SHAW	Miami
GEORGE STANLEY SMITZES	Tarpon Springs
CHARLES WALPER SNYDER	West Palm Beach
STEPHEN LOUIS SPERONIS	Tampa
GEORGE RICHARD SWARTZ	Leesburg
THOMAS RAY TAGGART	Tampa
HORACE WILLIAM THORNBURG	Melbourne
FRED RICHARD WAGNER	Tallahassee
HEWETT WALKER	Tampa
MAURICE WILLIAM WALTERS	Kissimmee
JOY OTIS WILLIAMSON	Bartow
EDWARD DENSMORE WOOTEN	United States Air Force
JAMES HOWARD YOUNG	St. Cloud

Figure 9-5. The listing of all 1965 Florida recipients of the Knight Commander of the Court of Honour, showing the name of James D. Shaw. Similar lists of recipients are published every odd year showing the newly elected K.C.C.H.s and Thirty-third Degree Masons. From *Transactions of the Supreme Council, 33°, S.J.* (Washington, D.C.: 1965), pp. 224–25.

Shaw's Fifth Claim

The 33° is an important and limited honor in the Scottish Rite. At any time, about 1–2 percent of all Scottish Rite Masons hold this honor in recognition of their service to the fraternity or to mankind. It cannot be applied for and must be denied if requested. Of course, it can be falsely claimed by anyone brazen enough to steal the title. Sadly, this is what Rev. Shaw has done.

Although he refused to provide an exact date, Rev. Shaw gave enough information to deduce the date of his alleged reception of the Thirty-third Degree:

> I had been a K.C.C.H. for only four years. A man cannot even be considered for the 33rd Degree until he has been a K.C.C.H. four years. I was being considered for the 33rd in the minimum time![5]

He received the KCCH in 1965 and resigned from Masonry on October 25, 1966, thirty-seven months before reaching the four-year mark (see figure 9-6). Simple arithmetic demonstrates that Rev. Shaw should have received the 33° in 1969, some three years after his resignation. Tom McKenney was aware of this date discrepancy, but ultimately chose to ignore the public record and support Rev. Shaw's untenable account. Any other conclusion by Mr. McKenney would have destroyed the credibility (and sales) of his book.

> Initially, I was greatly troubled by . . . the apparent problem in the time lapse between KCCH and 33rd Degree in Jim's case. When I discussed this problem with Jim, he replied simply that the Supreme Council can do whatever it chooses to do. . . . In the final analysis I must choose whom I will believe. Upon consideration of all of the above, and knowing Jim as I do, I accept and believe the testimony of Jim Shaw, including all his Masonic credentials, exactly as published in "*The Deadly Deception*."[6]

Further evidence of this lie appears in the printed pamphlet distributed at the Miami, Florida, ninety-seventh Convocation Memorial Reunion, held on May 8, 1966, just five months before Rev. Shaw resigned from Freemasonry. Page 33 lists "James D. Shaw, 32°, K.C.C.H." as the "Degree Master" (casting director) for the 25° performed at that time. Significantly, his photograph shows him wearing a KCCH cap, not a 33° cap.

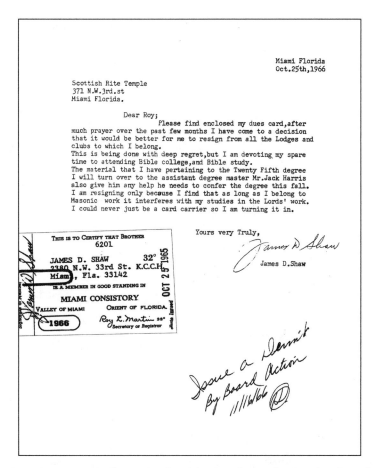

Figure 9-6. Rev. James D. Shaw's October 25, 1966, letter of resignation from the Scottish Rite with his attached 32°, K.C.C.H. dues card. The note below his signature says, "Issue a Demit [certificate of withdrawal] By Board Action 11/16/66." The tone of his letter is cordial and belies the deep hatred that later developed and led to so many malicious lies. Archives, Miami Scottish Rite, Miami, Florida.

It is important to note that in special circumstances, The Supreme Council, 33°, SJ, may indeed waive the traditional four-year period between the KCCH and its bestowal of the Thirty-third Degree. In such cases, the recipient has performed an extraordinary labor benefiting and/or honoring the fraternity. The Supreme Council, 33°, NMJ, may also waive its traditional period for similar reasons. An example of the latter was the bestowal of the Honorary Thirty-third Degree on John J. Robinson just before his death. Mr. Robinson was a popular author and lecturer who publicly defended Freemasonry, though not a Mason himself at the time. Shortly after joining the fraternity in 1993, it became known that Bro. Robinson was terminally ill and the Supreme Council, 33°, NMJ, exercised its right to confer the Honorary Thirty-third Degree on him in recognition of his extraordinary labors.

Although Rev. Shaw served decently in the minor positions he held while an active Mason, he was virtually unknown outside of his local circle and did nothing which would have warranted his reception of an Honorary Thirty-third Degree.

All Masons elected to the 33° have their names published in the *Transactions of the Supreme Council* like those elected KCCH. These volumes are easily available for inspection in any Scottish Rite body in the Southern Jurisdiction or in the Library of the Supreme Council, 33°, SJ, the oldest library open to the public in Washington, D.C. The name of James Dayton Shaw was never listed as the recipient of the 33°, despite his claims to the contrary.

The fifth claim is a lie.

Shaw's Sixth Claim

The upper right-hand corner of the book's cover has a bright red, eye-catching band with this come-on, "The 33rd Degree initiation ceremony revealed for the first time in history!" Rev. Shaw takes almost seven pages in the book to describe the events leading up to his so-called receipt of the 33°. The ceremony he describes is not based on his personal experience, but was plagiarized (or stolen) from another source. The source Rev. Shaw selected was an exposé of the "Cerneau" 33° ritual in Jonathan Blanchard's *Scotch Rite Masonry Illustrated*, which has been in print since 1887. Textual clues, such as drinking wine from a human skull, pinpoint Blanchard's work. It helped Rev. Shaw in his deception that such sources are easy to come by. A casual search shows that authors have "revealed" versions of the 33° initiation ceremony at least two dozen times since 1813, starting with Delaunay's *Thuileur des Trente-trois Degres de L'Ecossisme*. A partial listing of the exposés of this great "secret" is given at the end of this chapter.

A naïve anti-Mason might be forgiven for not knowing that various versions of the 33° initiation have been "exposed" for the better part of two centuries. Rev. Shaw obviously knew about at least Blanchard's "exposure" because he needed some source for describing the ceremonies in which he allegedly participated. Not only did Rev. Shaw lie about receiving the 33° himself, he did not have the moral integrity to cite the source he pilfered for his so-called description.

The sixth claim is a lie.

The lies cataloged above are not the result of simple misunderstandings; they were carefully calculated to deceive the trusting. Since at least 1976, Rev. Shaw made similar claims, perhaps to increase his importance in the eyes of his readers.

> I was not willing to be just a "card carrier." I was too eager for that. So I served in all the chairs and ultimately became Worshipful Master of the lodge. I pursued the degrees of the Scottish Rite and joined the Shrine in my quest for preeminence in the eyes of men. In time I became Past Master to all Scottish Rite Bodies. And finally was selected for the coveted 33rd Degree, and was made a 33rd Degree Mason in the House of the Temple in Washington, D.C.[7]

Before getting to even the first page of *The Deadly Deception*, the reader is deliberately deceived with four verifiable lies on the cover. They seem intended to boost the reputation of Rev. Shaw as an important former Mason, to reinforce the believability of his story, and to increase the sales of his book. They obviously are not intended to promote the truth.

FURTHER LIES IN THE BOOK

There is much more wrong with Rev. Shaw's and Mr. McKenney's book than the lies on the cover. As readers go through the book, they encounter a succession of charges, allegations, and subtle innuendo. Among other things, Rev. Shaw claims the cost of the Thirty-second Degree is exorbitant, Scottish Rite obligations have blood oaths, Masons are drunkards, and Masonry teaches reincarnation. Many of Rev. Shaw's other claims, however, cannot be confirmed by independent research. For example, how can anyone possibly confirm what unidentified Masons supposedly said in private conversations to Rev. Shaw?

Thus we reluctantly must address the issue of Rev. Shaw's general character: How many independently verifiable, deliberate lies about Freemasonry are needed before any statement made by Rev. Shaw must be questioned? We have found so many lies that we believe almost nothing Rev. Shaw or Mr. McKenney write about Freemasonry.

The Cost of the Thirty-second Degree

On page 59, Rev. Shaw describes joining the Scottish Rite. On page 63 (endnote 1), he greatly exaggerates the cost of "going all the way to the 32nd Degree."

> The Secretary greeted me and explained the nature and structure of the Scottish Rite. . . . He said that some men could not afford to take all of the degrees at one Reunion because of the cost.[1]

> [1] There is a price to be paid. in dollars, for all "earned" Masonic degrees, from Entered Apprentice to the 32nd Degree. Dollar values change with time and fees vary some from place to place. but the total cost of going all the way to the 32nd Degree can be very substantial, well into the thousands of dollars today.

It's not clear what the authors intended by this aside, unless it was to suggest an extravagant waste of money by Masons for initiation fees. A copy of Rev. Shaw's Scottish Rite petition, dated August 14, 1952, shows the true state of affairs (figure 9-7).

The cost in 1952 for the Fourth through Thirty-second Degrees, "including Patent [membership certificate], [gold 14°] Ring, and copy of *Morals and Dogma*" was $160. Rev. Shaw chose to purchase a 32° cap for $7.50, so his complete cost for joining the Miami Scottish Rite was $167.50. During his fifteen years of membership, he paid a total of $107.50 in annual dues: $7.50 dues annually for 1953 to 1966 plus $2.50 pro-rated dues for 1952 (figure 9-8).

The cost of joining the Scottish Rite in Miami has not kept pace with inflation. The fees in 2003 for the Fourth through the Thirty-second Degrees, including patent, 14° ring in a Lucite pyramid, and a 32° cap is $200. Rex Hutchens's *A Bridge to Light* (see Appendix, "Please Look a Little Closer," for information on *A Bridge to Light*) is now given to new members rather than Albert Pike's *Morals and Dogma*. Members wanting a 14° ring to wear must make a separate purchase. Annual dues in 2003 were $55.

ANCIENT AND ACCEPTED

Scottish Rite of Freemasonry

SOUTHERN JURISDICTION OF THE UNITED STATES
VALLEY OF MIAMI — ORIENT OF FLORIDA

PETITION FOR SCOTTISH RITE DEGREES

Date___AUGUST 14___195_2_

To the Officers and Members of

Mithra Lodge of Perfection   Utopia Council, Knights Kadosh
Acacia Chapter, Knights Rose Croix   Miami Consistory

I am a Master Mason in good standing in___ALLAPATTAH___Lodge No.__271__

Located at___Miami___under the Jurisdiction of the Grand Lodge of___Florida___

I have been a Master Mason six months yes or no._yes_). I hold a Certificate of Proficiency (yes or no_no_).

    The Grand Lodge of Florida requires that all members of Florida Lodges must have been Master Masons more than six months, or have passed a satisfactory examination in the catechism of the Master Mason Degree and hold a Certificate of Proficiency before applying for other Masonic Degrees.

I was born on the_27_ day of_Nov._, 19_11_, in_Indianapolis_State of_Indiana_

                                                Town or Nearest Post Office

I am married_X_My wife's name is_Bonnie Brice Shaw_

I am a registered voter in the State of Florida_yes_and have actually resided in this State since_Sept 15,45_

My residence is_2380 NW 33rd. street_____Miami_____37___Fla._
            Street   City   Zone   State

My mail address is_2380 NW. 33rd. street_____Miami_____37___Fla._
            Street   City   Zone   State

My Occupation is_Owner and operator of Bakery and Delicatessen._
                            (State fully character of business or occupation)

In employ of_self_Address_2305 NW.27th ave._

Residence Phone_64-3305_Business Phone_64-9277_Hat size_7-$\frac{1}{8}$_Ring size_11+_

Height_5_feet_11_inches. Color of eyes_grey_Color of Hair_brown_

I am a member of_____at_____
                    (State highest Scottish Rite Body to which advanced)

I have never previously applied for any of the Scottish Rite degrees except as noted here_X_

The Supreme Council announces as fundamental principles, the following:

    "The inculcation of patriotism, respect for law and order and undying loyalty to the Constitution of the United States of America."

    "The entire separation of church and state and opposition to every attempt to appropriate public monies —federal, state or local—directly or indirectly, for the support of sectarian or private institutions."

Do you approve wholeheartedly of these principles?_YES._Have you ever held or expressed opinions
                                    Yes or No

contrary to the foregoing or been affiliated with any organization which has,_NO._ If you answer this
                                             Yes or No

question in the affirmative, give particulars_____

I now respectfully petition to receive the degrees from the_4th._to the_32nd._inclusive, promising always to bear true faith and allegiance to the Supreme Council of the Thirty-third Degree for the Southern Jurisdiction of the United States.

Recommended by two members of Miami Bodies:

Hiram B Wadsworth   JAMES DAYTON SHAW
                                     Print Name in Full—Don't Use Initials

Roy L Martin   _James D Shaw_
                                                  Signature

At least $60.00 must accompany petition — Make Checks Payable to Miami Scottish Rite Bodies
SCHEDULE OF FEES AND DUES

Lodge of Perfection	. . . .	4 to 14 degrees	$ 60.00	Dues	$3.00
Chapter of Rose Croix	. . . .	15 to 18 degrees	30.00	Dues	1.50
Council of Kadosh	. . . .	19 to 30 degrees	30.00	Dues	1.50
Consistory	. . . .	31 to 32 degrees	40.00	Dues	1.50
	Total, including Patent, Ring, and Copy of Morals and Dogma	. . .	$160.00		$7.50

Figure 9-7. Rev. James Dayton Shaw's 1952 Scottish Rite petition showing his membership in Allapattah Lodge No. 271 at the top and the cost of fees and dues at the bottom. Archives, Miami, Florida Scottish Rite.

YEAR	DEBIT	PAYMENT DATE						DEBIT	PAYMENT DATE	FOLIO	CREDIT
1952	2.50	11/9/52			2.50	1967	-$10.00				
1953	7.50	11/9/52			7.50						
1954	7 50	*Oct*	12	53	67	2 50					
1955	7 50	11-22-54		119	7 50						
1956	7 10	*May*	14	56	39	7 50					
1957	7 50	*Sept.*	26	56	59	7 50					
1958	7.50	*Dec*	18	57	155	7 50					
1959	7 50	*Dec*	17	58	160	7 50					
1960	7 50	*Dec*	8	59	162	7 50					
1961	7 50	*Dec*	10	60	138	7 50					
1962	7 50	*Nov*	15	61	149	7 50					
1963	7 50	*Oct*	17	62	44	7 50					
1964	7 50	*Oct*	11	63	48	7 50					
1965	7 50	*Nov*	9	64	58	7 50					
1966	7.50	*Oct*	25	65	52	7 50					

SHAW, JAMES DAYTON

Figure 9-8. Member's record card of Rev. James Dayton Shaw showing total dues payments of $107.50 to the Miami Scottish Rite. Archives, Miami, Florida, Scottish Rite.

When joining Evergreen Lodge No. 713 in 1945, Rev. Shaw paid $50 in initiation fees for the First through the Third Degrees, Entered Apprentice to Master Mason; his annual dues then were $7. By 2003, Evergreen Lodge had merged with another lodge to become Evergreen-Oriental No. 500. Their initiation fees had risen to $125 and their annual dues to $65.

Rev. Shaw's entire cost for the First through Thirty-second Degrees was $217.50, and his total annual dues then were $14.50. In 2003 the cost for the First through Thirty-second Degrees was $325.00 and total annual dues are $120.00. This is far from being "well into the thousands of dollars" in 2003, and certainly wasn't even close in 1988 when *The Deadly Deception* was published.

Scottish Rite Obligations

As he continues his summary of joining the Scottish Rite, Rev. Shaw describes receiving the Fourth Degree on pages 60 to 61. Endnote 2 on page 63 amplifies the obligations of the degrees.

Is It True What They Say about Freemasonry?

The Fourth Degree was put on just like a play, with one candidate chosen from the class to represent us all as he participated.

The presentation went on until time to take the oath at the end. At this time we were told to stand, put our hands over our hearts and repeat the oath [2] of obligation. . . .

[2] There was a blood-oath of obligation for each degree, as in the Blue lodge.

This description of the twenty-nine Scottish Rite obligations certainly sounds ominous, but it overlooks a few niceties of fact. To start with, there have been no symbolic physical penalties in the Scottish Rite, Southern Jurisdiction, since about 1860, and there have never been any actual physical penalties. Here is what *Coil's Masonic Encyclopedia* says about the matter:

Albert Pike, in revising the rituals of the Southern Supreme Council of the Scottish Rite about 1855–1860, completely eradicated all such penalties from the degrees and substituted mental, moral, and symbolic condemnation, and that example was followed in the Northern Jurisdiction of the Scottish Rite about the middle of the 20th century.[8]

Rev. Shaw received the Scottish Rite degrees and conferred them for years. He knew as well as any Mason that there are no "blood oaths" in the Scottish Rite.

Why Must We Always Do So Much Drinking?

Rev. Shaw describes traveling to a Conclave in a "distant city" to be invested with the rank and decoration of a KCCH. In his story, he makes an aside about drinking, much like his comment about the cost of the Scottish Rite degrees. There is a subtle attempt by the authors to vilify Masons without the courage of making direct charges.

There was a great deal of drinking at the Conclave and it bothered me. "Why must we always do so much drinking?" I asked myself, but had no answer. I enjoyed a little drinking and did it regularly. But it bothered me that there was always so much of it and that it played such a major role in the Masonic life.[9]

The Grand Lodge of Florida, like many other American Grand Lodges, firmly forbids the sale or consumption of alcohol at any lodge function. Here is the 1954 regulation on alcoholic beverages that governed Florida lodges when Rev. Shaw joined:

28.06 (398) No particular Lodge shall allow its properties or any part thereof to be used for the purpose of conducting or carrying on a liquor business or for the dispensing of alcoholic beverages in any form.[10]

In 1975 the regulation was unchanged, though the following decision had been added to clarify the law. "The serving of any intoxicating beverage in Masonic Temples or Lodge Rooms or at Masonic banquets is forbidden by Masonic Law. (1969 Proc. 58, 212)"[11] Bro. William Wolf, Grand Secretary of the Grand Lodge of Florida, summarized the 1993 rules governing alcohol in Florida lodges:

> the Grand Lodge of Florida itself does not allow any alcoholic beverages in its ceremonies or the sale or dispensing of any alcoholic beverages on any property that it owns. Nor do we allow a function that is held in a particular lodge or in the Grand Lodge to have any alcoholic beverages for dispensing, such as Grand Master Homecomings, Grand Lodge Dinners, etc.[12]

Equally explicit are the 1953 *Statutes of the Supreme Council, Southern Jurisdiction,* to which the Scottish Rite Bodies of Miami hold allegiance. "Art. XV, §24. The use of any spirituous, vinous, or malt liquors by any Body is hereby prohibited."[13]

Neither the Grand Lodge of Florida nor the Supreme Council, SJ, permitted alcoholic beverages to be used by any of their subordinate bodies. Florida Masons are bewildered when asked how alcohol "played such a major role in the Masonic life" because there it has no role. What sort of meetings did Rev. Shaw attend where they "always do so much drinking"? It could not have been meetings of the lodges or the Scottish Rite bodies in Florida. His statement is cleverly designed to leave the reader with the impression that regular, heavy drinking is the norm at Masonic gatherings.

THE RESURRECTION OF HIRAM ABIF

One of the most subtle frauds of *The Deadly Deception* is Rev. Shaw's distortion of the legend of Hiram Abif. Rev. Shaw tries to convince his readers that he is a reliable expert on Masonry: "33rd Degree [*sic*], Knight Commander of the Court of Honour, Past Worshipful Master [*sic*], Blue Lodge, Past Master of all Scottish Rite bodies [*sic*]."[14] How could someone with these credentials not expose the plain truth about Masonic ritual?

The legend of Hiram Abif is a simple story, apparently based upon Hiram the metalworker, mentioned in 1 Kings 7:13. In the Masonic tale, Hiram is the Master Architect of King Solomon's Temple and one of only three Master Masons, the others being King Solomon and Hiram, King of Tyre. One day Hiram Abif is accosted by three Fellowcrafts (journeymen masons) who demand the secrets of a Master Mason. Hiram refuses to betray his trust and is murdered. The murderers are captured and executed. After a search, Hiram's body is removed from its temporary grave and re-interred in the Sanctum Sanctorum. (Such a burial never would have been allowed under Jewish law, but that didn't stop the authors of Masonic legend, who were familiar with the European practice of burying dignitaries beneath the floors of a cathedral.)

The legend is a simple vehicle for teaching fidelity to a trust; it has no basis in historical truth. It is a Biblically inspired morality play much like *Amahl and the Night Visitors*. It seems to have been introduced into Masonic ceremonies around 1726. The legend was first published in 1730 in *Masonry Dissected* by Samuel Prichard, an exposure of Masonic rituals.

In the Masonic legend the body of Hiram is taken from its temporary grave so it can be given a more suitable burial. Rev. Shaw's description, again, does not agree with the record: "Hiram was not only brought up out of the grave but restored to life."[15] Again, the purpose of this subtle distortion isn't entirely clear, but it seems to be to support Rev. Shaw's charge that Masonry teaches a doctrine of reincarnation to its members.[16] This teaching is offensive to Christians and, if true, would be ample reason for a Christian to leave the lodge.

> With the degree work and other Masonic writings as our source, we finally decided that the truth lay in reincarnation and that if we would try to live a good life now, be good to our brother Masons, help the sick and attend to good deeds in general, when we died we would enter the next life on a higher plane—just like going through a door.[17]

This lie is best discredited by Rev. Shaw's fellow anti-Masons who, in this case, have agreed with Masonic writers. Since at least 1723, Masonic ritual has been exposed in print, usually with the motives of trying to embarrass

Masons, closing lodges, and making money for the author. For over 250 years, these books have sought the same ends as Rev. Shaw, but they have told a story that stands in contrast to his. We quote several representative books to illustrate the consistent version of the Hiramic legend. Rev. Shaw's motives here are unknown but, like his version of the story of Hiram Abif, are not to be trusted.

Masonry Dissected, Samuel Prichard (London: 1730; reprint, Bloomington, Ill.: The Masonic Book Club, 1977), pp. 28, 29.

> Ex. What did King Solomon say to all this?
> R. He order'd him to be taken up and decently buried.
> Ex. Where was Hiram inter'd?
> R. In the Sanctum Sanctorum.

Three Distinct Knocks, anonymous (London: 1760; reprint, Bloomington, Ill.: The Masonic Book Club, 1981), p. 61.

> After this King Solomon sent those 12 Crafts to raise their Master Hiram, in order that he might be interred in Sanctum Sanctorum.

Jachin and Boaz, anonymous (London: 1762; reprint, Bloomington, Ill.: The Masonic Book Club, 1981), p. 45.

> When the Execution was over, King Solomon sent for the Twelve Crafts, and desired them to take the Body of Hiram up, in order that it might be interred in a solemn Manner in the Sanctum Sanctorum. . . .
> "What did they do with the body?"
> Ans. "Raised it in a Masonic form and carried it up to the temple for more decent interment."

Illustrations of Masonry by One of the Fraternity, William Morgan (Batavia, [New York]: Printed for the Author, 1826), pp. 88–89.

> Q. What did they do with the body?
> A. Raised it in a Masonic form and carried it up to the Temple for more decent interment.
> Q. Where was it buried?
> A. Under the sanctum sanctorum, or holy of holies of King Solomon's Temple. . . .

Secret Societies, Norman MacKenzie (London: George Redway, 1897), pp. 318, 319.

Is It True What They Say about Freemasonry?

[King Solomon], when the first emotions of his grief had subsided, ordered them to return and raise our Master to such a sepulture, as became his rank and exalted talents. . . . Our Master was ordered to be re-interred as near to the Sanctum Sanctorum as the Israelitish law would permit. . . .

The evidence is clear and consistent. Anti-Masonic authors, all with the intent of harming Masonry, have told the same story for over 250 years, which in this instance happens to agree with what Masons have said. Hiram Abif was murdered and buried in a hastily dug, temporary grave. His body was taken from the grave to be re-interred in or near (wordings vary) the Sanctum Sanctorum. There is no "resurrection" or doctrine of reincarnation. The legend of Hiram Abif is not the only thing Rev. Shaw misunderstood while he was a Mason—Freemasonry teaches a reverence for truth to its members.

"EXPOSURES" AND DESCRIPTIONS OF THE 33° INITIATION CEREMONY

1813—"Souverain-Grand-Inspecteur-General," in [François H. Stanislaus Delaunay], *Thuileur des Trente-trois Degres de L'Ecossisme di Rite Ancien, dit Accepte*, Paris: Delaunay, Libraire, Palais-Royal, 1813, 1821.

1829—"Sovereign Grand Inspector General," in David Bernard, *Light on Masonry*, Utica, N. Y.: William Williams, 1829.

1830—"Souverain Grand Inspecteur General," in Vuillaume, *Manuel Maçonnique ou Tuileur des Divers Rites de Trente-trois Degres de L'Ecossisme di Rite Ancien, Maçonnerie Practiques en France*, 1830 (reprint ed.; Paris: Dervy-Livres, 1975)

1843—"Reception au 33eme degre," in F. T. B. Clavel, *Histoire Pittoresque de la Franc-Maçonnerie*, Paris: N.p., 1843.

1857—"Sovereign Grand Inspector General," in Charles Laffon de Ladebat, *Thirty-Third Degree and Last of the Ancient and Accepted Scotch Rite: Sovereign Grand Inspector General*, New Orleans: 1857.

1860—"Sovereign Grand Inspector General," in Jabez Richardson, *Richardson's Monitor of Free-Masonry*, New York: Fitzgerald, 1860.

1860—"Sobrano Gran Inspector General," in Andres Cassard, *Manual de la Masoneria*, New York: Macoy, 1860.

1861—"Souverain Grand Inspecteur General," in Jean-Baptiste Marie Ragon, *Tuileur General de la Franc-Maçonnerie, ou Manuel de l'Initie*, Paris: Collignon, 1861.

1872—"Old Cahier of the 33rd Degree," in Albert Pike, *Grand Constitutions of Freemasonry, Ancient and Accepted Scottish Rite*, New York: Masonic Publishing Co., 1872.

1888—"Sovereign Grand Inspector General," in Jonathan Blanchard, *Scotch Rite Masonry Illustrated*, 2 vols., Chicago: Ezra A. Cook, 1887–1888.

1890—"Sovereign Grand Inspector General," in *Secret Societies Illustrated*, Chicago: Ezra A. Cook, ca. 1890.

1923—"Sovereign Grand Inspector-General," in Arthur Edward Waite, *A New Encyclopedia of Freemasonry*, 2 vols., rev. ed., London: Rider & Co., 1923.

1933—"Official Ritual of the 33rd and Last Degree of Ancient and Accepted Scottish Rite," in Paul Rosen, *Satan et Cie*, Paris: 1888, excerpted in Edith Starr Miller, *Occult Theocrasy*, 2 vols., 1933, reprint, Hawthorn, Calif.: Christian Book Club, 1968, 1976, 1980.

1933—"33d Degree-Knight Grand Inspector General," in W. J. Coombes, trans., E. J. Marconis de Negre, *The Sanctuary of Memphis or Hermes*, [N.C.]: Nocalore, 1933.

1946—S. Farina, "Sovrano Grande Ispettore Generale" in *Il Libro Completo dei Rituali Massonici Rito Scozzese Antico ed Accettato*. Rome: 1946.

1984—"Soverain Grand Inspecteur General," in Paul Naudon, *Histoire, Rituels et Tuileur des Haut Grades Maçonniques*, Paris: Dervy-Livres, 1984.

Chapter 10

T. N. Sampson:
Defending the Deception

FOR THE SPIRIT OF TRUTH

From the cowardice that dares not face new truth,
from the laziness that is contented with half-truth,
from the arrogance that thinks it knows all truth.
Good Lord, deliver me. Amen.

—Prayer from Kenya, United Methodist Hymnal

In the February 1993 issue of *The Scottish Rite Journal,* Dr. S. Brent Morris, then
Book Review Editor, reviewed *The Deadly Deception,* by Rev. James D. Shaw and
Tom McKenney. Several months after the review was published, Mr. T. N.
Sampson of Cornerstone Ministries sent Dr. Morris a letter challenging the
accuracy of his review. Thus began a correspondence that continued off and
on for two years. This chapter reproduces the initial book review and the
subsequent correspondence. Although sometimes tedious to read, these letters reveal the great lengths to which anti-Masons will go to defend their
prejudices.

THE SOUND AND THE FURY

[Book Review, Scottish Rite Journal, February 1993]

The Deadly Deception: Freemasonry Exposed by One of Its Top Leaders, by Rev. James D. Shaw and Tom McKenney

The Deadly Deception is a fine example of the level to which anti-Masons are willing to stoop in pursuing their vendetta against Freemasonry. The book is written in simple language, accessible to someone without a high school education. Co-author Tom McKenney tells the life story of Jim Shaw, emphasizing his Masonic career and religious conversion. The biography is engaging, empathetic, and scattered with clever, vicious lies.

Mr. McKenney is not to be faulted for confusing a 33° Sovereign Grand Inspector General with a 33° Inspector General Honorary as he does on page 8. Masonic nomenclature is charmingly baroque and can be confusing, even to the initiated. But someone must take responsibility for the lies that start on the front cover with the claim that Jim Shaw had attained the "33rd Degree." Mr. Shaw was invested with the Rank and Decoration of a Knight Commander of the Court of Honour on November 18, 1965, and resigned from Masonry on October 25, 1966, thirty-seven months before he would have been eligible for the Thirty-third Degree. He was neither nominated for nor elected to any Scottish Rite honors other than the KCCH. The *Transactions of The Supreme Council, 33°,* list all elected to Scottish Rite Honors and can be consulted in most Scottish Rite Valleys to verify this falsehood.

Jim Shaw was never a Thirty-third Degree Mason.

Continuing with the claims on the front cover, Jim Shaw is not "Past Master of all Scottish Rite Bodies"; he was elected Master of his lodge. The claim that he was "one of [Masonry's] top leaders" is laughable puffery, but within the bounds of acceptable self-promotion. He served in Mithra Lodge of Perfection in the appointive offices of Prelate, Captain of the Host, and Assistant Expert from 1961 to 1966, when he resigned.

134   *Is It True What They Say about Freemasonry?*

Jim Shaw never presided over any Scottish Rite body.

The book's cover tries to lure purchasers with this inducement: "The Thirty-third Degree initiation ceremony revealed for the first time in history!" It doesn't take much research to discover that many authors have claimed to reveal the Thirty-third Degree initiation ceremony. David Bernard's 1829 *Light on Masonry* offered its readers an "exposé" of the Degree of Sovereign Grand Inspector General. In 1887 Rev. Jonathan Blanchard published *Scotch Rite Masonry Illustrated* with what he claimed were the Thirty-third Degree ceremonies of the Cerneau Supreme Council for the United States of America (considered illegitimate by both the Northern and Southern Jurisdictions). *Deadly Deception* is certainly not the first book to try to pump up sales with this misleading enticement. The fragmentary ceremony described on pages 103 to 104 appears to be plagiarized from Blanchard's book, which at least offered its readers "passwords," illustrations, and full details.

Three of the five statements on the book's cover are deliberate lies.

Finding further deceptions inside the book is like shooting fish in a barrel. Masons are depicted as being drunkards (page 83), as believing Hiram Abif was "restored to life" when King Solomon raised his body from the grave (page 151), and as spending "well into the thousands of dollars today" to receive the Thirty-second Degree (page 63). Most of the deceits inside the book are clever distortions of the truth intended to subtly present an image of Masons as convivial, anti-Christian pagans.

Several facts can be established easily from published records.

1. Neither the Grand Lodge of Florida nor The Supreme Council, 33°, S.J., permit alcohol to be served at their functions.

2. The legend of Hiram Abif has been associated with Freemasonry for a little over 250 years; it is widely published and well studied. Hiram's body was re-interred; he was neither resurrected nor reincarnated.

3. Mr. Shaw's Scottish Rite initiation fees and Thirty-second Degree cap were $167.50 in 1952; the cost today in Miami is $200.

Identifying and exposing these pathetic inventions, however, is a task that must be ultimately fruitless. Anyone willing to overlook the easily verifiable lies on the book's cover will just rationalize away the corruption within. What is saddest about this book is the eagerness of the authors to cheat the public to achieve their twisted ends, all in the name of Jesus. Jesus told his disciples, "I am the way, the truth, and the life," but truth is only a minor obstacle in the authors' headlong rush to defame our gentle Craft. The "deadly deception" in the title best describes the contents of this book.

Mr. T. N. Sampson begins his correspondence with Dr. Morris in a cordial tone, but clearly disbelieves virtually anything written by Masons. He implies that Dr. Morris is deceptive (for example in quoting current Masonic regulations on alcohol but not those of Rev. Shaw's time), but stops just short of accusing Dr. Morris of outright lying.

[LETTER 1]

Cornerstone Ministries
Poquson, Virginia

August 28, 1993

Dr. S. Brent Morris, Book Review Editor
The Scottish Rite Journal
1733 16th Street, NW
Washington, DC 20009-3199

Dear Dr. Morris:

Cornerstone Ministries was formed by my wife and myself to provide information to Christians about non-Christian cults and religions. Not surprisingly, Freemasonry is a topic we are addressing. I have spent some time reading the various articles and books dealing with both sides of the issue and have found that the truth in the matter is somewhere between Dr. Holly and Mr. Robinson; however, falsehood abounds on both sides.

I read your article, "The Sound and the Fury," in the February 1993 edition of *The Scottish Rite Journal* and came away uncertain as to whether you were being truthful or not in your criticisms of Jim Shaw's book, *The Deadly Deception*. Since my attempt is to ascertain the truth, may I trouble you to respond to the following questions?

- You note that the book "is written in simple language, accessible to someone without a high school education." What is meant by that statement? Is that good or bad? My son has an

International Children's bible which is written to the third grade level; does that reflect badly on its content?

- You note that Mr. McKenney confused "a Thirty-third Degree Sovereign Grand Inspector General with a Thirty-third Degree Inspector General Honorary." I do not understand what the difference is. Mr. Shaw claims to be a Sovereign Grand Inspector General (pg 103) and Coil notes that is the proper title for the 33 degree (pg 608 of his *Encyclopedia*). I could not find the latter title so I cannot figure out what was being confused for what (though I am confused!).

- You say that Mr. Shaw was never a 33rd degree Mason. I have written a similar letter to Mr. Shaw asking him about this and will share his answer with you when it is received.

- You note that Blanchard claimed that his *Scotch Rite Masonry Illustrated* contained the ceremonies of the Cerneau Council. As I understand it, Blanchard did not claim that his book reflected Cerneau ceremonies; this is a claim made by Masons, and an unproven one at that.

In shooting fish in a barrel, you hit one or two that weren't in there:

- You say that Shaw depicts Masons as being drunkards (pg 83). On that page, Shaw merely notes that there was a great deal of drinking at the conclave, a statement which does not support your criticism. You further note that "neither the Grand Lodge of Florida nor The Supreme Council 33°, SJ permit alcohol to be served at their functions." That is nice, but you state current practice, not historical practice. Did either allow alcohol when Shaw was a member in the '60s? As well, Shaw notes going to a "distant city" to receive this high honor, which may or may not have been in Florida.

- You dispute Shaw's claim that Masons spend thousands to receive the 32nd degree; however, that's not what he claimed. On pg 63, he notes that "going all the way to the 32nd degree can be very substantial, well into the thousands of dollars today." Thus, the cost estimate goes from Entered Apprentice to the Master of the Royal Secret. Do you dispute his actual statement?

- Your comment about Hiram being restored to life by Solomon appears correct, based on what I know of the Master Mason ritual.

I am struck more by what you have chosen not to criticize than by what you do. Why do you not challenge Mr. Shaw's descriptions of the Maundy Thursday ritual? Or his linkage between the Hiram Abif legend and that of Isis and Osiris? Or any of the other significant charges that would give any Christian pause for thought?

Finally, I found it interesting to read in your article that you find the theory that Masonry "descended from the so-called 'Ancient Mysteries' and other forms of pagan worship" has been discredited, and that only anti-Masons continue to perpetuate this charge. How can this be true? To quote Rex Hutchens in *A Bridge to Light* "Whatever the truth of history, the contributions to the symbolism of Freemasonry by the religions, philosophies, mythologies and occult mysteries of the past lie upon its surface for all to see." Hutchens' book must be considered authoritative; how do you resolve the conflict between the two viewpoints?[1]

I am looking forward to hearing from you.

Sincerely,

T. N. Sampson

Mr. Sampson wrote politely enough that he was "uncertain as to whether [Dr. Morris was] being truthful or not in [his] criticisms of Jim Shaw's book." Dr. Morris's response tries to assure him that he was being truthful and to provide him with detailed references to support his contentions. At all times, Dr. Morris relies on publicly accessible records.

[LETTER 2]

1733 16th St., N.W.
Washington, DC 20009-3103

September 23, 1993

Mr. T. N. Sampson Cornerstone Ministries
PO Box 2183
Poquoson, VA 23662-0183

Dear Mr. Sampson,

Thank you for your letter of August 28 about my February 1993 book review column, "The Sound and the Fury." It is always satisfying to authors to get feedback on their writing. I am happy to answer your questions about the Reverend James Shaw.

Everything I wrote in my column was truthful to the best of my knowledge. One misstatement, however, did slip in, despite my best intentions. I made the embarrassing mistake of assuming that Rev. Shaw told the truth about being a Past Master. The record reveals that he was never elected to any office in Allapattah Lodge No. 271. I can find no evidence he ever belonged to another Florida Lodge; neither did he serve in any office in his mother Lodge, Evergreen No. 713 in Indiana. It appears I fell for one of Rev. Shaw's slickly packaged lies. *Mea culpa.*

The Deadly Deception is a well-written, entertaining book. As I said in my review, "The biography is engaging, empathetic, and scattered with clever, vicious lies." It is also written in "simple language, accessible to someone without a high school education." This is testimony to Mr. McKenney's abilities as a writer; he told a good story in simple language. For a much less accessible book on anti-Masonry, see Paul Goodman, *Towards a Christian Republic*, New York: Oxford University Press, 1988.

Mr. McKenney said "[Jim Shaw's] ardent quest carried him through . . . the *position* of Sovereign Grand Inspector General. . . ." (emphasis added) In the Southern Jurisdiction, "Sovereign Grand Inspector General" is both the name of a degree and of a position. Each state has one active member of the Supreme Council who has the position of "Sovereign Grand Inspector General" for that state. All other 33° Masons are honorary members of the Supreme Council and are called "Inspectors General Honorary." The nomenclature is somewhat different in the Northern Masonic Jurisdiction. For more information, see *Coil's Masonic Encyclopedia*, p. 313, s.v. "Honorary 33rd Degree Masons."

I stand by my statement that Rev. Shaw was never a 33° Mason. Rev. Shaw became a Knight Commander of the Court of Honour in December 1965 and resigned in October 1966, thirty-seven months before he would have been eligible even to be nominated for the Thirty-third Degree, much less elected. The names of every newly created 33° Mason are published in the *Transactions of the Supreme Council*, and thousands of copies are distributed. All Rev. Shaw has to do is to give the year; and you can easily check the record.

The title page of Rev. Blanchard's book claims to contain, "The Complete Ritual of the Ancient and Accepted Scottish Rite," and the rituals themselves abound with references to various clandestine Cerneau Supreme Councils. Rev. Blanchard was much too smart not to have known which Supreme Council he was dealing with, especially as he provided a detailed commentary on all aspects of each degree. I can only conclude he understood what he wrote.

Here is one reference to a Cerneau Supreme Council, vol. I, p. 124, ". . . under the auspices of the Supreme Council of the 33d degree of the Ancient and Accepted Scotch Rite, in and for the Sovereign and Independent State of New York. . . ." This name was used by H. C. Atwood's Supreme Council, circa 1852–54.

The name of a different Cerneau Supreme Council is found in vol. I, p. 303, ". . . under the auspices of the Supreme Grand Council of Sovereign Grand Inspectors General of the 33d degree for the Northern Jurisdiction of the Western Hemisphere. . . ." Edmund B. Hays, Atwood's successor, used this name circa 1860–1863. *Coil's Masonic Encyclopedia*, pp. 600–617, s.v. "Scottish Rite Masonry," gives many names of the Cerneau Supreme Councils.

For more evidence that *Scotch Rite Masonry Illustrated* contains Cerneau ceremonies, see the 1979 edition, vol. I, pp. 124, 145, 303, 358, 419, 436; vol.

2, pp. 137, 242, 287, 340, 388, 445, 462, 464, 470, 472, 475. I cannot think of better proof that the rituals are Cerneau ceremonies than this extensive, explicit, internal evidence. Confusing the regular and Cerneau Scottish Rites is like confusing the Church of Christ with the Church of Christ, Scientist.

Your reading of Rev. Shaw's comment on p. 83 differs from mine. He does begin by talking about the Conclave, but he then goes on to say, "Why must we always do so much drinking? . . . But it bothered me that there was always so much of it and that it played such a major role in the Masonic life." This is a general comment on normal Masonic behavior. My dictionary gives this definition for *drunkard*: "1. One who habitually drinks strong liquors immoderately." Rev. Shaw's comment clearly portrays Masons as habitually drinking strong liquors immoderately.

You questioned whether such restrictions were in place when Rev. Shaw was a member. He affiliated with Allapattah Lodge No. 271 in 1952. The 1954 *Digest of the Masonic Law of Florida F&AM* is pretty clear on the issue of alcohol:

> 28.06 (398) No particular Lodge shall allow its properties or any part thereof to be used for the purpose of conducting or carrying on a liquor business or for the dispensing of alcoholic beverages in any form.

In 1975 the regulation was unchanged, though the following decision had been added to clarify the law. "The serving of any intoxicating beverage in Masonic Temples or Lodge Rooms or at Masonic banquets is forbidden by Masonic Law. (1969 Proc. 58, 212)" Equally explicit are the 1953 *Statutes of the Supreme Council*, Southern Jurisdiction: "Art. XV §24. The use of any spirituous, vinous, or malt liquors by any Body is hereby prohibited." The prohibition is unchanged in the 1991 *Statutes*, though it has been renumbered as Art. XV §25.

Rev. Shaw received the KCCH on December 18, 1965, in the "distant city" of Orlando. Neither the Grand Lodge of Florida nor the Supreme Council, SJ, then permitted or now permits alcoholic beverages to be used by any of their subordinate bodies. Florida Masons are bewildered when asked how alcohol "played such a major role in the Masonic life," because it has no role. What sort of meetings did Rev. Shaw attend where they "always do so much drinking?" It could not have been meetings of Florida Blue Lodges or Scottish Rite.

I indeed dispute Rev. Shaw's statement that "... going all the way to the 32nd Degree can be very substantial, well into the thousands of dollars today." When joining Evergreen Lodge No. 713 in 1945, Rev. Shaw paid $50 in initiation fees for the 1°–3°; the cost in 1952 for the Fourth through Thirty-Second Degrees, was $160. Thus the total for him "going all the way" was $210. In 1993 the comparable fees were $125 and $200, respectively, for a total of $325. This is far from being "well into the thousands of dollars"; it's not even close to $1,000.

It is satisfying to know that you agree Rev. Shaw's comments about the resurrection of Hiram Abif appear incorrect, as in fact they are. Rev. Shaw's description is not the result of some simple misconception. He was a Mason for twenty-one years and claimed to be a Past Master. His malignant distortion of the legend of Hiram Abif was consciously designed to outrage Christians. He was not confused. His description is not some minor misstatement, like calling an IGH an SGIG. He carefully designed his story and its many amplifying details with the purpose of defaming Freemasonry.

I chose to criticize those parts of Rev. Shaw's book that could be verified by non-Masons; his lies concerning the Maundy Thursday ceremony cannot. The space assigned to my book review column further limited the number of lies I could expose.

The connection between Hiram Abif and the Isis-Osiris legend was quite popular some 100 years ago. Many of those writers also found connections between Isis-Osiris, Jesus, and Baldur. Shaw supports his case by citing "the most authoritative Masonic writers." Mackey and Sickles wrote a century ago, and I neither have heard of nor read Pierson. Mackey and Sickles wrote before the advent of the "authentic school" of Masonic historians; they accepted evidence that would be laughed at today. Coil discusses this pp. 310–311, s.v. *"History of Freemasonry."* Robert Freke Gould's 1885 *History of Freemasonry* is probably the best Masonic history. It isn't "authoritative," just accurately researched, carefully written, and conservative in its conclusions, the most that can ever be asked of history.

The theory of descent from the Ancient Mysteries has indeed been discredited among serious Masonic historians, including Gould; there is no evidence to support its fanciful ideas. You could compare Coil's opinion of the theory, pp. 432–433, s.v. "Mysteries, Ancient Pagan." The most serious Masonic history is published by Quatuor Coronati Lodge No. 2076, London, in their annual transactions, *Ars Quatuor Coronatorum*.

Your quote by Dr. Hutchens refers to the symbolism of Freemasonry, not its *organization*. Freemasonry uses some symbols that were used by earlier organizations. This borrowing of symbols is found in many organizations. For example, the cornucopia is a symbol of plenty used by many churches to represent the overflowing bounty of God's blessings. The symbol came from the magical horn that Zeus gave to Amalthea, the goat who nursed him as a child (legends vary as to details). While the symbol originated in a pagan religion, it would be ludicrous to suggest that churches perpetuate pagan worship if they decorate their Sunday schools with cornucopias at Thanksgiving. Similarly, the dove used by Christians to represent the Holy Spirit was used much earlier as a symbol of Aphrodite.

Dr. Hutchens's book, like Pike's *Morals and Dogma*, is an expression of personal opinion; neither represents dogmatic teachings. A printing oversight led to the omission from the current edition of *A Bridge to Light* of the disclaimer that Pike used for *Morals and Dogma* (and which still applies today): "Everyone is entirely free to reject and dissent from whatsoever herein may seem to him to be untrue or unsound." This disclaimer will be added with the next printing of *A Bridge to Light*.

I would be most interested in seeing your correspondence with Rev. Shaw. It will be easy for you to confirm if he received the Thirty-Third Degree, was a Past Master, or was Past Master of all Scottish Rite Bodies. Once he gives you the dates and places he served, you can check the records. If you can send me any evidence that I was wrong, I will correct my statements, as I intend to correct my misstatement that he is a Past Master.

I think part of my review of *The Deadly Deception* is still appropriate. "Identifying and exposing these pathetic inventions, however, is a task that must be ultimately fruitless. Anyone willing to overlook the easily verifiable lies on the book's cover will just rationalize away the corruption within. What is saddest about this book is the eagerness of the authors to cheat the public to achieve their twisted ends, all in the name of Jesus."

Sincerely yours,

S. Brent Morris, Ph.D.
Book Review Editor
The Scottish Rite Journal

cc: J. W. Boettjer, 33°, Editor

Mr. Sampson's next letter reveals the conclusions he has already reached about Freemasonry and how he handles anti-Masonic sources that don't support his verdict: If an anti-Masonic source is contradicted by other evidence, Mr. Sampson will not change his conclusions nor warn anyone else of the falsehoods, he just quietly drops that reference from his source list.

[LETTER 3]

Cornerstone Ministries
Poquson, Virginia

October 4, 1993

Dear Dr. Morris:

I was pleasantly surprised by your response to my earlier letter concerning Rev. Jim Shaw's *The Deadly Deception*. In my dealing with Masons, not all the responses I receive (verbally or via letter) maintain a proper degree of cordiality. You have probably experienced similar problems yourself with those who are against Masonry. At any rate, your response was far more detailed than I hoped to expect and I certainly appreciate the time you took in its composing. You were very considerate of a stranger's request.

I have not yet received a response from Rev. Shaw on my questions about his book. Should he respond, I will send along a copy to you. Should he choose not to respond, I would conclude that he has no answer to the charges you raised, that your criticisms are valid, and drop him from my source list. I find it hard to believe that he would falsely claim so many titles and Lodge offices, but people have done worse for what they considered to be a worthy goal. I have always felt that the ends do not justify the means; rather, the means must be worthy of the ends.

As to my own efforts, I have come to the conclusion that Masonry is indeed a religion, and that the god of Masonry is not the God of the Bible. One can quote Pike, Coil, and Hutchens, on these points, but the rituals speak eloquently for themselves. Purporting to convey a mystery, or hidden "knowledge," they teach concepts which are alien to Christianity and lead the Christian Mason to choose between the two Deities. Over time, his studies of Masonry replace his studies of Christianity and he begins to believe what those rituals teach. Finally, by his participation in them, he implicitly approves what is being taught.

I have enclosed a summary of what I have found concerning Masonry, which I use when answering questions about Masonry. I would appreciate learning of any errors I may have made. My primary references were Ankerberg's *The Secret Teachings of the Masonic Lodge*, Hutchens's *A Bridge to Light*, the Southern Baptist Convention's study on Masonry, and *Duncan's Ritual*. With respect to the latter, I have compared it to a much-censored version of the Oklahoma *Murrow Masonic Monitor* and find enough commonality to conclude that it accurately details Masonic rituals. Should there be errors, perhaps you could send a complete Monitor which would show where I have made mistakes. (I'm not serious; this is a little joke between us!)

I appreciate your position that Hutchens presents his own views and is not authoritative; however, that confounds reason. The fact that the Supreme Council endorsed his book (disclaimer or no disclaimer) and that it is given to Masons, in the Lodge, as part of the 14°, makes the book authoritative. Someone of his stature must know what Masonry teaches and can be considered authoritative until he is shown to be in error. If we extend the Masonic argument, if Coil is not authoritative when he says Masonry is a religion, then you are not authoritative when denying that statement. So where does the authority lie? It is clear to me that Masonry likes nothing to be authoritative except the Rituals, and then tries to ensure that no one outside Masonry can see them. As an analyst by profession, the logic of this escapes me.

Finally, I would like to state that in everything I say or write concerning Masonry, I try to stick to the facts and be nonjudgmental. This is hard, as you can imagine; however, both my father and father-in-law are Masons, and if I attack any Mason, I attack those I love as well. Yet by keeping silent, I also hurt them by not expressing my concerns and prodding them (or any) Mason into questioning what he does and why. The Mason's decision is his to make, for he accepts the consequences. This leads me to ask you: Is Masonry your religion? Is the Lodge more important to you than Jesus? Do you spend more time studying Masonic rituals than you do in Bible study? If these answers are yes, perhaps you should consider what you have accomplished in Masonry in the light of the instructions Jesus gave his disciples in the last chapter of Matthew.

Sincerely,

T. N. Sampson II

Dr. Morris's next letter addresses what seems to be one of Mr. Sampson's major misunderstandings of Freemasonry: Who speaks "authoritatively" for the fraternity? Dr. Morris also points out various errors in Cornerstone Ministries' pamphlet on Freemasonry. Typical of many anti-Masonic tracts, the pamphlet gave few citations that could be checked. It seems that Mr. Sampson wanted Dr. Morris to make the pamphlet as accurate as possible in terminology and history without any willingness to change its fundamentally wrong conclusion that Freemasonry is a religion antithetical to Christianity.

[LETTER 4]

1733 16th Street, NW
Washington, DC 20009-3103

February 12, 1994

Dear Mr. Sampson,

Personal and professional obligations have prevented me from answering your letter of October 4 in a more timely manner. I do appreciate the cordial tone of your letters; you are the only anti-Mason to communicate with me and to have the civility of identifying yourself. I usually receive anonymous mailings of tracts by Jack Chick or Ed Decker.

It is not surprising that Rev. Shaw has not responded to you. He is a pathetic liar caught in his web of deceit. As far as I know, no anti-Mason has ever expressed embarrassment or even chagrin at his lies (or those of Carlson, Schnoebelen, Chick, Decker, and so many others). Only Dr. Robert Morey has acknowledged the outlandishness of some attacks against Masonry. Most anti-Masons, if they can be convinced that one of their sources has engaged in premeditated fraud, just quietly drop the reference and move on to another "expert."

Rev. Shaw did much more than "falsely claim so many titles and Lodge office," as you narrowly acknowledged. He maliciously perverted the descriptions of his Lodge experience to slander Freemasonry, and his book is still in wide distribution, a wolf in sheep's clothing, duping the trusting.

Your summary of Freemasonry is interesting, but abounds with factual and interpretative errors. There are so many that I must decline your offer to correct them for you. I simply do not have the time to point out all of them, but I will show you some.

The only mysteries or hidden "knowledge" to be found in Freemasonry are the modes of recognition and the stories told in the degrees. Masons are encouraged to undertake a spiritual examination, but no answer is given or demanded. Each Mason must reach his own independent conclusions. Freemasonry, not being a religion, is incapable of providing an answer.

Your sources deserve some comment. Ankerberg's *The Secret Teachings of the Masonic Lodge* relies heavily on Blanchard's *Scotch Rite Masonry Illustrated* (which I hope I convinced you is inaccurate, but on which you haven't commented). I do not have Duncan's *Ritual*, but I presume it, like most exposés, is reasonably accurate. The problem comes with the inaccuracies. For example, Rev. Shaw gives a generally correct description of Freemasonry but slips in his twisted tales of reincarnation, resurrection, and phallic worship. I have a complete Monitor for you and will present it on the night you become a Master Mason. (This is a joke between us, but the offer is nonetheless serious.)

You are right that I am not authoritative when I deny Masonry is a religion. I, as well as Hutchens, Coil, et al., am an individual Mason speaking for myself. I am, however, consistent with most historians, the vast majority of Masons, the Southern Baptist Convention's study, and—most importantly above all others—with Grand Lodges.

Here's what the SBC said on p. 70 of their $100,000+ report. (Its final version was so negative towards Freemasonry that its principal author, Dr. Gary Leazer, asked that his name be removed.) It's confounding that you choose to ignore the consistent statements of Grand Lodges, the "overwhelming majority of Masonic Leaders," and the finding of the SBC.

- While some Masonic writers and some Masons consider Freemasonry a religion, even their religion, the overwhelming majority of Masons reject the idea that Freemasonry is a religion. The various Monitors of Grand Lodges and statements from the overwhelming majority of Masonic leaders in the past and today deny that Freemasonry is a religion.

- Since Freemasonry requires no doctrinal statement from members, other than the general affirmation concerning the existence of God, it is reasonable to expect that Masons profess a broad range of beliefs about religious matters. . . . While the vast majority of Masons are professing Christians, some Masons are non-Christians, a few are probably or have been anti-Christians.

It is illogical to insist that the beliefs of one or more Masons constitute the beliefs of all Masons.

- It was not found that Freemasonry is anti-Christian or Satanic, nor does it oppose the Christian church. While a few Masonic writers glorify non-Christian philosophy and religions, they are clearly a minor voice. Every organization, including the Christian church, has some individuals who espouse positions not held by the vast majority of members. Organizations must be judged by the positions of the majority, not those of a small minority.

Authority for Freemasonry lies with Grand Lodges, not independent writers, however respected they may be. Henry Wilson Coil was a California Mason; his encyclopedia was commercially published in New York. The only force his writings have on Maryland Masonry is that of a good, conservative historian.

Jim Baker and Jimmy Swaggart were (and perhaps still are) widely heard and read ordained ministers of the Assemblies of God (if my memory serves me). Their writings are not authoritative for the Assemblies of God, much less the Baptists or Presbyterians.

It is difficult to comment on your paper as you chose to give few citations and seem to rely almost exclusively on secondary research. I will offer a few corrections, but cannot give a comprehensive revision. [The following comments refer to Mr. Sampson's pamphlet.]

- I have never heard of a Grand Lodge named "Ancient *Order* of Free and Accepted Masons." Most commonly in the United States the Fraternity is known as "Ancient, Free and Accepted Masons," AF&AM, or "Free and Accepted Masons," F&AM.

- Masonry does not deny Christian beliefs any more than Rotary does. It is not a religion, it does not allow religious discussions at its meetings, and is thus incapable of accepting or denying the beliefs of any religion.

- The history of Masonry written prior to the twentieth century is indeed "almost totally fiction," but you ignore or are unaware of the "authentic school" of Masonic history that arose about 1880 and now comprises the majority of Masonic history writing. Robert Freke Gould exemplifies modern Masonic scholarship: scrupulous in facts, insistent on details, conservative in conclusions. There are abundant, accurate (and non-sensational) histories available for anyone who bothers to look. Good choices are Gould's *History of Freemasonry*, Coil's *Freemasonry Through Six Centuries*, John Hamill's *The Craft*, and almost anything published in *Ars Quatuor Coronatorum*, the transactions of Quatuor Coronati Lodge No. 2076, London, the premier Lodge of Masonic research.

- There is no Masonic doctrine to keep pure. Thus the idea of central enforcement is meaningless. Freemasonry, not being a religion nor having a doctrine, does not care how much or how little its members believe, as long as they believe in God.

- The Worshipful Master is *not* a symbol of deity, any more than the "Right Worshipful Lord Mayor of London." The title preserves an archaic word form, as found in the Wycliffe Bible, "worschipe thi fadir. . . ." [Matthew 19:19. The King James' translation has, "Honour thy father. . . ."]

- There is no part of the Lodge called the "Holy of Holies." During parts of the ceremonies, the room indeed represents King Solomon's Temple, with the porch, steps, middle chamber, and Holy of Holies. This usage is similar to a church front lawn at Christmas representing the manger in Bethlehem.

- Master Masons are not symbolically raised from the dead. The Hiramic Legend has the body of Hiram removed from a temporary grave for re-interring.

- Masonry does believe in the Fatherhood of God and the Brotherhood of Man. It says nothing about "all men [being]

His spiritual sons in good standing with Him." To belabor a point (which you have chosen not to accept), Freemasonry is not a religion and is incapable of such pronouncements.

- Freemasonry does not teach "that self-improvement and good works will secure God's favor and guarantee entry into heaven." It offers no path of salvation nor sacraments of any sort. It only presents symbols for the individual Mason to interpret for himself. My lambskin apron reminds me of St. James's admonition that "Faith, if it has not works, is dead." [James 2:17]

- Contrary to your assertion that Masonry teaches "God is an unreachable, uncaring Spirit," Masons are taught the vital importance of regular prayer.

- Masonry does not teach that the Name of God is lost. The Royal Arch Degree in particular reaffirms that His name is יהוה (the pronunciation of which is indeed lost).

- The York Rite does not teach that "Jahbulon" is the secret name of God. This lie originated with Walter Hannah's *Darkness Visible*, 1952. (A little more attention to original sources would greatly improve the accuracy of your paper.)

- The name of Jesus is not forbidden in Lodge prayers. His name is used widely in Lodges around the world.

- The legend of Hiram Abif is not presented as Biblical history; its analysis is available for anyone to read. I suppose some Masons may think it is history, but then again many Christians probably believe the Bible says there were three wise men and their names are Balthazar, Melchior, and Gaspar.

- I am particularly disappointed in the way you subtly misused my statistics on 1990 Masonic charity. The source of your figures is my book, *Masonic Philanthropies*, which you did not choose to acknowledge. When I compiled the figures I tried

Is It True What They Say about Freemasonry?

to be scrupulously accurate in all categories, so there was no possibility of misinterpretation by fair-minded readers. Your quote is "42% of the $525 million collected by Masonic charities went to non-public (i.e., Lodge) purposes." This could be easily read as going for refreshments, entertainment, or Lodge operating expenses. The money went to orphanages and retirement homes, which I think can be appropriately called philanthropy. The Methodist Church maintains a retirement home in Baltimore and the Church considers it a part of their ministry, even though the residents are all Methodists. Is this true charity? The Methodist Church thinks so, I think so, but you may not. If you don't, then by all means discount this aspect of Masonic philanthropy, but your readers deserve a more accurate treatment of the facts. Tell them where the money goes and why you don't think it counts as charity.

At this point I must stop correcting your errors; I do not have the time. My efforts, though, would be ultimately fruitless as you have reached a verdict, passed sentence, and now seek only to sift through the evidence to support your conclusions. I have neither the time nor interest to continue our correspondence.

In closing, let me answer your final questions.

- Masonry is not my religion.

- Jesus is infinitely more important to me than the Lodge.

- I study the Bible more than Masonic ritual.

In fact it was through Masonic ritual that I increased my interest in and study of the Bible. This led to a two-year Bible teacher training program with a commitment to teach a two-year Bible course. I have ten weeks left teaching my original course and am making plans for another when this is done. Regular Bible study is essential to Christian growth.

It is important to me to be challenged in my response to God's love, to be reminded of the impossibility of ever repaying or of being worthy of His great gift. The most I as a repentant sinner can be is what I am now: forgiven.

When given a challenge to my Christian faith and responsibilities, such as contained in your last paragraph, I am grateful for the reminder of my debt and of my failures in repaying it. I gladly turn my other cheek to you.

Sincerely yours,

S. Brent Morris, Ph.D.

The initial correspondence comes to an end with this letter. Note that Mr. Sampson is willing to rely on Dr. Morris to make his pamphlet sound accurate, but is unwilling to correct his erroneous conclusions. In keeping with his fellow anti-Masons, Mr. Sampson vaguely refers to "many Masons" without giving any further information. It would be easy to find "many Christians" who would cite baptism, church attendance, or tithing as "evidence" that a person was "saved." This is profoundly at odds with orthodox Christian doctrine but would not be accepted by fair-minded people as evidence against a church's teachings.

[LETTER 5]

Cornerstone Ministries
Poquson, Virginia

February 27, 1994

Dear Dr. Morris:

Thank you for your response. I appreciate the time expended in compiling the response, and I find your sense of humor delightful and your letters a real pleasure to read. However, I will respect your decision to discontinue our correspondence.

To wrap up our exchanges, I have taken the following actions pertinent to your letter:

- Changed the title to "Ancient, Free and Accepted Masons."

- Rewrote the statement about doctrine and lack of central enforcement, as the latter is indeed meaningless.

- Deleted the reference to the W[orshipful] M[aster] being a symbol of Deity. This came out of *The Scottish Rite Journal* (Crabbe, Summer, 1993).[2] I had assumed since it is published by the Supreme Council that it must be factual. No other Mason has subsequently supported that position.

- Deleted the reference to the Master Mason's Lodge being called the "Holy of Holies." This came from Duncan's Monitor, but no Mason I have talked to is aware of it.

- Rewrote the Masonic charity comment. I was not aware that you were the source. I'll get a copy and ensure my statements are consistent with yours. I drew the data from the *Journal* (Hinton, Feb. '93), which did not address the remainder of the equation.

- Will get a copy of Gould's *History of Freemasonry*.

As to your other comments:

- Blanchard is inaccurate. I am matching it against *A Bridge to Light* to see what commonalities there are. I have also asked Masons who have demitted to comment on some of the rituals quoted by Blanchard.

- Masonry is not a religion. At the worst, include me in a minority Masonic opinion. Masonry's practices and rituals are proof enough to support such a conclusion. FYI, the PR campaign about Masonry not being a religion has been successful. Masons mention that right up front, though many have never heard of Masonic writers who support that viewpoint (Pike, Coil, etc.). Coil is undergoing revision, and his view will not survive the update by the purity group. Of interest to you, one Mason noted that Pike and Hutchens were outdated, and no longer applicable. I pointed out that you had done a review of Hutchens book [*A Bridge to Light*] in the Nov. '93 issue of the *Journal*, thus undercutting his argument. His vague response was not flattering to you, and I found myself in the strange position of defending your integrity.

- No symbolic raise from the dead. I can see no other meaning of the candidate being "raised" in the 3rd Degree. The candidate has been doing a great job of imitating a corpse for almost an hour; I think the act we are addressing has no other practical teaching. Several Masons have confirmed that viewpoint.

- "All men in good standing with Him." You will not be surprised how many Masons have expressed exactly that sentiment to me.

- Name of God lost/no Jahbulon. Both have been confirmed by other Masons. With many of the rituals being given in very compressed times, it is quite believable that many have not understood the impact of this part. However, those who choose to study the rituals for moral and spiritual lessons seem to find the oddest things there. "Self-improvement." As before, I find that viewpoint over and over again when talking to Masons.

- Jesus, name used in Lodge? Again, many Masons have explained to me very carefully why His name cannot be used in the lodge.

- The SBC study. I have indeed read it, and several times at that. Did Dr. Leazer remove his name? Others have said he was fired for his lack of impartiality. At any rate, I found the study flawed in some key areas, but, as I have stated before, agreed with the conclusion.

Is It True What They Say about Freemasonry?

Your comment about authoritative writers contained a nugget that you perhaps did not intend. Both Baker and Swaggart, before or after their respective Waterloos, were authoritative only when their writings or comments were consistent with the Bible, which is the source of Christian doctrine. By the same token, Coil, Hutchens, and Pike are authoritative only when consistent with Masonic doctrine. This doctrine does not exist in clear written form, but exists nonetheless in the Ritual and in the Lodge. I have dealt with enough Masons to hear the same comments over and over again to finally understand that such doctrine does indeed exist, and covers four main points:

> the Bible is one of several books of Divine Will, and no better or worse than the others;
>
> all religions are part of one Religion;
>
> all gods merely reflect one God;
>
> good works, tolerance of all religious beliefs, and personal improvement are all one needs to enter the Celestial Lodge above.

I think that this doctrine extends to many Masons' spiritual life, and contributes to their strange view of Christianity.

Sincerely,

T. N. Sampson II

P.S. You may be interested to know that Ed Decker recently stepped on his sword in a very large and public fashion. His Mormon video, *Godmakers II*, used sources that were questionable at best. As a result, it has been condemned by the most reliable sources of data on Mormonism. He retains little credibility because of that work and his very negative reaction to criticism.

Mr. Sampson now writes to the author of the article referred to in his last letter, Mr. Norman Crabbe, to verify Dr. Morris's answer that the Master of a lodge does not symbolize Deity. He disingenuously tells Mr. Crabbe he is not an "anti-Mason" but only a researcher. Webster's Revised Unabridged Dictionary gives a simple definition: "anti-Mason: One opposed to Freemasonry."

[LETTER 6]

Cornerstone Ministries
Poquson, Virginia

March 5, 1994

Norman Williams Crabbe
Edgewater, Maryland

Dear Mr. Crabbe:

Your interesting article appearing in the summer '93 issue of *The Royal Arch Mason Magazine* contained a statement that has been rejected by Scottish Rite gentlemen of the Supreme Council of the Southern Jurisdiction. I wonder if I could impose upon you to clarify the matter?

The question was whether the Master symbolized Deity, as your article claimed. I used that comment in an article I passed along to Dr. S. Brent Morris at the Supreme Council and he specifically said that the Master symbolized no such thing. I realize that many may see different things in Masonic symbolism, but your comment seemed pretty clear and, appearing as it did in an "official" magazine, I thought that it reflected a body of opinion.

My question, therefore, is: Does the Master symbolize Deity; in what way does he do this; is this reinforced by other Masonic writings? While on the subject, does your comment that Masons are "Holy Men" draw from the fact that they swear their vows on holy texts, or was another meaning intended?

By way of explanation, I am not a Mason, nor am I an "anti-Mason" (whatever that phrase may really mean). I have been researching Masonry for about four years to see what it really is and does, and have been surprised by the amount of misinformation on both sides of the issue. Articles such as yours are an important element in my research as it is far better to hear the views of someone who has first-hand familiarity with the subject matter than one who is "guessing" from the outside.

I thank you in advance for taking the time to explain this matter to me.

Cordially,

T. N. Sampson II

Mr. Crabbe confirms for Mr. Sampson that the interpretation of Masonic symbolism is left to personal investigation. He also explains what all Masons know: Articles in Masonic magazines represent personal views of individual Masons.

[LETTER 7]

Norman Williams Crabbe
Edgewater, Maryland

March 12th, 1994

Dear Mr. T. N. Sampson:

Thank you for your letter. I will do my best to answer you, but I'm not sure this answer will be of much help to you.

I would expect that Brent and I would have different opinions given the democratic nature of Masonry. The science of Freemasonry is exact but the art of the Craft is left up to one's personal interpretation. I'm sorry, but I am unable to offer you any substantiating evidence that my statements are in agreement with even one other Mason; living or dead. Please don't feel slighted. I have never intended to substantiate my statements to anyone either within the Craft or without the Craft. These views are personal, subjective observations accumulated over years of study; not only of Masonry, but of religions and philosophies in general. They are my own.

The Royal Arch Magazine to my knowledge is a vehicle where Royal Arch Masons can air their personal views on Masonic topics. For clarification, please contact the Editor of the *RAM*.

I am enclosing a reading list that I hope you may find interesting. I hope that you are able to spend the time required to read at least some of these works.

Masonry is for many men a starting point on their quest for Knowledge. Masonry in and of itself is never the "End" of the quest for Knowledge. This is one of the many reasons why Masonry is not nor can it ever be a "religion". There is no dogma or theology in Freemasonry. True Freemasonry is inclusive not exclusive when dealing with the religions of the world.

Yours in Faith,

Norman W. Crabbe

Dr. Morris renews the correspondence with Mr. Sampson to get his permission to reprint his letters in an article that eventually became this book. He also sought clarification of the terminology used by Cornerstone Ministries and further information on Rev. Shaw.

[LETTER 8]

1733 16th Street, NW
Washington, DC 20009-3103

May 31, 1994

Dear Mr. Sampson,

Please forgive me for troubling you after I asked that our correspondence cease.

1. May I have your permission to reprint your correspondence in an article I am preparing on arguments used against Freemasonry?

2. What definition of "cult" does Cornerstone Ministries use?

3. Can you furnish me with a list of the organizations against which Cornerstone Ministries cautions Christians?

4. Have you ever received a reply from Rev. Shaw responding to the evidence that he lied about his Masonic experiences? (I understand that his publishers are aware of the evidence and that they have contacted him and Mr. McKenney. I do not know what answer they may have received from Rev. Shaw or Mr. McKenney.)

Thank you for considering my requests.

Sincerely yours,

S. Brent Morris, Ph.D.

Mr. Sampson explains that he has decided to drop Rev. Shaw from his bibliography because he is unable to assess the truth about him, but he has no problems with deciding what is "true" about Freemasonry.

[LETTER 9]

Cornerstone Ministries
Poquson, Virginia

June 2, 1994

Dear Dr. Morris,

With respect to your questions:

1. You have my unrestricted permission to quote from my correspondence for any purpose you wish. I would be interested to know for which forum the article is intended, for the obvious reason. If it is *The Scottish Rite Journal,* perhaps you would forward my request for a subscription?

2. Generally speaking, a "cult" can describe any group that deviates significantly from a "norm." Therefore, any group (Christian, Mormon, Islam, or even Masonry) can have cults in their midst. If Catholicism is considered the norm, one could brand the Protestant movement as being a cult. A cult differs from a religion in that it usually features faith in one person's teachings, an autocratic control structure, and an absolute control over members' salvation. Having said all this, my own definition of a cult follows that used by Dr. Walter Martin: "a group of people gathered about a specific person or person's misinterpretation of the Bible." A cult then "embraces, teaches, or practices religious doctrine contrary to the

accepted and established truth of Biblical Christianity." (*The Kingdom of the Cults*, Bethany House, 1986)

3. We primarily address the beliefs of two cults (Mormonism and Jehovah's Witnesses) and two religions (Freemasonry and New Age), though we also offer information on the beliefs of other religions, such as Catholicism, Islam, Hinduism, and Buddhism. We are also a member of the Cult Awareness Network (a secular group) and are available to answer questions on any religious belief. We neither charge for our services nor do we solicit support from those who consult us.

4. Neither Rev. Shaw nor his spokesman has responded to our letter. As noted earlier, I have removed his book from our bibliography due to the charges you raised. I am in no position to assess the truth, but you have made the better case.

Of possible interest to you is a current discussion on the Masonry forum in CompuServe on Masonic spirituality. I have found it a fascinating discussion, given the public declarations that Masonry is not a religion. There has also been much discussion about possible legal action against those who "libel" Masonry. An interesting reaction, though I think it is more "spleen venting" than a plan of action. Finally, in yet another discussion, one of the correspondents ended his note with "in the faith . . ."; I wonder what faith he was referring to? At any rate, you would find the forum very interesting.

I am including the most recent copy of our booklet. You will find that the chapter of Masonry has been updated to reflect additional information learned since the initial printing. The first chapter on Christianity should provide sufficient background to understand my perspective on writing the booklet. Should you have additional questions, please let me know.

Cordially,

T. N. Sampson II

The crux of the differences between Mr. Sampson and Dr. Morris is clarified here. Dr. Morris believes that it is significant that Rev. Shaw has published verifiable lies about his Masonic experience and that anti-Masons still rely upon his testimony.

[LETTER 10]

1733 16th Street, NW
Washington, DC 20009-3103

August 10, 1994

Dear Mr. Sampson,

Thank you for your letter of June 2, 1994, agreeing to let me quote from your correspondence. My article is intended as an additional chapter in a revised and expanded version of the book I coauthored with Art de Hoyos, *Is It True What They Say About Freemasonry?* (Silver Spring, Md.: MSA, 1994). It may be published separately as an article in its own right. I would not expect the revised book to be published for another year or so, but I will send you copies of anything in which I quote you.

It is satisfying to hear you say that I make a better case than Rev. Shaw, but I am disappointed that you feel you are in no position to assess the truth. The issues I raise are objective statements of fact that require no judgment or opinion. Rev. Shaw's publisher has sternly assured me that he can refute all of my charges, but so far he hasn't bothered to send me any data.[3]

What would it take to convince you that Rev. Shaw is a liar? I have a copy of his resignation letter plus his dues card at the time which shows him to be a 32°, KCCH, not a 33°. I can send you copies of lists of every Master of every Lodge in Florida from 1952 to 1966 (when Rev. Shaw was a member in Florida). I can also send you copies of lists of every new 33° Mason from Florida during the same period. Is there any amount of objective, independently verifiable evidence that will sway your opinion of Rev. Shaw? Knowing this will help me revise my book.

Sincerely yours,

S. Brent Morris, Ph.D.

Mr. Sampson is willing to alter his position, but only in a limited and incremental way. He will concede that Rev. Shaw lied about the 33°, but only about that facet of his Masonic life (apparently leaving open the possibility that there is some truth somewhere in something that Rev. Shaw wrote about the Masons).

[LETTER 11]

Cornerstone Ministries
Poquson, Virginia

August 20, 1994

Dear Dr. Morris:

I look forward to your book and will obtain a copy for my library upon its publication. Good sources can be hard to find.

As to Rev. Shaw, I am somewhat curious why my opinion would matter. I am a "cowan"[4] on the Masonry forum on CompuServe, and it is clear from their conversations that anyone who dares criticize Masonry for any reason is a bigoted, intolerant fool who is in it only for financial reasons. That there may be those who have solid reasons for questioning Masonic practices, and who do so honestly, is not even considered a possibility. Given that standing definition, I do not see how any agreement we reach in this matter is useful to either of us.

Having said that, you have asked a fair question, and it deserves an answer. Rev. Shaw has made a specific claim about being selected to receive the 33°. You have stated that this is untrue. I would consider a letter from the Supreme Council, on letterhead, signed by C. Fred Kleinknecht, stating that Rev. Shaw was neither invited to receive, nor received, the 33° honor at any time sufficient proof that Shaw lied about this facet of his Masonic life.[5] And, since it is such a critical part of his book, I would consider it be sufficient to reject him as a source of information (something, in fact, I have already done).

Since it has been somewhat over three years since I first started writing on Masonry, you may be interested to know how I have changed my own views. First, I no longer bring Albert Pike into the equation, as the main fact of his Luciferian viewpoints has indeed shown to be a lie (though there is a slight hint of this in *Morals and Dogma*, p. 321). As well, I note a change in the ritual over the years, meaning that what is listed in Blanchard, Duncan, and Richardson do not completely reflect today's Masonry. I also believe you did yourselves no favor by not sitting down with the foremost of Masonry's critics and *let them see the ritual used.* The honest ones would not then have relied on data listed in other sources, and you would have avoided some of the harshest charges. For example, what if Ankerberg had seen the actual rituals and not relied on Blanchard's work? Finally, I note the fact that Masonry changes slowly, but indeed changes. Perhaps the criticism raised has forced some of that change. But with these modifications I have not changed my view that Masonry offers an alien god to those who fall for the stage props indicating that the Biblical God resides in the Lodge or is somehow connected to Him via Solomon. Nor have I changed my view that the tolerance so stressed in Masonic lessons highlights the underlying assumption that, since all religions are the same, one must be tolerant, as it is the same God in all. These I continue to find objectionable.

Sincerely,

T. N. Sampson II

Because Mr. Sampson refused to accept the accuracy of the public records of the Supreme Council, Mr. C. Fred Kleinknecht, Sovereign Grand Commander of the Supreme Council, 33°, SJ, confirms that Rev. Shaw was never invited to receive nor received the 33° honor at any time.

[LETTER 12]

Supreme Council, 33°, SJ
1733 Sixteenth Street, NW
Washington, DC 20009-3199

August 29, 1994

Dear Mr. Sampson,

Dr. S. Brent Morris, who reviews books for *The Scottish Rite Journal*, has forwarded to me a copy of your letter to him of August 20, 1994. In this letter, you say: "I would consider a letter from the Supreme Council, on letterhead, signed by C. Fred Kleinknecht, stating that Rev. Shaw was neither invited to receive, nor received, the 33° honor at any time sufficient proof that Shaw lied about this facet of his Masonic life." I am a little surprised you require such a letter to convince you Mr. Shaw has grossly and deliberately misrepresented the facts of his alleged Thirty-Third Degree status in the Scottish Rite of Freemasonry in his book *The Deadly Deception*, coauthored with Tom McKenney. I understand you have received a copy of *Is It True What They Say About Freemasonry?* by Dr. Morris and Art de Hoyos. In this book, pages 38 to 52, you have read specific facts and seen photocopied records directly refuting Mr. Shaw's claims.

Nevertheless, I am pleased to cooperate with your request and state unequivocally that Mr. Shaw was neither invited to receive, nor received, the 33° honor at any time. Rather, it is my opinion, Mr. Shaw has yielded to religious enthusiasm to such an extent that he is willing to lie in what he has come to believe is a good cause. This is putting the best light on his actions. Less charitable souls might point to the profits he, Mr. McKenney, and the book's publisher have gained by distributing this book. I hope Mr. Shaw, all

T. N. Sampson   167

concerned with *The Deadly Deception*, and you will pause to reconsider James 1:26 which states: "If any think they are religious, and do not bridle their tongues but deceive their heart, their religion is worthless."

Sincerely,

C. Fred Kleinknecht
Sovereign Grand Commander

Having painted himself into a corner, Mr. Sampson finally concedes that Rev. Shaw has lied— in one area.

[LETTER 13]

Cornerstone Ministries
Poquson, Virginia

September 5, 1994

Dear Sir [C. Fred Kleinknecht]:

Many thanks for your letter of August 29. That you are willing to state in print that Rev. Shaw never held the [33rd] degree [as he] claimed tells me that the claim is false.

Let me put your mind at rest concerning my reason for the request. I do not have a copy of Dr. Morris' book *Is It True What They Say About Freemasonry?* Rather, I intend to buy a copy next year when the updated version is ready. I was also unaware that Dr. Morris had presented photocopied evidence refuting Rev. Shaw's claims in that book. With no such proof in hand, I felt the letter as requested would be sufficient, and certainly appreciate Dr. Morris's offer of "proof positive." I continue to find it illuminating that Rev. Shaw would lie in an area that could be so easily disproved.

Of interest, I recently talked to a woman who had persuaded her husband not to join Masonry. She had used Rev. Shaw's book to buttress her discussion. I told her that there was much disagreement about Rev. Shaw's veracity, but that I agreed with her that there were good reasons for avoiding the Lodge.

In any event, I do not use the book since Dr. Morris's concerns were raised, and certainly would not recommend it based on the facts at hand.

Sincerely,

T. N. Sampson

Dr. Morris replies to Mr. Sampson, commenting on his methods used in studying Freemasonry.

[LETTER 14]

1733 16th Street, NW
Washington, DC 20009-3101

September 3, 1994

Dear Mr. Sampson,

Thank you for answering my question about Rev. Shaw [in your letter of August 20, 1994]. You should now have a letter from Mr. C. Fred Kleinknecht stating that Rev. Shaw was neither invited to receive, nor received, the 33° honor at any time.

You have been a courteous correspondent, even if you carefully came just short of calling me a liar about Rev. Shaw. I asked what would convince you, because you have so doggedly dismissed any evidence offered in the case of Rev. Shaw. I wanted to know if there was any amount of testimony that would convince you or other critics of Masonry. Even with the unequivocal statement from Mr. Kleinknecht, I note that you will only consider this "proof that Shaw lied about *this facet* of his Masonic life."

Rev. Shaw did not tell the truth about being a 33° [Mason], a Past Master, Past Master of all Scottish Rite bodies, or about revealing the "secrets" of the 33° for the first time in history. Further, he distorted the cost of joining, as well as drinking in Florida Lodges. Each of these prevarications can be independently verified with public records.

There is no "minimum donation of a very large amount of money" to receive the 33°. There is no interview before receiving the 33°, and there is absolutely no discussion of a member's religion before, after, or during the 33° ceremonies. These are among the many other fabrications that Rev. Shaw concocted about his Masonic experience, but none of these can be independently confirmed. I will not impose on your credulity by asking you to believe the word of a Mason.

However, there is plenty of objective evidence that doesn't require you to take the word of a Mason. Rather than only "doubt[ing] this facet of Shaw's Masonic life," you might have doubted more of his statements, perhaps even that nothing he said should be trusted without corroboration. Your loyalty to Rev. Shaw is very touching.

With the exception of Dr. Robert Morey, I have never read an anti-Masonic writer who had any concern about the venomous lies that are repeated about Masonry. Jack Chick's vile comic, *The Curse of Baphomet*, comes to mind as an example, as well as the publications of Texe Marrs, Ed Decker, and Ron Carlson.

It is interesting that you think we should share our rituals with our critics. When Rev. Pat Robertson repeated the Pike-Lucifer hoax in *The New World Order*, Mr. Kleinknecht wrote to him on May 12, 1992, pointed out the error, and said, "If we must disagree let us base our disagreement upon the truth." He further said, "All of [Pike's] writings are in the Library of The Supreme Council, 33°, at the House of the Temple, in Washington, DC. They are available for public inspection, and you are welcome to read them." I am not sure what more could be offered. Rev. Robertson has not given Mr. Kleinknecht the courtesy of a reply. There seems to be little interest on Rev. Robertson's part in correcting factual errors, at least as long as only Masons are being defamed. I do not share your idealism about the good intentions of anti-Masons, especially those with a profitable line of lurid publications.

Sincerely yours,

S. Brent Morris, PhD

Mr. Sampson explains that "it is not [his] function to document and publish errors in books on Masonry." He then raises unsubstantiated charges by an unnamed Mason to challenge Dr. Morris's assertion that there is no minimum donation required to receive the Thirty-third Degree.

[LETTER 15]

Cornerstone Ministries
Poquson, Virginia

September 9, 1994

Dear Dr. Morris:

I did indeed receive the requested statement from Mr. Kleinknecht, who noted his surprise at the request. He had the mistaken impression I had already read your book *Is It True What They Say About Freemasonry?* and had seen the documentary evidence therein. I noted that I had not seen the book, but looked forward to buying the updated version next year. As to the letter itself, it was all I had asked for, and I consider the case closed on Rev. Shaw.

I do remain somewhat curious as to why my opinion of Rev. Shaw's book, or his veracity, is of such apparent interest to you. I get the impression that there is something you wish me to say, but I cannot fathom what that might be. Rather than being loyal to Rev. Shaw, as you have charged, I have dropped him from my list of references and do not use any of his material. I informed you of this as early as Oct. '93 and again in June '94. Further, it is not my function to document and publish errors in books on Masonry, pro or con; rather, it is to find credible sources to use in developing my own opinions. I use this technique in any area of study, be it Mormonism, Jehovah's Witnesses, or Christianity. Based on our correspondence, I do not find Rev. Shaw a credible source. Period.

Of possible interest to you is that a Mason recently noted to me that one selected to the Thirty-third Degree was required to pay $1,000 to cover the cost of his ring, dinner, hotel, and other related expenses incident to his selection. Now you and I can quibble over what constitutes a "minimum donation," but clearly money is required from the candidate, a fact which you appear to deny. Another Mason noted that drinking was allowed in the rooms adjacent to the lodge when a new W[orshipful] M[aster] was installed. Yet you have flatly denied that drinking is allowed. Since the truth is not totally clear in either case, I do not accuse you of being a liar; however, I do think that you have been less than forthcoming in some key areas. As you quite correctly point out, nothing requires me to take the word of a Mason, or any other person, in matters of fact. Sufficient objective evidence can always be found to determine what is true and what is not.

As to sharing your rituals, the example I had in mind was John Ankerberg, who noted that failure to obtain the approved rituals resulted in using Blanchard. As I noted, a little "horse trading" on both sides would have resulted in more of the truth being known, and less of the unjust criticism. I found Ankerberg's books pretty well thought through, though he did overly rely on Blanchard, which you have convinced me does not reflect current Masonic rituals.

Finally, it is surprising that you would mention Jack Chick's *The Curse of Baphomet*, as I found a copy waiting for me the day I received your letter. A neighbor had ordered several such booklets and asked me about them. I found it somewhat overheated, and its conclusions do not agree with my own. I would neither endorse it nor distribute it based on its contents; however, it did raise an interesting question about the symbol on your cap. I have nothing on that symbol or its origination. Perhaps you could identify a source which explains such Masonic symbols? And rest assured: I do not accuse Masons of worshipping Baphomet!

Sincerely,

T. N. Sampson II

Mr. Sampson has yet again carefully avoided condemning Rev. Shaw. Dr. Morris responds to Mr. Sampson's alleged anonymous contacts with references to his own experiences and to public sources that can be independently confirmed. Dr. Morris then ends this second series of correspondence.

[LETTER 16]

1733 16th Street, NW
Washington, DC 20009-3103

November 29, 1994

Dear Mr. Sampson,

Your letter of September 9 was received. I resent your suggestion that I have not been forthcoming with you. I have answered you with statements you can verify for yourself. In contrast, you present anonymous anecdotes, but I will try to respond fairly.

There is nothing more you need to say about Rev. Shaw; your many previous statements speak loudly and clearly.

On page 101 of *The Deadly Deception*, Rev. Shaw described the alleged "minimum donation" required to receive the 33rd Degree.

> She then told me that in order to receive the [33rd] degree, I would be expected to make a "minimum donation" of a very large amount of money

(at least it was a "very large" amount for me). This took me completely by surprise for there had not been a word about any such "minimum donation" in my letter sent me by the Supreme Council.

It would seem that Rev. Shaw is trying to create an unflattering image of the Supreme Council luring 33rd Degree candidates to Washington and then surprising them with an unwritten requirement of a substantial donation. In my letter to you of September 3, I referred to this and other falsifications of Rev. Shaw concerning his alleged receipt of the 33rd Degree. There is a fee for the Degree, but it is well known and published in the *Statutes of the Supreme Council*, "Art. XI, Sec. 4.E. For the Thirty-third Degree, Patent included—$200.00." Anyone who bothers to read the *Statutes* knows about the fee; every other expense associated with the degree is voluntary. There is no charge to new 33rd Degree Masons for the Supreme Council banquet, despite what your unnamed informant may have told you.

The Supreme Council [SJ] normally elects new 33° members on a Monday morning, and the degree is conferred Tuesday afternoon. If a newly elected 33° Mason chooses to receive the degree in Washington, there is indeed the expense of travel and lodging. However, the degree is conferred many times around the country in regional meetings.

In 1991, Wilkins Jewelers, Inc. of Vero Beach, Florida charged $120.75 to $280.50 for a gold 33° ring, depending on weight and karat, and $275 for a 33° jewel. Neither a ring nor a jewel is required to receive the degree, just as a senior class ring is not required to graduate from high school or college.

A new 33° Mason could spend $755.50 for the fee, ring, and jewel. On the other hand, I spent nothing when I received the degree. The Valley of Baltimore paid my initiation fee; I chose to continue wearing my 32° ring; and I have not bought a jewel.

I do not deny nor have I denied there are expenses associated with receiving the Thirty-third Degree. However, they are either well-known and published or entirely voluntary. What I do deny is Rev. Shaw's allegation that there is any sort of unexpected "minimum donation." That is simply not true.

I never said "drinking is not allowed." That would be as foolish as saying, "No one professing to follow Christ drinks." What I did point out is that the Grand Lodge of Florida and the Supreme Council, SJ, completely forbid alcohol at the functions of their subordinate lodges.[6] Rev. Shaw's description of drinking by Florida Masons is as phony as the idea that a Seventh Day Adventist church would sponsor a wine tasting.

Different Grand Lodges have different rules concerning alcohol—some stricter and some more lenient than Florida. I cannot say anything about your other anonymous story, since you don't share the year, state, or other pertinent details. I can say, however, that Rev. Shaw's pious pronouncement on drinking in Florida is another of his slick fabrications: "But it bothered me that there was always so much [drinking] and that it played such a major role in the Masonic life."

The question you raise about the 33° emblem is an interesting one, but I do not have the time to do research for you. Thank you for answering my questions. This letter, so far as I am concerned, concludes our correspondence.

Sincerely Yours,

S. Brent Morris, PhD

Once again the Morris-Sampson correspondence is revived, this time when Mr. Sampson fulfills an earlier promise to share further information about Rev. Shaw, a position paper from Tom McKenney, coauthor of The Deadly Deception. *Mr. Sampson also offers editorial suggestions on Dr. Morris's writings.*

[LETTER 17]

Cornerstone Ministries
Poquson, Virginia

November 24, 1995

Dear Dr. Morris:

This letter is not to restart old arguments, but rather to fulfill an old promise. Two years ago, I said that if I ever received any information on Rev. Shaw's claims from the writer of *The Deadly Deception*, I would pass them along. Mr. McKenney has sent along a position paper on the subject, which I have enclosed for your review. Rev. Shaw, as you know, passed away.

While I have your attention, may I recommend finding another editor? In rereading your book, *Is It True What They Say About Freemasonry?*, I noted that on pages 41 and 43 you have extracts from the references being used to rebut Rev. Shaw's claims; however, you've used the 1989 examples, when Shaw left the Craft in 1966. Unless I've missed something, it would have made more sense to show the extracts from the year in which Rev. Shaw made his claims, not extracts some 20 years after the event. A second instance is in your article in the October '95 issue of *The Philalethes* entitled "Misrepresentations of Freemasonry."[7] In this article, I had a difficult time separating your comments from quotes by Enchanter! For example, refer to the paragraphs under the heading "The Difficulty of Dialog" (p. 104). How is the reader to tell which paragraphs are yours and which are quotes? In rereading, I assume the odd paragraphs are yours (1, 3, and 5) and the even by Enchanter! Otherwise, the article has you saying "[you] have taken vows to uphold certain secrets, even if it means telling lies." (Was that indeed what Enchanter! said? Is that a true statement?) The same problem occurs in the quotes from Dr. Morey's book, where quotation marks were not used, nor was a colon used in the preceding paragraph to introduce the quotes. Ditto the quotes under the heading "Deficient Research." Seems to me that any good editor would have ensured that quotes were properly indicated. Finally, and a very minor point, Grand Lodges are capitalized except once in your quote from the de Hoyos and Morris book. In that quote, one "lodge" appears with a lower case "l." Again, a good editor would have caught this. I bring this to your attention because arguments for or against Masonry are sometimes discarded for editorial reasons, vice incorrect factual statements. I hope we both support the view that this argument should be based on facts.

While on my soapbox, I did find consistent your attempts to separate Albert Pike from the Scottish Rite. It's certainly true that he is not the "guiding force" behind Masonry, but he certainly was that force behind the Scottish Rite, southern variant. One cannot separate him as easily as Masonic writers would have us believe. I also found it interesting that you noted that Pike's tome has not been distributed in the Scottish Rite since ca. 1971, but did not bother to mention that *A Bridge to Light* is distributed in its place. Since the latter is based mainly on the former, one easily (and correctly) concludes that Pike's thoughts remain in force in the Scottish Rite, SJ.

Since you are interested in the "online world," among the interesting opinions expressed on our electronic highways these days was one entitled "The Damning of Spiritual Masonry"[8] by Norman Williams Crabbe, MPS, (claimed to be reprinted from *The Philalethes*, April 1994). An intriguing article, to be sure. It told me much about Masonic thinking (minority view, I assume) and of the quality of writing that *The Philalethes* is willing to publish (assuming the claim is true).

Finally, the next Leadership Conference on Masonry will be in Indianapolis next June and I extended an invitation to Allen Roberts, via Nelson King, to attend. Mr. Roberts had a few comments on the last conference, and I thought that he might wish to attend the next and present his own views. You should consider attending yourself if nothing else, it would get us all together for an open discussion of viewpoints (we all trust riot control measures will not be needed).

Cordially,

T. N. Sampson II

Here follows the position paper prepared by Mr. Tom McKenney presumably in response to Dr. Morris's book review of The Deadly Deception *and the first edition of* Is It True What They Say About Freemasonry?

POSITION PAPER: JAMES D. SHAW AND THE 33RD DEGREE

[By Tom McKenney]

22 February 1995

1. The Issue. Subsequent to the publication of *"The Deadly Deception: Freemasonry Exposed by one of Its Top Leaders"* (Huntington House, Lafayette, La.), charges have been made by Scottish Rite Masonry that Jim Shaw was never a 33rd Degree Mason; the charges were subsequently expanded to allege that Jim also was never Worshipful Master of his Blue Lodge or Master of any Scottish Rite Body, and that he was not "one of (Masonry's) top leaders."

2. Evidence in Support of the Charges.

A. Scottish Rite Masonry presents that it has no records of Jim's having held the offices or degree in question.

B. Scottish Rite Masonry presents records appearing to show that Jim was made Knight Commander of the Court of Honor (KCCH), the prerequisite honor and "final stepping stone" to the 33rd Degree, in October 1965 but resigned from Masonry one year later, effective October 1966, before becoming eligible for the 33rd Degree. (Theoretically a man must be KCCH for 4 years before being considered for 33rd Degree.)

3. Evidence in Support of Jim Shaw's Testimony.

A. *Jim Shaw's Character and Reputation.* Jim Shaw has been a dedicated Christian for 30 years, a man of unquestioned character until these charges were brought by Masonic officialdom.

B. *Masonry's Attitude Toward Truth.* Freemasonry is a system built upon lies and deception (for only one of many references, see *Morals and Dogma*, p. 819).

C. *My Own Pre-Publication Investigation.* Before I wrote Jim's story, on advice of a friend experienced in such matters, I investigated Jim's story. The only non-Masonic sources who could verify Jim's story were

Is It True What They Say about Freemasonry?

Jim's friend, Mike; Dr. Swords, the ophthalmologist who had led Jim to the Lord; and Mrs. Swords. I couldn't speak with Mike for he had died of cancer years before. I found Dr. Swords in semi-retirement as a physician/surgeon and extremely active in Christian affairs. He is a man of sterling reputation and almost radically correct Christian character, a man who would never compromise, especially with the truth (yes, I checked on Dr. Swords, also). Dr. Swords got out Jim's medical records to refresh his memory, and I found that Jim's story was meticulously accurate, according to Dr. Swords's records and his very precise memory. Both Dr. Swords and his wife stated, emphatically and without hesitation, that Jim was 33rd Degree when he left the Lodge. They, of course, had not seen the Scottish Rite records, but knew him and his Masonic identity at the time of leaving the Lodge in 1966 extremely well.

D. *His Credentials Never Challenged Before.* Jim Shaw has openly presented himself to the world as "Rev James D. Shaw, ex-33rd Degree Mason" in his published tracts, pamphlets and cassette tapes for more than 20 years. In addition, he has had published forewords as an ex-33rd Degree Mason in two widely distributed major anti-Masonic books for many years. Never, during all those 20-plus years, was any question or challenge to his credentials or testimony raised by Masonic officialdom, either privately or publicly, until after publication of *"Deadly Deception."*

E. *Most of His Masonic Records Were Burned.* When Jim became a Christian, he burned his Masonic apron, regalia, certificates, etc., according to the Scriptures. The only items surviving the burning were some that his wife hid; significant among these are Scottish Rite Reunion programs which show Jim as "32°, KCCH" and "Degree Master," the program from the ceremony making him KCCH, and a 33rd Degree Medal with purple ribbon, still in its original plastic case. (The medal is not personalized or dated.)

F. *Acknowledged as 33° by the Universal League of Freemasons.* There also survives a membership card in The Universal League of Freemasons, an international Masonic order, issued to Jim without his request by Sigmund Holsjen, Universal Grand Master, identifying Jim as "Bro. Rev. James D. Shaw, 33°" (photocopy, obverse and reverse, attached). Jim continued to pay dues to this order for some time after leaving the Lodge in order to receive its literature for research.

G. *The Opinion of Another Christian 33° Mason.* F. Evans Crary, Esq., who was made KCCH in the same program with Jim Shaw, and who subsequently became 33rd Degree and held the highest office in Masonry, Grand Master of Masons, Grand Lodge of Florida, believes that Jim Shaw was 33rd Degree.

H. *They Possess the Records.* The Scottish Rite has possessed the records for nearly 30 years; what reason have we to believe that a system based on lies and deception, with that much time, hasn't "lost" or altered the records prior to their recent, late-in-the-game charges? As possessors of the records, we certainly can't expect them to verify such a damaging testimony.

I. *"One of (Masonry's) Top Leaders."* Concerning Masonry's denial that Jim was ever one of Masonry's "top leaders," let me say first that this has never been Jim Shaw's claim. Those are the publisher's words, not Jim's. Before publication of *"Deadly Deception,"* I argued against the word "top" but the publisher prevailed. At any rate this point is moot; it could mean that in the 1960s Jim was one of Masonry's top 3 leaders, or one of the top 3,000, or it could mean that he was one of the top 300,000; surely, if only Degree Master and KCCH in the Scottish Rite, he was at least that.

J. *Jim's Testimony Is NOT "Impossible."* Theoretically, one must be a Master Mason for 6 months before becoming eligible for the Scottish Rite Degrees (4°–32°), then one must be a 32° Mason for 4 years before being eligible for KCCH, and then be KCCH for 4 more years before becoming eligible for the 33°. Concerning the argument that Jim wasn't KCCH long enough even to be considered for the 33rd Degree, let alone receive it, the fact is that the Supreme Council, which selects men for both KCCH and the 33rd Degree, can coronet men when they please.

A Case in Point. A recent example of this is that of the late John J. Robinson. As a non-Mason, Mr. Robinson wrote a sympathetic history of Masonry, *Born in Blood,* followed by two more pro-Masonic books. Mr. Robinson was made a Master Mason in November 1992, a Scottish Rite Mason of the 32nd Degree on 24 April 1993 (Northern Jurisdiction) and 4 May 1993 (Southern Jurisdiction). On 3 Sept 1993, three days before his death, Robinson was made a 33rd Degree Mason. After going all the way from non-Mason to 33rd Degree in only 10 months, Mr. Robinson died on 6 Sept 1993. It is certainly conceivable that Jim Shaw, after 20 years as a Mason, after more than 19 years as 32° and a year as KCCH, could have been made 33° just before he resigned from Masonry.

K. *When Unable to Refute the Message, Attack the Messenger.* Although *The Scottish Rite Journal* has publicly called me a liar and Jim Shaw a phony, first in a feature article and later in a special issue book, not one word of our charges against Masonry has been refuted. It appears to be a classic case of damaging charges which can't be refuted, so the attack is made on the source instead; since they can't refute the message, they attack the messenger. This obscures the real issue (for which they have no defense), by creating a false issue (concerning which they hold all the records). This is exactly what has been done in Arkansas, incidentally, to everyone who has spoken damaging truth against the Clintons' circle of power (those who haven't died in the process).

4. My Conclusion.

Initially, I was greatly troubled by certain aspects of the charges by Scottish Rite officialdom, especially the apparent problem in the time lapse between KCCH and 33rd Degree in Jim's case. When I discussed this problem with Jim, he replied simply that the Supreme Council can do whatever it chooses to do; this has proved to be the case.

In the final analysis I must choose whom I will believe. Upon consideration of all the above, and knowing Jim as I do, I accept and believe the testimony of Jim Shaw, including all his Masonic credentials, exactly as published in *The Deadly Deception.*

[Tom C. McKenney]

Tom C. McKenney
PO Box 413 Marion, KY 42064
Co-author, *The Deadly Deception*; author, *Please Tell Me*

Dr. Morris provides Mr. Sampson with a point-by-point response to Mr. McKenney's position paper. Dr. Morris clearly raises the fundamental issue here, which no supporter of Rev. Shaw has addressed: What are the dates of Rev. Shaw's Masonic service?

[LETTER 18]

1733 16th Street, NW
Washington, DC 20009-3103

December 29, 1995

Dear Mr. Sampson:

Thank you for forwarding me a copy of "James D. Shaw and the 33rd Degree" by Mr. Tom C. McKenney. This document confirms my opinion of Mr. McKenney and Rev. Shaw. Your observations about the editing of my articles are noted.

A computer glitch seems to have destroyed the formatting of "Misrepresentations of Freemasonry"; I have enclosed a correctly formatted copy for you. I am responsible for the choice of reproductions in *Is It True What They Say About Freemasonry?* As Rev. Shaw is never listed as an officer of Allapattah Lodge, I chose the 1989 listing as an example of what an independent researcher could find; I thought reproducing every listing of officers during Rev. Shaw's membership in the Lodge would be tedious.

Because of the confusion this has caused for you, we will consider adding a summary of all officers published in the Grand Lodge *Proceedings* in the next edition. We could include tables of Scottish Rite officers during Rev. Shaw's membership and a sampling of souvenir programs listing dignitaries, and so on.[9] At some time, however, this becomes pointless if Mr. McKenney and his ilk ignore the facts by stating that "Freemasonry is a system built upon lies and deception."

You said you enclosed the position paper for my review, and so I will give you a brief one, addressing the points made by Mr. McKenney. It is first worth noting, sadly, that the issue of Rev. Shaw has been reduced to ad hominem arguments. Rev. Shaw makes many claims about Freemasonry in his book that we cannot verify objectively. The reader is left to rely upon his veracity in judging his witness about Freemasonry. The way to counter Rev. Shaw's false statements is to show a general pattern of deliberate deceit.

For example, Rev. Shaw claims that candidates drink wine from a human skull in the 33° ceremony. This is plagiarized directly from Blanchard's *Scotch Rite Masonry*, vol. 2, p. 470, and is in fact an identifying characteristic of Cerneau ritual. I imagine if I produced a copy of the 33° ritual to counter this claim, Mr. McKenney would declare the document a forgery. Similarly, neither members of the Supreme Council nor anyone else interview 33° candidates (pp. 102–103), but how could a researcher confirm this statement? We are reluctantly left with addressing the general pattern of Rev. Shaw's claims that can be tested.

3A. *Jim Shaw's Character and Reputation.* I have no doubt Rev. Shaw's friends and colleagues regarded him as a good Christian who tried to share the good news of grace through Jesus Christ's sacrifice. However, none of this addresses the factual evidence.

3B. *Masonry's Attitude Toward Truth.* Whether Freemasonry is based upon lies or truth is not the issue. Mr. McKenney makes claims that he cannot or will not substantiate.

3C. *My Own Pre-Publication Investigation.* I am confident Rev. Shaw told Dr. and Mrs. Swords that he was a 33° Mason, but, as Mr. McKenney admits, they never saw the records. We cannot verify their emphatic statement of Rev. Shaw's membership.

3D. *His Credentials Never Challenged Before.* This is an interesting argument— something of a statute of limitations for lying. The fact that no one has bothered to point out Rev. Shaw's lies does not give any greater credence to Rev. Shaw's statements.

3E. *Most of His Masonic Records Were Burned.* A cynic could argue this is much too convenient for Mr. McKenney's case. He says Rev. Shaw's records are not available and then argues (in 3H) that Scottish Rite records cannot be trusted. His only evidence is a reunion program that lists Rev. Shaw as "32°, KCCH," an honor we have never questioned. The undated and non-personalized 33° Medal established nothing; anyone can buy one in a pawn shop.[10]

3F. *Acknowledged as 33° by the Universal League of Freemasons.* The ULF is a clandestine organization, membership in which usually results in expulsion for regular Masons. I know of no regular Grand Lodge that acknowledges the ULF. The question of whether membership in the ULF proves one is a Mason is similar to the question of whether membership in the Mormon Church proves one is a Christian. It is my understanding the ULF will accept anyone who claims to be a Mason. It might be amusing for you to join, or for me to get a membership for my cat. What the dues card does prove is that Rev. Shaw had no compunction about deceiving the ULF and claiming Masonic membership for nearly twenty years after his 1965 resignation.

3G. *The Opinion of Another Christian 33° Mason.* F. Evans Crary received the rank and decoration of KCCH with Rev. Shaw, but Mr. Crary offers no evidence that Rev. Shaw ever received the Thirty-third Degree. It is nice that Mr. Crary *believes* that Rev. Shaw received the Thirty-third Degree, but a lawyer should offer better corroboration than hearsay. Was Mr. Crary present when Rev. Shaw received the degree? Can he give us a date? Does he have any document— program, newsletter, or *Transactions*—that can be independently verified?

3H. *They Possess the Records.* Indeed we do, but we base our arguments on public not archival documents. The Supreme Council publishes its *Transactions* biennially and distributes hundreds of copies around the world. The *Transactions* list every 33° Mason when he receives the degree. Further, the Valley of Miami publishes a newsletter that lists officers, and their reunion programs list their "Honor Men," the KCCHs and 33° Masons. Thousands of these documents have been distributed. Any of these documents would establish Mr. McKenney's case and produce a public acknowledgment of error by me. Rather than call the Scottish Rite liars, Mr. McKenney should point to some fact that can be independently confirmed.

3I. *"One of (Masonry's) Top Leaders."* This question is moot, as we conceded that this is well within the allowable limits of advertising.

3J. *Jim's Testimony is NOT "impossible."* Here we made a technical error. We stated that Rev. Shaw resigned from Masonry "thirty-seven months before he would have been eligible to even be nominated for the 33°." This is much the same as saying, "The US Constitution prevents the election of a President and Vice-President from different parties." In the latter case, one has to add, "Unless no majority is obtained in the electoral college, and the election is moved to the Congress, and the House elects the President from one party, and the Senate elects the Vice-President from another."

Of course, the Supreme Council can make exceptions, as it did for John Robinson, but these cases are exceedingly rare and are always published. Mr. McKenney need not speculate how Rev. Shaw might have received his 33rd Degree in less than eleven months. We can rely on Rev. Shaw's own words that he waited four years: "I had been a KCCH for only four years. A man cannot even be considered for the 33rd Degree until he has been a KCCH four years. I was being considered for the 33rd in the minimum time!" (*Deadly Deception*, p. 90) Mr. McKenney continues to avoid the central issue (at least to us): When did Rev. Shaw receive his 33rd Degree? Mr. McKenney says, "I accept and believe the testimony of Jim Shaw, including all his Masonic credentials, exactly as published in *The Deadly Deception*. We should be able confidently to add four years to 1965, the date Shaw and Crary received the KCCH, and check the records for Shaw's 33rd. The check is in vain.

3K. *When Unable to Refute the Message, Attack the Messenger.* Mr. McKenney suggests we have not answered his charges against Masonry. In his book, he accuses the Scottish Rite of being drunkards, of having exorbitant initiation fees, of having bloody oaths, and of teaching resurrection and reincarnation. I think we refuted these rather well. As I noted above, Rev. Shaw makes many claims about Freemasonry in his book that cannot be verified objectively. Either you believe Rev. Shaw or you don't. We have gone to public documents to show that Rev. Shaw was not truthful about his membership claims. Mr. McKenney refuses to address the problem of there being no records to examine—Supreme Council *Transactions*, Grand Lodge *Proceedings*, Lodge or Scottish Rite newsletters, reunion programs, photographs.

He tries misdirection when he says, "The Supreme Council can do whatever it chooses to do; this has proved to be the case."

Please excuse me for taking so long to review Mr. McKenney's position for you. I think we will include this analysis in the second edition of *Is It True?* Your invitation to attend the next Leadership Conference on Masonry is thoughtful, but I decline. Consider, as just one example, the chasm that exists between what Mr. McKenney thinks is evidence and what I do. I cannot imagine any productive discussion occurring at the Conference. Enjoy yourself there.

Sincerely yours,

S. Brent Morris, Ph.D.

Dr. Morris, still trying to establish the veracity of Rev. Shaw's claims, wrote to Mr. McKenney requesting information on Rev. Shaw's Masonic credentials.

[LETTER 19]

1733 16th Street, NW
Washington, DC 20009-3103

October 9, 1996

Mr. Tom McKenney
Words for Living Ministries
PO Box 413
Marion, KY 42064

Dear Mr. McKenney:

I understand you have published a supplement to *The Deadly Deception* in which you address the factual record of Rev. Shaw's Masonic credentials. I would like to obtain a copy and have enclosed $2 and a stamped self-addressed envelope. Please let me know if this is not enough to cover reproduction and shipping.

I look forward to learning more about Rev. Shaw's Masonic career.

Sincerely Yours,

S. Brent Morris, PhD

Mr. McKenney replied to Dr. Morris and sent him a copy of the position paper on Rev. Shaw which Mr. Sampson had already shared.

[LETTER 20]

Words for Living Ministries
Marion, Kentucky

31 October 1996

Dear Brent,

Your letter was forwarded to me here in Ocean Springs, [Mississippi].

You have been misinformed; there has been no supplement to *Deadly Deception* published (at least none of which I'm aware).

I have, however, written a position paper on Jim's claims, which I provide on request. A copy is enclosed, with your $2.00; there is no charge for it.

I would like to explain to you that disputed "one of Masonry's top leaders" statement in the subtitle. That was insisted upon by the publisher; I argued against the word "top" for at least an hour on the phone, but he had his way. At any rate, it is a completely imprecise term; it could mean he was one of the top two, or one of the top two million, but I'd like for you to know how it arrived in the subtitle, which I thought was much too lurid. (I also argued against "exposed," but lost that one too.)

You may not know that Jim died in April '94. He is survived only by his wife, Bonnie, who is in a nursing home in Florida.

With Jesus' love,

Tom C. McKenney

Dr. Morris replied to Mr. McKenney and sent him a copy of his letter to Mr. Sampson [Letter 18] with the point-by-point response to the position paper as well as copies of many of the public records concerning Rev. Shaw's Masonic career. Dr. Morris concludes this letter to Mr. McKenney with two simple options and the evidence for each: 1) Rev. Shaw is telling the truth or 2) Rev. Shaw is lying.

[LETTER 21]

1733 16th Street, NW
Washington, DC 20009-3103

January 2, 1997

Dear Mr. McKenney:

Thank you for your letter of October 31, 1996, and for a copy of your position paper, "James D. Shaw and the 33rd Degree." I had already received a copy of the paper from Mr. T. N. Sampson who has an anti-Masonic ministry in Poquoson, Virginia. Enclosed is a letter I sent to Mr. Sampson commenting on your position paper. Mr. Sampson no longer recommends *The Deadly Deception* in his ministry.

I can sympathize with your frustration with your publisher (I have had similar problems myself). However, Huntington House's insistence on using

Is It True What They Say about Freemasonry?

the subtitle "Freemasonry exposed by one of its top leaders" only supports the contention of Art de Hoyos and me: greed motivates the publication of anti-Masonic books. Why else would the publisher use a subtitle that an author thinks is "much too lurid"? Why highlight in eye-catching red the demonstrably false claim, "The 33° initiation ceremony revealed for the first time in history"?

You are indeed correct that Supreme Councils can waive the normal waiting period for the Thirty-third Degree, as with John J. Robinson, 33°. We will correct this misstatement in the upcoming revision to our book. What is consistent with Supreme Councils is careful public documentation of all recipients of the Thirty-third Degree. I have enclosed a copy of the public record of Bro. Robinson's degree (*1993 Proceedings of the Supreme Council, NMJ*, p. 72).

It is not necessary, as you suggest, to search for a special meeting of the Supreme Council for Rev. Shaw's 33rd, since we can deduce the date he claims to have received the degree. He was elected to receive the rank and decoration of a Knight Commander of the Court of Honor on October 19, 1965 (*1965 Transactions of the Supreme Council*, SJ, pp. 218, 225); the ceremony was held on December 18, 1965. He later said, "I had been a KCCH for only four years. A man cannot even be considered for the 33rd Degree until he has been a KCCH four years. I was being considered for the 33rd in minimum time!" (*Deadly Deception*, p. 90). Thus, Rev. Shaw claims to have been elected to the 33rd Degree in 1969. I have enclosed a list of the twenty-nine 33rd-Degree Masons elected from Florida in 1969; Rev. Shaw's name is not included (*1969 Transactions of the Supreme Council*, SJ, pp. 5, 42, 43). This is not surprising since Rev. Shaw submitted his letter of resignation on October 25, 1966 (copy enclosed).

Rev. Shaw received the 32nd Degree on November 9, 1952. He says, "I didn't enter the Shrine after the Spring Reunion [1953] when I became eligible. . . . In the Blue Lodge I was Senior Deacon and preparing to be the Junior Warden, only two chairs away from the office of Worshipful Master. . . . The following fall [1953] however, after Reunion, I decided it was time to enter the Shrine" (*Deadly Deception*, p. 74). One can infer from this that Rev. Shaw was elected Junior Warden for 1954. He says, "I continued my progression 'through the chairs,' from office to higher office in the Blue Lodge . . ." (*Deadly Deception*, p. 77). Again, one can infer that Rev. Shaw was elected Master of his

Lodge (Allapatah No. 271) in 1956. The Grand Lodge of Florida publishes annual *Proceedings* of its meetings, which include a listing of the elected officers of every Florida Lodge. Rev. Shaw is not listed as Junior Warden for 1954, nor Master for 1956, nor for any office during 1952 to 1966, the years he was a member (copies enclosed).

Rev. Shaw's story about his experience in Freemasonry abounds with inconsistencies, but I won't bore you with more details. It is difficult to carry on a civil discussion about objective, public facts when you say, "Freemasonry is a system built upon lies and deception" and "What reason have we to believe that a system based on lies and deception, with that much time, hasn't 'lost' or altered the records prior to their recent late-in-the-game charges? As possessors of the records, we certainly can't expect them to verify such a damaging testimony." The *Proceedings of the Grand Lodge of Florida* and the *Transactions of the Supreme Council, SJ* are public documents. Hundreds of copies were published. They are distributed to each of their constituent bodies, to officers, and to other Masonic bodies around the world. Masonry makes these records available to anyone.

You cannot produce any public records to support Rev. Shaw's 33rd Degree or his being Master of Allapattah Lodge, much less give us the dates when these events occurred so we can verify them ourselves. You ask that Rev. Shaw's testimony be trusted completely, and yet you accuse us of lying, deceiving, and altering documents when we present our public records.

I see two possible explanations for the situation here:

> 1. Rev. Shaw is telling the truth. This means the Grand Lodge of Florida recalled and altered every copy of its *Proceedings* that list Rev. Shaw as Junior Warden, Senior Warden, and Master. Allapattah Lodge recalled and altered every monthly bulletin that listed Rev. Shaw as Master as well as every membership certificate he signed during his year in office, and every letter he wrote as Master. Similarly, the Scottish Rite Valley of Miami must have recalled every bulletin, reunion, banquet program, and document that lists Rev. Shaw among their 33° members. Besides this, all Florida Masons must have been instructed to deny Rev. Shaw's accomplishments,

all photographs that show Rev. Shaw in his regalia have been destroyed, and every local newspaper article that may have mentioned Rev. Shaw has been altered.

2. Rev. Shaw is lying.

I am willing to let our readers check the public records and make up their own minds.

Sincerely Yours,

S. Brent Morris, PhD

[EPILOGUE]

On August 14, 1997, Mr. McKenney wrote to Dr. Morris, "Jim Shaw told me, and continued to so state until his death, that Billy Graham participated [at his 33° ceremony]. Also present, he said, were the King of Denmark, Harry Truman, Dwight Eisenhower (a non-Mason), Norman Vincent Peale, Daniel Polling, and J. Edgar Hoover." Dr. Morris repeatedly requested evidence of Rev. Shaw's receipt of the Thirty-third Degree and attendance by any of these distinguished men, or Shaw's service as Master of his lodge. Mr. McKenney's health and general over-commitment have prevented him from finding independently verifiable information. However, the Supreme Council's published Transactions, which prints the names of all visitors, fails to notice the alleged attendance of these prestigious persons.

On July 11, 2003, eight years after his last letter to Dr. Morris, Mr. Sampson begrudgingly posted a message to the website of Ephesians 5:11, an anti-Masonic ministry, which read: "Mr. Shaw got carried away and lied about his accomplishments in the Craft."

Thus we see that in spite of overwhelming and substantive evidence to the contrary, Mr. Sampson, who remains Rev. Shaw's disciple, still struggles to free himself from Rev. Shaw's many lies, rejecting only his exaggerated accomplishments in the Craft. However, there is no question that Rev. Shaw did get one thing right. He understood the gullibility of human nature expressed by the old Latin phrase, Mundus vult decipi, ergo decipiatur, "The world wishes to be deceived, therefore deceive!"

[LETTER 22]

Skip_sampson (Skip_sampson)
Moderator
Username: Skip_sampson

Post Number: 286
Registered: 01-2003
Posted From: 205.188.209.80
Posted on Friday, July 11, 2003 - 06:15 pm:

To all:
QUOTE
James D. Shaw was indeed a Mason, although he never was Worshipful Master in the Lodge as claimed.
UNQUOTE
Mr. Pyle needs no support from me in these matters, but it is an issue I am very familiar with. I've seen the officer lists of Mr. Shaw's lodge and he did not hold the offices he claims. He did hold one office (JD?), but was never Master of his Lodge or any other that I could uncover. And I looked real hard.

I also have a letter from Mr. Kleinknecht (SR/SJ) noting that Mr. Shaw was never a 33 degree SR Mason. From the facts of the matter, Mr. Shaw got carried away and lied about his accomplishments in the Craft. Cordially, Skip

http://www.ephesians5-11.org/discus/messages/15/631.html#POST4100 (accessed June 30, 2009)

Chapter 11

Falsus in Multis, Falsus in Omnibus

> Whoever can be trusted with very little can also be trusted with much, and whoever is dishonest with very little will also be dishonest with much.
>
> **—Luke 16:10**

An old Roman legal maxim holds *Falsus in uno, falsus in omnibus*—False in one, false in all. In other words, if one of several claims is found false, then all are assumed to be false. This is a high standard, perhaps unreasonably high for men dedicated to "saving" the world from Freemasonry. It may be that their zeal has overwhelmed their sense of fair play or what exactly constitutes bearing false witness.

Possibly a more lenient measure of truth would be better suited for anti-Masons, something like handicapping for horse races. If we adopt *Falsus in quinque, falsus in omnibus*, then it would take five false statements to bring all of an author's statements into question. With this relaxed standard, the lies on the cover of Rev. Shaw's book wouldn't condemn his text. Of course, Rev. Shaw then would have no room for his insinuations about the cost of membership or Masonic drinking. The problem could be solved if we didn't count insinuations as out-and-out lies. Another solution would be to adopt *Falsus in multis, falsus in omnibus*—False in many, false in all. Then each could set his own standard for what constitutes "many."

The real problem, though, is deeper than quibbling over how many lies are too many. (For *most* Christians, one lie is too many.) Many anti-Masons are willing to accept negative statements about Freemasonry without question. They are so zealous in their cause that they ignore normal standards of decency and research.

Revs. Ankerberg, Carlson, and Shaw, who proudly boast of their knowledge about Freemasonry, are pathetic liars who bear false witness in the name of the Christian religion. We have not bothered exposing all of their frauds because the exercise is ultimately futile. If someone is willing to overlook the lies we have catalogued, then why would they be convinced if we show them five or ten or twenty more?

Is it true what they say about Freemasonry? Absolutely not! . . . If they say Freemasonry is a satanic cult, or if they say Masons are taught to hate Christianity, or if they say lodges are organized for sex worship. These are but a few examples of the absurd and lurid lies used by those who despise our fraternity. Their hatred is so great that they can rationalize any fantasy, fraud, or deceit to accomplish their ends.

What is true is that Freemasonry is a fraternity of God-fearing men. Masons are men who strive to be better—not better than others, but better than themselves. Lodges give Masons the opportunity to join together for friendship, to serve their neighbors through community service, and to help the less fortunate through scores of Masonic philanthropies. In 1995, American Masonic philanthropy was $750 million or $2 million per day, of which 70 percent went to the general American public.[1]

Masons believe that all men are brothers under the fatherhood of God and Masons agree while in lodge not to discuss religion beyond this simple belief. Masons would agree with this definition of religion from James 1:27, "Religion that is pure and undefiled before God, the Father, is this: To care for orphans and widows in their distress, and to keep oneself unstained by the world."

If this is what they say about Freemasonry, then it is indeed true.

Appendix 1

The Confession of Léo Taxil

Translated by Alain Bernheim, 32°,
A. William Samii, 32°, and Eric Serejski, 32°

A good practical joke can produce weeks of laughter; a grand joke is retold as the centerpiece of later get-togethers; a few jokes become legendary. Gabriel Jogand-Pagès, better known as Léo Taxil, played a legendary practical joke a century ago. He chose to ridicule the Roman Catholic Church's credulity about Freemasonry, and he seemed to have thought it all good fun. He invented an elaborate hoax of "Luciferian High Masonry" with Albert Pike as the "Sovereign Pontiff of Universal Masonry." On April 19, 1897, Taxil confessed everything at a public meeting in Paris. His confession, however, hasn't stopped anti-Masons from rediscovering the hoax and reusing it to attack the Craft. Monsieur Taxil, like Dr. Frankenstein, could not foresee what his creation would do.

A transcript of Taxil's confession was published in the weekly Parisian newspaper, *Le Frondeur*, on April 25, 1897 (figure AI-I). It is a long, rambling speech that was first published in English in *Heredom*, the transactions of the Scottish Rite Research Society, vol. 5 (1996), pp. 137 to 168. It is reprinted here with the permission of the Scottish Rite Research Society. Taxil's confession is both amusing and appalling and gives the reader a glimpse of the magnitude of his deceit. Taxil's text was colloquial and ungrammatical in many places, as well as taken from a verbal presentation. The translators have tried to be faithful to the original format while producing a readable text.

DEUXIÈME ANNÉE (Nouvelle Série).   Le Numéro : 10 centimes   N° 13. — 25 AVRIL. 1897.

LE FRONDEUR

HEBDOMADAIRE

Tuons-les par le Rire !

ABONNEMENTS :

France et Algérie, un an ..... 5 fr.
Étranger, un an .... 8 fr.
Les Abonnements se paient d'avance

Directeur : Alfred MOURLON
Rédaction et Administration :
9, Cité Condorcet — Paris

PUBLICITÉ :

Faits divers .... 3 fr. la ligne.
Réclames .... 2 » —
Annonces .... 1 » —

Douze ans sous la Bannière de l'Eglise
LA FUMISTERIE DU PALLADISME
MISS DIANA VAUGHAN — LE DIABLE CHEZ LES FRANCS-MAÇONS
Conférence de M. Léo TAXIL
à la Salle de la Société de Géographie, à Paris

Tous les journaux ont rendu compte, plus ou moins impartialement, de la soirée mémorable du 19 avril, à la Société de Géographie. Nous avons pensé que le plus simple était de donner in-extenso la conférence de M. Léo Taxil.

Disons tout d'abord que l'assistance, fort nombreuse, se composait surtout de représentants de la presse des divers pays et de toutes les opinions, beaucoup de prêtres, religieux, un grand nombre de dames, des libres-penseurs, des francs-maçons. La Nonciature avait envoyé deux délégués ; l'Archevêché s'était également fait représenter. Toutes les entrées étaient gratuites ; mais on n'était admis qu'avec les cartes d'invitation personnelle qui avaient été envoyées depuis un mois.

À l'ouverture de la séance, eut lieu le tirage au sort d'une superbe machine à écrire, offerte par Miss Diana Vaughan. L'heureux gagnant a été M. Ali Kemal, rédacteur du *Ikdam*, de Constantinople.

M. Léo Taxil a pris ensuite la parole :

Mes Révérends Pères,
Mesdames,
Messieurs,

Il importe, tout d'abord, d'adresser des remerciements à ceux de mes confrères de la presse catholique, qui, — entreprenant *tout-à-coup*, il y a six ou sept mois, une campagne d'attaques retentissantes, — ont produit un merveilleux résultat, celui que nous constatons dès ce soir, et que l'on constatera mieux encore demain . L'éclat tout-à-fait exceptionnel de la manifestation de la vérité dans une question, dont la solution aurait pu peut-être, sans eux, passer absolument inaperçue.

À ces chers confrères, donc, mes premières félicitations ! et, dans un instant, ils vont comprendre combien ces remerciements sont sincères et justifiés.

LÉO TAXIL

Dans cette allocution, je m'attacherai à oublier ce qui a été publié d'injuste et de blessant contre ma personne, au cours de la polémique à laquelle je viens de faire allusion ; ou du moins, si je suis amené à éclairer certains faits d'une lumière qui, pour beaucoup, est inattendue, je dirai la vérité en écartant de ma pensée l'ombre même du plus léger ressentiment .

Peut-être, après ces explications, dont l'heure a enfin sonné, ces confrères catholiques ne désarmeront pas devant ma pacifique philosophie ; mais, si un

bonne humeur, au lieu de les calmer, les irrite, je les assure que rien ne me fera abandonner cette placidité d'âme que j'ai acquise depuis douze ans et dont je suis infiniment heureux.

D'ailleurs, s'il est vrai que cet auditoire d'élite est composé des éléments les plus disparates, — puisqu'on a fait appel indistinctement à toutes les opinions, — cet auditoire n'en a pas moins, j'en suis convaincu, le sentiment de la plus douce tolérance en matière d'examen. Disons le mot : nous sommes ici entre gens de bonne compagnie. Tous, nous savons faire la part de ce qui est sérieux, et nous l'examinons avec la gravité nécessaire, sans emportement ; mais aussi, quand un fait qui nous est soumis est avant tout amusant, nous ne nous fâchons pas davantage. Mieux vaut rire que pleurer, dit la sagesse des nations.

**

Maintenant, je m'adresse aux catholiques.

Je leur dis : — Quand vous avez su que le docteur Bataille, se disant dévoué à la cause catholique, avait passé onze années de sa vie à explorer les antres les plus ténébreux des sociétés secrètes, Loges et Arrière-Loges, et même Triangles lucifériens, vous l'avez carrément approuvé, vous avez trouvé sa conduite admirable. Il a reçu une véritable pluie de félicitations. Des articles élogieux, il en a eu même dans les journaux du parti qui aujourd'hui n'ont pas assez de foudres pour pulvériser Miss Diana Vaughan, la traitant tantôt de mythe et tantôt d'aventurière et de tireuse de cartes.

On peut revenir à présent sur ces acclamations qui ont accueilli le docteur Bataille : mais elles n'en ont pas moins eu lieu, et elles ont été éclatantes. Illustres théologiens, éloquents prédicateurs, éminents

Figure A1-1. The April 25, 1897, issue of the Parisian weekly newspaper, *Le Frondeur*, carried a transcript of Léo Taxil's confession.

Twelve Years Under the Banner of the Church

THE PRANK OF PALLADISM

MISS DIANA VAUGHAN— THE DEVIL AT THE FREEMASONS

A Conference held by M. Léo TAXIL at the Hall of the Geographic Society in Paris

With more or less impartiality, all newspapers reported the memorable evening at the Geographic Society on April 19. We thought the best thing to do was to reproduce the full text of M. Léo Taxil's conference.

Let us say first that the very numerous audience consisted mainly of press representatives from various countries and of all opinions, many priests, monks, very many ladies, some free-thinkers, some freemasons. The nunciature had sent two delegates; the archdiocese was also represented. Entrance was free, but one could get in only by showing nominal invitation cards which had been sent one month in advance.

First thing in the evening, a splendid typewriter offered by Miss Diana Vaughan was raffled. Its lucky winner was M. Ali Kental, Editor of the *Ikdam*, at Constantinople

Then M. Léo Taxil addressed the audience:

MY REVEREND FATHERS,

LADIES,

GENTLEMEN,

First of all, it is appropriate to convey some thanks to those of my colleagues of the Catholic press who—*suddenly* undertaking a campaign of vociferous attacks six or seven months ago—produced a marvelous result; we already witness it tonight and tomorrow will witness it even better, I mean the quite exceptional explosion of the manifestation of truth in a question whose solution might possibly have passed completely unnoticed without them.

To these dear colleagues, accordingly, my first congratulations! And they will understand in a moment how much these thanks are sincere and justified.

This evening, I shall strive to forget all the unjust and offensive things which have been published against me during the polemic I just mentioned. Or, at any rate, if I come to elucidate specific facts in a way unexpected for many, I shall merely tell the truth, setting aside the very shadow of the lightest resentment from my thoughts.

After the explanations whose time has come at last, maybe these Catholic colleagues will not disarm before my peaceful philosophy. However, should my good dispositions annoy them instead of calming them down, I assure them that nothing will induce me to set aside the equanimity I acquired over the last twelve years and which makes me infinitely happy.

Besides, if this exceptional audience is truly made of the most disparate elements—since all opinions were indiscriminately invited—, nevertheless I am convinced that this audience is possessed of the sweetest tolerance, as far as survey is concerned. To call things by their proper name: we are here among well-educated people. All of us are all able to make allowance for what is earnest and to take it under consideration with the required seriousness and without passion. However when a fact submitted to us is above all on the witty side, we do not get excited either. Better to laugh than cry, as the nations' wisdom goes.

The Prank Outlined

Now, I address myself to the Catholics.

I tell them:—When you were told that Doctor Bataille, pretending to be devoted to the Catholic cause, spent eleven years of his life exploring the darkest dens of secret societies, Lodges and Back-Lodges,[1] and even Luciferian Triangles, you fully approved him, you found his behavior admirable. He was overwhelmed with congratulations. Laudatory articles were written even in the publications of the party which, today, can't hurl enough thunderbolts to reduce Miss Diana Vaughan to ashes, here calling her a myth, there an adventuress and a fortune-teller.

Should the cheers which greeted Doctor Bataille be now reconsidered, they existed nonetheless and were thunderous. Illustrious theologians, eloquent preachers, eminent prelates congratulated him, each louder than the other. And I do not say they were wrong.

I merely and simply determine a fact.

And the purpose of this determination is to allow me to say forthrightly:

"Do not get angry, my reverend fathers, but do laugh heartily when you are told now that what did happen is the very opposite of what you expected. There wasn't the shadow of a dedicated Catholic exploring the High-Masonry of Palladism under a false nose. But, on the contrary, there has been a free-thinker who, for his own edification, *not because of any hostility*, came into your camp and strolled, not during eleven years but during twelve, and . . . it is your servant." (Various reactions: murmuring, laughter).

There wasn't the least Masonic plot in this story, which I shall prove to you shortly. We must leave to Homer, singing the exploits of Ulysses, the adventure of the legendary Trojan Horse; that formidable horse has nothing to do in this case. Today's tale is much less intricate.

Your servant told himself once that having gone for irreligion too young and possibly with much too much spirit, it was well possible that he might not be aware of the true situation. Then, not acting in anybody's name, willing to change his mind if there were reasons to do so, entrusting no one at first with his decision, he thought he had found the means of knowing better, of ascertaining better, for his own instruction.

Add to this, if you wish, a touch of prank at the back of his temper—he wasn't born in Marseille in vain![2] (Laughter)—Yes, add the lovely pleasure, that most people ignore but which is quite real, the intimate joy of playing a good turn on an opponent, without malice, just for fun and to have some laughs.

Well, I must say so at once, this twelve-year long prank taught me something valuable from the start, namely that I had acted without moderation indeed, that I better should have stayed on the ground of ideas, and that in most cases, it had been a mistake to make personal attacks.

I feel bound to make such a statement and I also admit that I make it easily. During these twelve years spent under the banner of the Church and although I registered as a prankster, I realized how wrong it is to impute the malice of some people to doctrines. It results from mankind itself. A bad man remains bad, just like a good man acts with goodness, whether he keeps his faith or loses it. Dishonest people as well as honest ones are found everywhere. (Marks of approval.)

Accordingly, I made for myself a study which has born fruit. That study gave me the equanimity, the inner philosophy mentioned before.

I came at first as a curious person, a bit at random,—but of course intending to withdraw once the experience had come to its end.—Then, the sweet pleasure of pranking took over, overwhelming everything, I lingered in the Catholic camp, gradually developing my plan of an altogether amusing and instructive mystification, and giving it ever broader proportions as things went along.

In the course of time, I happened to secure two collaborators, not more than two: one was a fellow I knew since childhood, whom I took at first for a ride and to whom I ascribed the pseudonym of Dr. Bataille; the other was Miss Diana Vaughan, a French Protestant, rather on the free-thinking side, a professional typist and the representative of one of the typewriter manufacturers in the United States. I needed both to achieve the success of the last episode of this joyful prank, which American newspapers call "the biggest hoax of modern times." (Many laughs. Murmurs.)

The Origins of a Prankster

Of course, this last episode had to end in April, the month of gaiety, the month of pranks,—and let us not forget that the hoax also started in April, on April 23, 1885,—this last episode is the only one which has to be explained today, though in broad terms only; because if everything was to be told and secret aspects disclosed from the start, it would take many days. This April Fools catch brought home a gigantic whale. (Explosion of laughter.)

However, it is necessary to illuminate the starting point with a few rays of gentle light.

Among the maxims of the culinary art, an often-quoted one says: "One becomes cook, but one is born a roaster." Perfection in the science of roasting cannot be learned. I believe the same can be said of pranksterism: one is born a prankster.

Here are some admissions concerning my outset in this noble career:

The Sharks of Marseille

Let us begin with my native town. In Marseille, nobody has forgotten the celebrated story of the coves ravaged by a school of sharks. Letters from local fishermen describing their escape from the most awful dangers began to flow in. Panic spread among swimmers, and beaches were deserted for several weeks from les Catalans to the Prado beach. The municipal Commission felt upset; the mayor suggested, quite judiciously, that the sharks, plague of the coves, likely came from Corsica, following a ship which, no doubt, must have thrown overboard a spoiled cargo of smoked meat. The municipal Commission voted an address to General Espivent de la Villeboisnet—martial law was then in force—requesting a company armed with Chassepot-rifles for an expedition on a tugboat. The worthy general, only wanting to please the administrators he had picked out himself for the dear and good city where I was born (Laughter), General Espivent, presently a senator, thus granted one hundred well-armed men, with an ample stock of ammunition. The rescuing ship left the harbor under the cheers of the mayor and his deputies, coves were explored in all directions, but the tugboat returned empty-handed; no more sharks than here in this room! (General laughter) A later inquiry showed all letters of complaint from various local fishermen to be fanciful. Such fishermen did not exist in the localities where these letters were posted; and once the letters were collected, one noticed that they all seemed to have been written by the same hand. The author of the hoax was not found out. Here he stands before you. All this happened in 1873; I was then nineteen years old.

I do hope that General Espivent will forgive me for having once compromised his prestige in the eyes of the population with a prank. He had suppressed my paper, *La Marotte, journal des fous*.[3] The stuff about the sharks was a most harmless vengeance, wasn't it?

The Underwater City

Some years later, I was in Geneva, absconding from a few press sentences. In the mean time, La Fronde, then *Le Frondeur*,[4] succeeded *La Marotte*. One fine day, the scientific world was thrilled to hear of a wonderful discovery. Someone in the audience may remember what it was about: an underwater city was said to have been perceived rather confusedly on the bottom of Lake Geneva between Nyon and Coppet. Letters were dispatched to the four corners of Europe, keeping the papers informed of the alleged searches. They relied upon a most scientific explanation founded upon the *Commentaries of Julius Caesar*: this city must have been built during the Roman conquest, at a time when the lake was so narrow that the Rhone traversed it without disturbing its waters. Well, the discovery made lots of noise everywhere—everywhere, except of course in Switzerland. The inhabitants of Nyon and Coppet were not a little astounded when tourists, arriving every now and then, asked to see the underwater city. The local boatmen ended by resolving to take the most insistent ones on the Lake. Oil was spread over the water in order to see better and, indeed, there were some who did manage to perceive something . . . (General laughter) remnants of streets rather well set in a line, crossings, what do I know? A Polish archaeologist who made the trip returned contented and issued a report in which he asserted he had very well recognized the remainder of a place in the middle of which a nondescript object might well be the remnant of an equestrian statue. An Institute delegated two of its members; but upon their arrival, they got in touch with the authorities and being told that the underwater city was a pure humbug, they returned from whence they came and, alas, did not see anything!

The underwater city did not survive their scientific proceedings (Prolonged laughter). The father of the city under the Lake of Geneva—presently speaking—had a precious auxiliary for the spreading of the legend in the person of one of his fellow exiles—it is hardly necessary to stress that he too was born in Marseilles—, my colleague and friend Henry Chabrier, presently residing on the borders of the Seine, just as I am. Both anecdotes, among a hundred that I might quote, are told merely to assert that your servant's inclination for great and joyous pranks goes back more than twelve years ago.

The Most Grandiose Prank

I come now to the most grandiose prank of my existence. It comes to an end today and will evidently be the last because, after this, I doubt whether any colleague, even belonging to the Icelandic or Patagonia press, would confidently accept the report of any extraordinary event upon my recommendation or that of one of my friends! . . . (*A voice*: Obviously!— Laughter.)

One will easily understand that the formidable fame of my irreligious writings didn't make it easy for me to be accepted in the bosom of the Church without being met with an even more formidable mistrust. I needed, however, to get there and to be greeted, so that once the mistrust had faded away completely, at least in high quarters, I could organize and lead the prodigious prank of contemporary devilry. (*A voice*: Distasteful! How can one admit to being such a prankster?)

In order to reach the goal I had set to myself, it was necessary, indispensable, to entrust no one with my secret, absolutely no one, not even my most intimate friends, not even my wife, at least in the beginning. It was better to be deemed to have turned crazy in the eyes of those who approached me. The least indiscretion could ruin everything. And I was playing for high stakes because I faced a powerful opponent. (*A voice*: Oh! yes!) On the contrary, the hostility of some, the saddened and vexed annoyance of others, were my best trumps since—as was to be expected—I was set under close scrutiny during the first years.

Nevertheless, a few particulars will strike a bell for my old friends if I recall them now.

Expulsion from the Anticlerical League

Thus, after the publication of the letter in which I disowned all my former irreligious writings, the Parisian groups of the Anticlerical League gathered in a general assembly to vote upon my expulsion. People were surprised to see me arrive there; the Leaguers were baffled, and my presence was incomprehensible indeed, since I had not come to defy those from whom I seceded, and didn't say a word either to try and gain them over, as a convert would have done in his neophyte's fervor. No! I came to the meeting under the pretense of making my farewells—though having demitted for more than three months!—but in fact in order to seek and find the opportunity to place a word I could remind them of later, when time would be ripe.

Most of these anticlerical leaguers were my friends. Some of them cried and I was moved myself. . . .

A Catholic journalist: You, moved? . . . Come on now! . . . You made fun of them like you make fun of us!

M. Léo Taxil—I assure you that I was not taking leave from them unconcerned. Well, take it as you wish. Though I felt affected, I kept cool in the middle of a true tempest; I refer you to contemporary newspapers.

In order to close the meeting, the president submitted the following resolution which was agreed upon through an unanimous vote:

> Considering that the individual named Gabriel Jogand-Pagès, called Léo Taxil, one of the founders of the Anticlerical League, has disowned all the principles he stood up for, has betrayed free-thinking and all his fellow-unbelievers:
>
> The leaguers attending the meeting of July 27, 1885, without taking into consideration the motives which dictated such an infamous behavior to the individual named Léo Taxil, expel him from the Anticlerical League as a traitor and renegade.

I objected then against one word, one single word of that resolution.

Presumably, old friends who attended the July 1885 meeting are in this room. I shall remind them of the formulation of my protest.

I said the following in a most peaceful voice: "—My friends, I accept this resolution, except one word. . . ."

The president interrupted me and exclaimed: "—Indeed, this is cheeky!"

I kept on undisturbed: "—You have the right to say that I am a renegade, since I just published, four days ago, a letter in which I expressly retracted and disowned all my writings against religion. But I beg you to cross out the word traitor which in no ways applies to my case; there is not the shadow of treason in what I do today. *What I tell you here, you cannot understand at the present moment; but you shall understand it later.*"

I refrained from putting too much insistence on this last sentence, because I could not let them get suspicious of my secret. But I said it clearly enough so that it would stick in their memories, though it laid itself open to various interpretations.

And, when I had the opportunity to issue a report of that meeting, I took great care to omit this declaration which indeed could have put people on their guards.

Faithful Friends

Second fact. Between the day in April when I came to a priest and trusted him with my conversion, and the day of the meeting when I was expelled from the free-thinkers, an anticlerical congress took place in Rome, of which I had been one of the organizers. Nothing was easier for me than to disorganize it and to make it fail completely. This congress took place in the first days of June. All the leaguers know that, until the end, I devoted all my strength for its success; only the death of Victor Hugo, which happened at that time, turned public attention from this congress.

Later, when it was learned that since April I had seen priests again, it was said and printed that, under the pretense of this congress, I had gone to Rome to negotiate my betrayal and was received secretly at the Vatican. It was even inserted in my biography that I was given a large sum, it was said "one million." (Laughter)

I let it go because I didn't care much and laughed inside myself.

But today I have the right to say that things were quite different. Amongst the guests of the present evening, there is an old friend who made the trip with me, who accompanied me everywhere, who did not leave me for a minute. He is here and will not contradict me. Did he leave me a minute? Did I leave him to undertake anything suspicious: No!

This is not all. During the same trip, while returning to France, we stopped in Genoa. I insisted on visiting someone with whom I was bound by friendship: general Canzio-Garibaldi, Garibaldi's son-in-law.

During this visit, I was accompanied by the friend I just mentioned and another one, he is still alive, was with us: Doctor Baudon who was recently elected Deputy of Beauvais.

Both can testify to the fact that during the visit, I withdrew one moment aside with Canzio. And then Canzio can testify to what I told him:

"—My dear Canzio, I have to tell you, under the seal of secrecy, that in a short while, I shall make a complete and public break. Be surprised at nothing, and keep your trust in me in your heart."

I did not insist much with him either, and later I was even afraid of having said too much. For the next two or three years, Canzio sent me his card on New Year's Day, in spite of our break. Then, likely estimating that things took too much time, he must have gotten tired and stopped manifesting himself.

Lastly, one of my former co-workers who liked me a lot, kept on seeing me in spite of everything. He is now dead: his name was Alfred Paulon, a former magistrate.[5] (*A voice*: He is dead! So he won't disown you.) Please wait. I know that through his shrewd and constant observation, he reached the conclusion that I was hoaxing people. (Various reactions.)

A voice: Then you boast about deceiving Catholics! . . . It's a scandal!

M. LÉO TAXIL—Paulon, my former co-worker who kept on associating with me, had a way of defending me which was often in my way.

This is what he said of me to his friends: "Léo is hard to get. I thought first that he had turned crazy but when I resumed relations with him, I noticed on the contrary that he is in full possession of his mental faculties. I don't get it: something tells me he is still with us in his heart and mind; I can feel it. I never touch religious matters with him, because I noticed he doesn't want to let the cat out of the bag, but I would stake my life on it, he does not work for the clerics; one of these days, we shall have a big surprise."

Alfred Paulon cannot testify to what he noticed; but he mentioned it to many friends. And if there are any in this room, I ask them: "Is it true that when he spoke of me, Paulon expressed himself that way?" *Various voices.*— It's true! It's true!

Penance and Confession

Let's now come to the hoax itself, to this funny as well as instructive hoax. In high quarters, they did not rely upon that good man of a vicar, a priest with a simple soul, to whom I confided how I had been struck by grace, like Saul on the road to Damascus.

"This block covered with flour somehow looks suspicious,"[6] it was thought among the "big hats" of the church. (Laughter)

Accordingly, it was decided that the day after my letter of retraction, they would let me make a good little retreat at the reverend Jesuit fathers' house, and one of the most expert ones in the art of turning over souls and searching them was picked out to take care of me. The choice was not made immediately. They let me wait a good week for the great searcher who was to be my lot.

He turned out to be a former military chaplain who became a Jesuit, a sly one among the sly! His appreciation was to be weighty.

Ah! It was a tough game that the two of us played! . . . I still have a headache when I think of it . . . Among other things, the dear director made me practice the *Spiritual Exercises of Saint Ignatius*. I thought little of these exercises, but at least I had to skim through the pages, so as to look as if I had gone deeply into these extraordinary meditations. It was not the right time to be caught.

My general confession let me win the battle. This general confession did not last less than three days. (Prolonged laughter) My last crushing blow came at the end of it.

I said everything, this, that, and other things, but my *partner* suspected there was a further big sin, very big, very big, which was hard to confess, a sin more painful to come out with than the admission of thousands and thousands of impieties.

At last, it had to come out, this monstrous sin.

Ladies and gentlemen, I don't want to keep you waiting as long as he had to: my big sin was a murder, a first-class murder, one of the best downright assassinations. No, I had not slaughtered an entire family, but without being a Tropmann or a Dumolard,[7] I was good for the guillotine, no doubt, had I been found out.

I had taken care to investigate a few disappearances reported three years before by newspapers, and had imagined a little fairy-tale based upon one of them. But my reverend father didn't let me tell it all in details. He thought me capable of the most dreadful sacrileges, and found grounds to be pleasantly surprised. He did not however expect an assassin at his knees. (New laughter)

When the first words of admission fell from my lips, the reverend father jumped backwards in a most significant way. Ah! Now he understood my embarrassment, my difficulties, my way of discussing certain sins of less significance at such length . . . And how ashamed I was when I confessed my crime! . . . Not only ashamed, but disconcerted, frightened. . . . A widow was part of the story, the reverend father let me promise that, in an indirect and indeed most ingenious way, I would bestow a rent on my victim's widow. . . . He did not want to hear any name, but what he was interested in was to know whether I had murdered with or without premeditation. After beating around the bush and falling under the weight of shame, I admitted premeditation, a true ambush.

A churchman: What you are doing right now is abominable, Sir.

Another listener: For your punishment, a priest will never receive your confession. You are an utmost rascal! (Tumult)

Other listener: All priests in this hall ought to leave at once!

Abbott Garnier: No! We must listen to the scoundrel to the end! (Some people in the audience stand up and leave.)

M. LÉO TAXIL—Whether you leave or not doesn't matter. I proceed. . . .

It is my true duty to pay tribute to this reverend Jesuit father. I never got into troubles with the law. My prank thus allowed me to test the secrecy of confession. If one day I tell the story of these twelve years in details, I will do it just as today, with the strictest impartiality and with calm, Abbot Garnier! (Approval)

The main point at this stage was my first victory in the opening of the battle. Had anyone dared and told the reverend father I was not the most earnest convert, he would have gotten a strong rebuke. (Laughter)

Into the Vatican

It was not part of my plans to hurry and see the Sovereign Pontiff.[8]

My confession of assassination was indeed a fantastic success; but the director of my retreat at Clamart had kept it secret. Evidently, what else could he tell the hierarchical authority who entrusted him to inspect the depths of my soul, except: "Léo Taxil? . . . I vouch for him!"

Once the mistrust of the Vatican was set aside, how could I make myself agreeable? In order to bring the hoax to the heights I dreamed of and which I had the inexpressible joy to reach, I had to make good a point most cherished by the Holy See within the program of the Church.

This part of my plan was settled from the start, as soon as I decided to inquire into Catholicism.

One year earlier, the Sovereign Pontiff had made himself notorious with the encyclical *Humanum Genus*, and this encyclical agreed with a well-established idea of the militant Catholics. Gambetta[9] had said, "Clericalism, there is the enemy!" The Church, on the other side, said, "The enemy is Freemasonry!"

Accordingly, slandering Freemasons was the best way to establish the foundations of the colossal prank of which I savored all the suave happiness in advance.

At first, Freemasons were indignant; they did not foresee that the patiently prepared conclusion of the hoax would result in a worldwide outburst of laughter. They actually thought I had joined for good. It was said and repeated that it was a way of avenging myself for having been expelled from my Lodge in 1881, a well-known story which was not in the least dishonorable for me, but the mere consequence of a little row initiated by two men having nowadays disappeared, and disappeared under sad circumstances.

No! I was not avenging myself, I was having fun. And if one examines now the undersides of this campaign, even the Freemasons who were most hostile to me will acknowledge that I did not harm anyone. I would go as far as to say that I did a good turn to French Masonry. (*Interruption*: You go too far! . . .) Pardon me, wait until I explain myself, and I am sure you will agree with me. I mean that my publication of the rituals was certainly not irrelevant to reforms which resulted in suppressing outmoded practices which had become ridiculous in the eyes of all masons befriended with the notion of progress.

A Good Canon of Fribourg

Let us leave this aside and summarize facts. Since my goal was to invent all the elements of contemporary devilry—which was a good bit stronger than the city under the Lake of Geneva—it was necessary to proceed step by step, foundations had to be set, the egg from which Palladism was to be born had to be laid and incubated. A prank of this size cannot be created in one day. (*A voice*: Obviously!)

From the first moment of my conversion, I had found out that a certain number of Catholics strongly believed that the name "Grand Architect of the Universe," adopted by Freemasonry to designate the Supreme Being without relating it to the particular way of any specific religion, that this name, as I say, is used in fact to skillfully conceal Master Lucifer or Satan, the devil!

Various voices:—Enough is enough! He has become a freemason again! (Laughter)

Other listeners:—Keep on! . . . It's interesting.

M. Léo Taxil—Stories are told here and there in which the devil suddenly appeared in a Masonic Lodge and presided over the meeting. This is admitted among Catholics.

More good men than can be imagined believe that the laws of nature are sometimes set aside by good or bad spirits, and even by simple mortals. I was amazed myself to be asked to perform a miracle.

A good canon of Fribourg[10] once dropped by like a hurricane at my house and told me literally: "—Ah! You, Mister Taxil, you are a saint! Because God rescued you from so deep an abyss, you must have a mountain of graces upon your head [*sic*]. As soon as I heard of your conversion, I took the train and here I am. On my return, I must be able to say not only that I saw you, but that you performed a miracle in front of me." (Laughter)

I was not expecting such a request.

"—A miracle! I answered: I don't understand you, Mister Canon.

"—Yes, a miracle, he repeated, it does not matter which, just so that I can bear witness to it! . . . Whatever miracle you wish! . . . What do I know? . . . Here, for example . . . This chair . . . turn it into a cane, an umbrella. . . ." (Prolonged laughter)

I had gotten his point. I gently declined to perform such a wonder. And my Canon returned to Fribourg saying that if I was not performing miracles, it was out of humility.

Several months later, he sent me an gigantic Gruyère cheese on the crust of which he carved pious inscriptions, wild mystic hieroglyphs, with a knife—an excellent cheese by all means, which seemed never to come to an end and which I ate with infinite respect. (Laughter increases. Some Catholic listeners protest.)

Accordingly, my first books on Freemasonry consisted in a mixture of rituals, with short innocent parts inserted, apparently harmlessly interpreted. Each time an obscure passage occurred, I explained it in a way agreeable to Catholics who see Master Lucifer as the supreme grand-master of Freemasons. But only with a touch of suggestion. I was slowly smoothing the field first, in order to plough it later on, and then scatter the mystifying seeds which were to sprout so well.

An Audience with the Holy Father

After two years of this preparatory work, I went to Rome. (*A voice*: Ah! Here we are!)

Received at first by Cardinals Rampolia and Parocchi, I had the pleasure of hearing them, one as well as the other, tell me my books were perfect. Yes indeed, the books unveiled exactly what was so well known in the Vatican, and it was truly fortunate that a convert published these famous rituals. (Laughter.)

Cardinal Rampolia called me "my dear," thick as thieves. And how much he regretted that I had been only a mere Apprentice in Masonry! But since I succeeded in getting at the rituals, nothing was more legitimate than printing them. He said he could identify therein all his previous readings from documents in the Holy See's possessions. He identified everything, even that which, by my doings, had the same worth as the sharks of Marseilles or the city under the Lake of Geneva. (*A voice*: Rascal! Scoundrel! Blackguard! Rogue!)

As for Cardinal Parocchi, what interested him most, was the question of Masonic Sisters. My precious revelations had taught him nothing new either. (Murmurs on one side; laughter on the other.)

I had come to Rome unexpected, unaware of the fact that a request for a private audience with the Sovereign Pontiff must be made a long time in advance, but I had the pleasant surprise of not waiting at all, and the Holy Father received me for three quarters of an hour. (*A voice*: You are a ruffian.)

To win this new game, I had played it safe during the first evening I spent alone with the Cardinal Secretary of State. Evidently, he had been entrusted with my preliminary examination. But the impression I wished to give him was that I was somehow exalted—not quite as much however as the good Canon of Fribourg. (Laughter)

The verbal report which Cardinal Rampolla must have given to the Holy Father granted me the reception I desired.

Since the time of my admission under the banner of the Church, I had convinced myself of a basic truth, namely that one could not become a good author[11] if one does not put oneself in the body of the person one represents, if one does not believe—at least momentarily—that all of it is true. When a scene of despair is played on the stage, tears should not be faked: the third-rate actor wipes dry eyes with his handkerchief; the artist cries actually. (*A voice*: Rascal! Rascal!)

Which is why, along the morning before my reception, I filled myself so completely with the situation that I became ready for anything and incapable of flinching despite any kind of surprise. (Speaker's voice gets momentarily lost in tumult.)

When the Pope asked me:—My son, what do you wish?

I answered:—Holy Father, to die at your feet, right now! . . . This would be my greatest happiness. (Laughter)

A listener: Respect Léo XIII. You have no right to utter his name!

M. Léo Taxil—Smiling, Léo XIII deigned to tell me that my life was still very useful in the fight for faith. Then he touched upon the question of Freemasonry. He owned all my new works in his personal library. He had read them from one end to the other and insisted upon the satanic guidance of the sect.

Having been an Apprentice only, I had great merit to have understood that "the devil is there." And the Sovereign Pontiff stressed on the word *devil* with an inflection which is easy for me to render. It seems that I can still hear him repeating: "The devil! The devil!"

When I left, I was sure that my plan could be carried out to the end. The important thing was not to stand out any more, once the fruit was ripe.

Now, the tree of contemporary luciferianism began to grow. I gave it all my care for a few more years . . . Then I re-wrote one of my books, introducing a Palladian ritual in it, allegedly obtained in communication, in fact prettily fabricated by me from beginning to end.

A listener.—And we have to hear that! . . . It is disgusting!

M. Léo Taxil—Now, Palladism or Luciferian High-Masonry was born. The new book had the most enthusiastic reception, including all the magazines issued by the Fathers of the Society of Jesus.

Appendix 1

The Search for Collaborators

The time had come now for me to step aside, otherwise the most fantastic hoax of modern times would have failed sadly.

I started looking for the first collaborator I needed. It had to be someone who had traveled a lot and who might be able to describe a mysterious investigation in the Luciferian Triangles, in the dens of this Palladism described as secretly directing all the Lodges and Back-Lodges of the entire world.

I happened then to meet again in Paris with an old college friend of mine, who had been a doctor aboard ships.

At first, I did not put him on to the secret of the hoax at all.

I let him read various books of authors enthralled at my wonderful revelations. The most extraordinary one was authored by a Jesuit bishop, Msgr. Meurin, bishop of Port-Louis (Mauritius), who came to Paris in order to consult me. One can imagine how well informed he became! . . . (Laughter)

This excellent Msgr. Meurin, an erudite Orientalist, came out equal with the Polish archeologist who had recognized a fragment of an equestrian statue in the middle of a place in my underwater city. (New laughter)

Starting from the determined idea that Freemasons worship the devil, and convinced of the existence of Palladism, he discovered the most extraordinary things behind the Hebrew words used as passwords, etc., in the innumerable degrees of Masonic rites.

Sashes, aprons, ritualistic tools, he scrutinized everything. He examined the smallest embroidered figures on the most insignificant pieces of material having belonged to a Freemason and, in the best faith in the world, he found my Palladism everywhere.

Among the most joyous times of my life, I will always recall the hours during which he read his manuscript to me. His thick volume, *Freemasonry, Synagogue of Satan,* was a wonderful help in convincing my doctor friend that there truly was a secret Luciferian meaning in all of the Masonic symbolism.

In fact, the doctor did not care a rap. But he had really studied spiritualism out of curiosity as an amateur. He knew that believers in supernatural manifestations, phantoms, ghosts, werewolves, etc. existed throughout the world. He knew that within small groups of occultists, likable pranksters let specters appear to good people who forgot all of Robert-Houdin's[12] technique. But he did not know that such operations ever occurred in freemasonry. He did not know that there was a specific rite of Luciferian and Masonic occultism. He knew nothing of Palladism and of its triangles, of the Elected Wizards and of Templar Mistresses, and of all the astounding supreme organization imagined by me, the existence of which became scientifically established through the productions of Msgr. Meurin and others.

Sophia Walder, Grand Mistress of Palladism

In my book, *Are There any Women in Freemasonry?*, I created the part of a Grand Mistress of Palladism, a Sophia-Sapho, disclosing only the initial letter of her alleged true name: a *W.* I confided the whole name to my doctor friend. He believed in the existence of Sophie Walder.

Let us understand each other right. Because of books such as Msgr. Meurin's, the doctor believed in Palladism and in the various individuals, heroes of my hoax, who began to appear therein. But I did not try in the least to make him believe in the reality of the supernatural manifestations which had to be told.

(Renewed tumult. A monk bursts out laughing and begins to applaud. There is deep amazement by priests who sit next to him.)

This is how I asked my friend the doctor to work together with me.

"—Do you want to collaborate on a work on Palladism? . . . As for me, I am thoroughly familiar with the subject, but the issue of rituals is far less interesting than recounting adventures as a witness, especially unbelievable ones . . . Besides, to move good souls best, the narrator must himself be a hero. Not a convinced Palladist, but a zealous Catholic having put on the Luciferian mask in order to make this mysterious inquiry at the peril of his life . . . I will give you a pseudonym, because we shall say that for all sorts of reasons, the author cannot surrender his name to publicity: for example, he still has to write an inquiry about the nihilists . . . (Laughter) You will be known only to a small group of ecclesiastics, that will be enough . . . You will hand over to me the route of your voyages whereupon I shall design an outline which you will only have to embellish. Then I shall recopy your manuscript, correct it, cut out some parts and above all add a few ones. . . . Yours will be the medical part, the description of towns and some narratives. Mine will be the technical aspects of Palladism, information on all the individuals who are going to appear, and most of the added episodes. . . . I need your collaboration for some thirty or forty installments altogether . . . Now don't worry about denials . . . As you noticed in the works I gave you to read, there are two kinds of Palladists: nuts who really believe that Lucifer is the Good-God whose cult must be kept secret for a few more years still, and the wire-pullers who use the nutty ones as excellent subjects for their occultist experiments . . . Neither sort will be able to protest publicly, since the first condition of belonging to Palladism is the most rigorous secrecy. Besides, should some of them protest, their denials would be without effect, since they would appear to have been made in self-defense."

My doctor friend agreed and in order to strengthen his own belief in the existence of Palladism in spite of the hoax of marvelous facts attributed by us to its Triangles, I let him receive several letters from Sophie Walder. Sophie was indignant that he pretended to have met her.

The doctor faithfully related these letters to me.

After receiving three or four of them, he told me: "—I am afraid that this woman is going to make a scandal and demonstrate that the load of crap we spout about her is sheer nonsense." (Laughter.)

I answered: "Calm down. She protests for form's sake; in reality, she is thrilled to read that she has the talent of walking through walls and owns a snake who writes prophecies on her back with the tip of its tail. (Laughter) I got in touch with her and was introduced to her. She is a good girl. She is a Palladist hoaxster. She laughs her head off about all that. Do you want me to introduce you to her?"

He wanted to indeed! Boy! Was he happy to strike up an acquaintance with Sophie Walder! Several days later, I forwarded to my friend a letter from the Palladist grand-mistress. She agreed with the introduction. We were to meet at my house, and go from there to Sophia-Sapho who even invited us for dinner. . . . My friend came to my house in ceremonial full dress as if he was invited at the Elysée.[13] I showed him the table in my house and then told him everything . . . or, at least, almost everything.

Sophie Walder, a myth! Palladism, my most beautiful creation, only existed on paper and in a few thousand brains! He could not believe it. I had to show him some proof. Once convinced, he found the hoax even funnier and kept on working with me.

The Creation of Dr. Bataille

Among the things I forgot to tell him, there is one which he will learn at this conference, namely the reason why I picked *Dr. Bataille*[14] as his pseudonym.— Allegedly, it was to stress the offensive character of war against Palladism. But my own true reason, my intimate reason as a dilettante hoaxster, was this: one of my oldest friends, deceased by now, a hoaxster of the supreme category, was the illustrious Sapeck, prince of hoaxterism in the Latin Quarter.[15] In a way I was bringing him to life again without anybody's notice. Then Sapeck's true name was Bataille. (Long laughter.)

However my doctor friend was not enough to work my plan out. In *The Devil in the 19th Century*, my plan was to set the stage for the conversion of a Luciferian Grand-Mistress.

The book I had authored introduced Sophia-Sapho under the blackest colors. I had taken pains to make her as distasteful as possible for the Catholics: the accomplished type of an incarnate she-devil, wallowing in sacrilege, a true Satanist, such as one meets in Hymens' books.

The Birth of Diana Vaughan

Sophia-Sapho, or Miss Sophie Walder, was there only to serve as a contrast to another Luciferian, a sympathetic one, an angelic creature living in Palladist hell through the chance of birth. Her existence was to be revealed to the Catholic public through a work signed by Bataille. (*A voice*: Oh! The rogue! ... Oh! The base villain!)

Now, since this exceptional Luciferian woman was to convert at a given moment, I had to have someone in flesh and blood on hand, should it become necessary to produce her.

A little while before meeting again with my childhood friend, the doctor, the necessities of my profession let me meet a typist who was a European representative of one of the large typewriter manufacturers in the United States.

At that time, I gave her lots of manuscripts to type. I met with a woman who was intelligent, active, sometimes traveling for business. She was further gifted with a playful humor and an elegant simplicity, as in most of our Protestant families. One knows that Lutheran and Calvinist women, although proscribing luxury in the way they dress, nevertheless make concessions to fashion. Her family was French, father and mother French but deceased, the American origin went back to her great-grandfather only. In spite of the similarity in names, she had no family ties with Ernest Vaughan, former administrator of *L'Intransigeant.*[16] There are several Vaughans in France. In England and in the United States, Vaughans are innumerable. I have to say that, because one might believe that Mr. Ernest Vaughan, with whom I was acquainted in the past and whose brother-in-law always remained one of my best friends, one might believe, as I say, that Mr. Ernest Vaughan was more or less indirectly an accomplice in my hoax. Such a misunderstanding should be avoided at all cost. Miss Diana Vaughan is in no way related to him, the homonymy is no more than sheer coincidence.

My luck could not have been better. Nobody was better qualified than Miss Vaughan to assist me. The question was: would she accept?

Diana Vaughan

I could not ask her point-blank. I studied her first. Little by little, I interested her in devilry, which greatly amused her. She is, as I said, rather a freethinker than a Protestant. Consequently, she was amazed to find out that in this century of progress, there are still people who believe seriously in all the nonsense of the Middle Ages.

A voice: But we didn't come to listen to these things!

Other voices: Keep on! Keep on!

M. LÉO TAXIL—It is surprising that those who get mad at what I am saying now are precisely the same persons who, in their newspapers, urged me to speak. . . . I proceed. . . .

My first approach to Miss Vaughan was on the subject of the letters of Sophie Walder. She agreed to let them be written by one of her friends. I had the proof, thusly, that women are much less talkative than one says and that if their weak point is curiosity, on the other hand one can count on their discretion. Miss Vaughan's friend never boasted to anybody to have written Sophie Walder's letters. Besides, there weren't many.

Finally, I convinced Miss Vaughan to become my accomplice for the final success of my hoax. I drew a fixed agreement with her: 150 francs per month for typing manuscripts as well as for letters which should be copied by hand. It goes without saying that should trips be necessary, all her expenses would be defrayed; but she never accepted any money as a gift. In fact, she enjoyed the prank quite a lot and took a liking to it. Corresponding with Bishops, Cardinals, receiving letters from the private secretary of the Sovereign Pontiff, telling them fairy tales, informing the Vatican about the dark plots of Luciferians, all this set her in an inexpressible gaiety, she thanked me for associating her with this huge prank. Had she possessed the great wealth we attributed to her to make her prestige greater, she would have never accepted the price agreed for her collaboration, and further she would have paid for all the costs wholeheartedly.

She was the one who let us discover the existence of private postal agencies in order to reduce expenses. She had had the opportunity to have recourse to one of them in London, and told us about it. She also told me about the *Alibi-Office* in New York.

The Devil in the 19th Century was mainly written to introduce the existence of Miss Vaughan who was to play the main part in the hoax. Had her name been Campbell or Thompson, we would have given our sympathetic Luciferian the name of Miss Campbell or Miss Thompson. We merely turned her into an American, born by chance in Paris. We let her family originate in Kentucky. This allowed us to make her part as interesting as possible by multiplying extraordinary wonders concerning her, which nobody was able to check. (Laughter) Another reason was that we located the center of Palladism at Charleston in the United States, with the late General Albert Pike, Grand Master of the Scottish Rite in South Carolina, as Founder. This celebrated Freemason, endowed with vast erudition, had been one of the highlights of the order. Through us, he became the first Luciferian Pope, supreme chief of all freemasons of the globe, conferring regularly each Friday, at 3 p.m., with Master Lucifer in person. (Explosion of laughter)

A most curious point in the story is that some freemasons joined in the prank without in the least being asked to. Compared with the tugboat I had dispatched hunting for sharks in the coves of Marseille in my early years, the boat of Palladism was a true battleship.

With the help of Dr. Bataille, the battleship turned into a squadron. And when Miss Diana Vaughan became my auxiliary, the squadron grew into a full navy.[17] (New laughter)

We saw indeed some Masonic journals, such as *La Renaissance Symbolique*, swallow a dogmatic circular about Luciferian occultism, a circular dated July 14, 1889, written by myself in Paris, and which I disclosed as having been brought from Charleston to Europe by Miss Diana Vaughan on behalf of Albert Pike, its author.

When I named Adriano Lemmi second successor to Albert Pike as Luciferian Sovereign Pontiff—then Lemmi was not elected pope of the Freemasons in the Borghese palace, but in my office—, when this imaginary election became known, some Italian Masons, among which a Deputy at the Parliament, took it seriously. They were annoyed to learn through indiscretions of the profane press that Lemmi was secretive toward them, that he kept them aloof from the famous Palladism which the whole world spoke about. They met in Congress in Palermo, constituted in Sicily, Naples and Florence, three independent Supreme Councils, and named Miss Vaughan an honorary member and protectress of their federation.

A voice.—That was a successful prank!

Another listener.—These freemasons were your accomplices!

M. LÉO TAXIL—You bet! . . . May I say again that I had only two auxiliaries who were in the secret of the prank: my doctor friend and Miss Diana Vaughan.

An unexpected auxiliary—though by no means an accomplice, in spite of what he said—is Mr. Margiotta, a Freemason from Palmi, in Calabria. He began as one of the hoaxed, became more hoaxed than all the others and, what is most amusing, he told us he had met the Palladist grand-mistress during one of her trips to Italy. (Laughter) It is true that I had gently induced him to entrust me with this confidence. I had put in his head that the trip had really taken place; I had created around it an atmosphere of Palladism; I let him meet a chamberlain of Léo XIII in Rome who had dined with Miss Diana some times before. (Loud laughter and protests) Then I mentioned that during Miss Vaughan's imagined trip of 1889, when she was supposed to have brought the alleged dogmatic Albert Pike's circular letter to Europe, she had entertained many Freemasons in groups, in the course of two evenings in Naples, at Hotel Victoria. I knew that Mr. Margiotta, who is a poet, had dedicated a volume of verse to Bovio, and I had taken the trouble to tell him that the Freemasons were introduced to Miss Vaughan in 1889 by Bovio and by Cosma Panunzi. I added that these brothers had taken tea with her but were so many that she couldn't remember their names or faces. Timidly at first, Mr. Margiotta risked some allusions about this former meeting. Then, seeing that it seemed to work and that Miss Diana did not contradict him, he went all the way. He went indeed much too far.—Later, when I decided to prevent the mystification from collapsing under the silence of a Commission, our prank having been unmasked in the mean time in Germany, when I agreed with the doctor to tally-ho the panic of the mystified Cardinals, when Bataille and I, *always in agreement*, faked shooting at each other, Mr. Margiotta, having at last opened his eyes, feared ridicule and chose to declare himself an accomplice rather than a blind volunteer in our navy.

But we shouldn't appear more numerous than we actually were. We were three and that was enough. The editors themselves were mystified all the way. Anyway, they have nothing to complain about. First of all because our marvelous revelations brought them the most encouraging Episcopal congratulations, not counting those of the grave theologians who didn't bat an eyelid when our crocodile played the piano, and Miss Vaughan traveled to various planets. Then, because our triple collaboration let them give two works to the public, which can compete with *A Thousand and One Nights*, works which have been devoured with delight and will still be read for a long time, not with conviction any more, possibly, but out of curiosity.

Elaborations on a Theme

It is a bit unusual indeed, that we managed to get our staggering stories swallowed in our 19th century.

I ask myself however to what extent the high approvers of unmasked Palladism have the right to get angry today. When one understands that one was fooled, the best thing to do is to laugh with the audience. Yes, Mister Abbot Garnier! And your getting cross will make you even more laughed at.

Abbott Garnier.—You are a scoundrel! (attempts are made to try and calm down Abbott Garnier.)

M. LÉO TAXIL (when the tumult calmed down)—Those hoaxed by Palladism can be divided into two categories.

Firstly, those who were in good faith, entirely in good faith. They were the victims of their theological science and of their eagerly pursued studies of all that touches on Freemasonry. I had to immerse myself in these two sciences in order to imagine everything and in such a way that they wouldn't realize it was a prank. Can one believe, for instance, that it was easy to take M. de la Rive for a ride, he, the embodiment of an inquiring mind, who examines the slightest trifles with a microscope and who could beat our best investigating judges? He can boast of having given me trouble! . . . My whole Palladism had been solidly constructed as far as its Masonic part is concerned, since some Freemasons—even "thirty-thirds" if you please!—did not take it for a shadowy mirage and asked to become members. (Laughter) The impossibility of Palladism becomes plain as the nose on one's face only because of the supernatural elements we filled it with. But these devilries were a warning only for those who do not believe in those devilries described in other books, in pious books. Asmodeus carrying Miss Diana Vaughan to the Garden of Eden is no more extraordinary than Master Satan taking up Jesus Christ himself on top of a mountain and showing him all the kingdoms of the Earth . . . which is round! (*Various voices*: Bravo!)—Either one has faith or one has not. (Laughter)

Besides this first category of hoaxed people, however, there is a second one, and members of the latter one were not fully hoaxed. The good abbots and monks who admired Miss Vaughan because she was a converted Masonic Luciferian Sister have the right to think that such female Masons exist. They have never seen or encountered any, but they may think that it is because there are none in their diocese. In Rome, it's another story. In Rome, all information is centralized. In Rome one cannot ignore that there are no female Masons other than the wives, daughters, or sisters of Freemasons, admitted to banquets, public feasts, or those who meet separately, very decently, in private societies comprising feminine elements only, such as the Sisters of the Eastern Star or the Daughters of the American Revolution. (Signs of approval)

When one thinks about it, it is easy to understand that if Masonic sisters exist, such as the anti-Masons imagine, there would have been conversions and confessions a long time ago! The eagerness with which Miss Vaughan's alleged conversion was received in Rome is significant. Please notice that Msgr. Lazzareschi, delegate of the Holy See to the Anti-Masonic Union's central Committee, let a Thanksgiving *Triduum*[18] be celebrated at the Church of the Sacred Heart in Rome!

The Hymn to Joan of Arc, supposedly composed by Miss Diana, words and music, was performed at the anti-Masonic feasts of the Roman Committee. This music became nearly sacred and sounded with grand solemnity in the basilicas of the Holy City. Its tune is that of the *Philharmonic Syringe*, a musical jest written for the entertainments of the harem by one of my friends, conductor of the orchestra of Sultan Abdul Aziz. (Prolonged laughter. *Cries*: It is abominable! Oh! The blackguard!)

Such Roman enthusiasm sets one thinking.

I shall recall two typical facts.

Under the pen-name "Dr. Bataille" I related—and under that of "Miss Vaughan" I confirmed—that the Masonic temple in Charleston contained a maze at the center of which stands the chapel of Lucifer . . .

(*Interruptions*).

M. Oscar Havard.—The bishop of Charleston declared this to be an imposture.

M. LÉO TAXIL—So it is. I was going to say so in a moment. But do not triumph yet. Wait a little! . . . I said that in the Masonic temple in Charleston one of the rooms, triangular in shape, called the *Sanctum Regnum*, has as its main ornament a monstrous statue of Baphomet, which the High-Masons worship. That in another room, a statue of Eve comes alive when a Templar Mistress is especially agreeable to Master Satan, and that this statue then turns into the demon Astarte, for a moment alive, and gives a kiss to the preferred Templar Mistress. I published the alleged map of this Masonic building, a plan which I designed myself. Now, Msgr. Northrop, Catholic bishop of Charleston, went to Rome expressly to assure the Sovereign Pontiff of the highest fantasy of these writings. This journey would have remained unknown if Msgr. Northrop, on his way to Rome, had not let himself be interviewed. Which is how what he came to tell the Pope became public. He had come to say: "It is false, absolutely false, that the Freemasons of Charleston are the chiefs of a supreme Luciferian rite. I am especially well acquainted with the most important ones. They are Protestants, inspired by the best intentions. Not one of them considers practicing occultism. I visited their temple, none of the rooms indicated by Doctor Bataille or Miss Vaughan are to be found there. The map is a hoax." On his return from Rome, Msgr. Northrup did not protest any more and has kept silent ever since. Miss Diana Vaughan, on the contrary, replied to Msgr. Northrop's interview; she said the Bishop of Charleston was himself a Freemason and she received the Pope's blessing. (Sensation)

Second fact. Under the signatures of Bataille and Vaughan, I recounted and confirmed that immense secret workshops were located in Gibraltar under the English fortress, in which men-monsters fabricated all the instruments used in the ceremonies of Palladism, and Miss Diana Vaughan, asked about this by Roman high ecclesiastical dignitaries, enjoyed herself answering in her cutest style that nothing was more true and that the forges of the mysterious workshops of Gibraltar were fed by the very fires of Hell. (Laughter) Msgr. the Apostolic Vicar of Gibraltar wrote, on the other hand, that he confirmed what he had been forced to declare to various people, namely that the story of the secret workshops was an audacious invention, resting on no foundation whatsoever, nothing whatsoever, and that he was indignant to witness the creation of such legends. The Vatican did not publish the letter of the Apostolic Vicar of Gibraltar, and Miss Vaughan received the blessing of the Pope. (Applause.—*Many voices*: Bravo Taxil!)

Should I recall some of the letters of approval received by Miss Vaughan?

Various voices among the Catholic journalists—It's not true! There was no approval.

Letters of Approval

M. LÉO TAXIL—What! You dare deny it! Well, here is one, a letter of assent, and a weighty one! . . . It is from Cardinal Parocchi, Vicar of His Holiness; it is dated December 16, 1895:

Miss and dear Daughter in Our Lord,

It is with a lively but quite soft emotion that I received your good letter of 29 November, together with the copy of the Neuvaine Eucharistique . . . His Holiness has entrusted me with bestowing upon you, on his behalf, a very special blessing . . .

My sympathies have been all yours for a long time. Your conversion is one of the most magnificent triumphs of grace that I am aware of. Right now, I am reading your Memoirs which are just fascinating.

Be assured that I have not forgotten you in the mean time, especially in my prayers to the Holy Sacrifice. As for you, do not cease to thank Our Savior Jesus Christ for the great mercy which He bestowed upon you and the magnificent token of love which He gave you.

Do accept my blessing and believe me,

All yours in the heart of Jesus.

L.M. Cardinal-Vicar.

Here is another one written on the official letterhead of the general leading Council of the Anti-Masonic Union, which is the highest action committee against freemasonry, a committee constituted by the Pope himself, a committee whose leader is an official representative of the Holy See, Msgr. Lazzareschi. Listen:

Rome, May 27, 1896.

Miss,

Monsignor Vincenzo Sardi, who is one of the private secretaries of the Holy Father, has entrusted me with writing to you, by the order of His Holiness himself.

I should also tell you that His Holiness read with great pleasure your *Neuvaine Eucharistique*.

Commander Alliata had an interview with the Cardinal Vicar concerning the veracity of your conversion. His Eminence is convinced; but He declared to our president that He cannot bear witness of it publicly. *"I cannot betray the secrets of the Holy Office,"* is what His Eminence answered to Commander Alliata.

I am all yours, very devoted in Our Lord,

Rodolfo Verzichi,
Secretary General

The private secretary of Léo XIII, the same Mister Vincenzo Sardi who was mentioned above, writes among other things:

Rome, July 11, 1896.

Miss,

I hasten to express the thanks which are due to you for sending your last book on Crispi. . . .

This is a book in which, under the signature of Miss Diana Vaughan, I recounted that Crispi had a pact with a devil named Haborym, that Crispi was present in 1885 at a Palladistic meeting during which a devil named Bitru, introducing Sophie Walder to a certain number of Italian political men, announced to them that the said Sophie, on September 19, 1896, would give birth to a girl who was to become the grandmother of the Antichrist. I had sent the book to the Vatican. The private secretary of the Pope was expressing his thanks for it accordingly and added:

> Keep on, Miss, keep on writing and unmasking the iniquitous sect! Which is the reason why Providence has permitted that you belonged to it for such a long time . . .
> I recommend myself, with all my heart, to your prayers, and with a perfect esteem I declare myself your very devoted
>
> Msgr. Vincenzo Sardi.

The *Civiltà Cattolica*, the most important of all Catholic reviews in the world, the official organ of the Jesuits' General, a review published in Rome, issued the following lines in its issue no. 1,110 in September 1896:

> We want at least once to give ourselves the pleasure of blessing publicly the names of the valorous champions who entered first the glorious arena, among them the noble Miss Diana Vaughan.
> Miss Diana Vaughan, called from the depths of darkness to the light of God, prepared by divine Providence, armed with science and personal experience, turns towards the Church to serve it, and appears inexhaustible in her valuable publications which are unparalleled for accuracy and usefulness.

In the entourage of the Sovereign Pontiff, Miss Vaughan was not merely considered as a heroic polemicist; she was set on the same level as the Saints. When she started to be attacked, the secretary of Cardinal Parocchi wrote her from Rome, October 19, 1886:

> Keep on, Miss, through your pen and your piety, despite the efforts of hell, furnishing weapons to overwhelm the Enemy of mankind. All the Saints' deeds have been fought against; no wonder then that yours are not spared. . . .

Please accept, Miss, the expression of my liveliest feelings of admiration and respect.

A. Villard
Prelate of the Residence of His Holiness
Secretary to H. E. Cardinal Parocchi

You know well, gentlemen Catholic journalists, that these letters have been actually sent to Miss Vaughan. They may embarrass you today; but they are historical documents; these have not been forged, and their eminent authors will not disown them.

And not only did they patronize this hoax; but believing the woman with whom they corresponded to have an exalted head, they urged her to enter their game for preparing their miracles.

Time is short today; nevertheless, I want to acquaint you with a fact along the same lines. Everybody knows that *according to the Catholic legend*, once Joan of Arc had been burned, the executioner was shocked to find out that, alone, the heart of the heroine had not been consumed; in vain, he threw more burning pitch and sulfur upon it, the heart would not burn. Finally, on the injunction of the bailiff who directed the torment, Joan's heart was thrown in the Seine. Now, the French clergy requests the canonization of Joan of Arc; but it is Rome which canonizes, and Rome is in Italy. The French clergy has already found a relic of the girl they put to death, namely a carbonized rib. In Italy, they are preparing something better than that. They support a nun of the third order in the extraordinary idea that she is the one who will retrieve the heart of Joan of Arc; no doubt an angel will bring it to her. This ultra-mystical nun of the third order has said so in a letter she wrote to Miss Vaughan, and the very secretary of the Cardinal Vicar recommended to Miss Vaughan to correspond with this pious person, to exchange with her impressions about the supernatural facts concerning Joan of Arc. It is easy to get what that means. Be sure that one day an angel will carry the heart, not to France, but to Italy, the same as angels carried the house of Nazareth to Lorette.[19] Joan of Arc will be canonized, and all the French pilgrims who will come to Italy will not fail to make a visit to the Italian possessor of the miraculously retrieved heart; and their visits will be fruitful, won't they? (Laughter)

Indeed, Miss Vaughan has seen the favors of the princes of the Church fall upon her.

The masons of France, of Italy, of England, laughed in their sleeves and right they were. On the other hand, a German Mason, Findel,[20] got real mad and thundered forth a very well written pamphlet. Great excitement. That pamphlet was like a paving stone in a frogs' pond.[21]

A strong reaction appeared necessary. Findel endangered the final success of my hoax: his grand mistake was to think that it was a plot set up by the Jesuits—unfortunate Jesuits! I had sent them a fragment of the Moloch's tail, as a piece of evidence of Palladism! (Explosion of laughter)

Disquiet crept into the Vatican. Jumping from one extreme to another they got into a panic. They wondered whether they were not confronted with a hoax about to smash the Church instead of serving it. They named a secret commission of inquiry in order to ascertain what they were to believe.

Since then, the danger becoming great, my work was endangered, and I did not want to get shipwrecked. The danger was silence, strangling the hoax in the oubliettes[22] of the Roman Commission, preventing Catholic papers from breathing a word.

My friend the doctor went to Cologne; from there, he put me in the picture. And forewarned I left for the Congress of Trent, well forewarned. When I came back, the first person I saw was my friend. I told him of my fear of silent strangling.

Then we agreed upon all that was to be done and written. If the editors of the *Universe* doubt it, I can name them parts they left out of the letters of Dr. Bataille. It was I who stoked their fire that way, then it was necessary for the world press to be made aware of this grand and bizarre epic. And a good deal of time was necessary so that the uproar of furious Catholics, the polemic with those in favor of Miss Diana Vaughan would catch the notice of the major newspapers, those who walk along with progress and count millions of readers.

The Conclusion

Before ending, I must pay my respects to an unknown hoaxster, a shrewd American colleague. Among hoaxsters, one understands each other from one end of the world to the other without needing to exchange letters, without even having to drop a call. Respects therefore to the dear citizen of Kentucky who had the friendly thought of helping us without any prior agreement, who confirmed the revelations of Miss Diana Vaughan to the Louisville *Courier-Journal,* who certified to whoever wanted to hear that he had known Miss Diana Vaughan intimately for seven or eight years and that he often met her in the various secret societies of Europe and America . . . where she never set foot.

LADIES,

GENTLEMEN,

You were told that Palladism would be knocked down today. Better still, it is annihilated, it is no more.

In my general confession to the Jesuit father of Clamart, I had accused myself of an imaginary murder. Well, I will admit to a further crime. I committed infanticide. Palladism is now dead for good. Its father just murdered it.

(*An indescribable tumult meets this conclusion. Some laugh more and more and applaud the lecturer. Catholics scream and hiss. Abbot Garnier steps on a chair and attempts to address the audience, but he is hindered by the hoot. A few listeners strike up the comic song by Meusy:* O Sacred Heart of Jesus!)

Appendix 1

Appendix 2

The Fruits of Anti-Masonry

Wherefore by their fruits ye shall know them.
—Jesus Christ, Matthew 7:20

PART ONE: GARDEN OF EVIL?[1]

Purification? Vandalism? Pagan ritual rooted in superstition? Take your pick. These appear to be the three main attitudes toward a local memorial garden in Virginia. In late April 1996, five members of Westwood Hill Baptist Church of Kempsville, near Virginia Beach, Virginia, believed there was a powerful evil on the grounds of their church.

They consulted with their pastor, the Reverend Jess Jackson, two associate pastors, and several other church members. It was agreed that the evil lurked in a garden area between the old and new sanctuaries. Telltale clues, they thought, were a large cross fashioned from old basketball goal stanchions, a rose bush planted beneath the cross, and a cobblestone path with unusual patterns. Most incriminating of all, a stone carried a plaque dedicating the garden to "The loving memory of our teacher and friend, Arthur S. Ward."

There was the key! Arthur Sedrick Ward, a Mason. Worse yet, the cross and rose in the garden suggested he could have been a Scottish Rite Mason. Clearly, the garden had to go.

What are the facts? First, when he died of a heart attack on April 28, 1979, Arthur S. Ward was a member of Corinthian Lodge No. 266 in Norfolk, Virginia. There is no record, however, of any Scottish Rite membership, be it in the Southern or Northern Masonic Jurisdictions. Arthur Ward's widow, Donna Ward Meekins, said, "There was never an evil bone in Arthur

229

Ward's body. Yes, he was a Mason, but after our two sons, well, he got so involved in their sports and school and things, he just didn't have the time."

Ward's younger son, Gary, a Virginia Beach schoolteacher, said, "I don't recall him being in it [Masonry], going to meetings and that type of thing. He never spoke of it much. And it certainly wasn't an important part of his life."[2]

By all descriptions, Ward was a devout man, his life centered on his family and church. A retired supervisor for the Norfolk & Western Railway Company, he was a founding member of the Westwood Hill Baptist Church and turned the first spade of earth for the new sanctuary which was under construction when he died at the age of 64. The Sunday School class he taught for many years dedicated their donations and labor to creating the garden in his memory.

Yet on April 23, 1996, 17 years after Ward's death, ten members of the Westwood Hill Baptist Church, believing the garden was endowed with Masonic symbols, tore up every plant, removed every cobblestone (each a collector's item over 100 years old from streets in Norfolk), burned the wooden cross, and broke the stone on which the garden's memorial plaque was mounted.

What could not be burned was hauled away as trash. "Then, according to church members, they reconsecrated the ground by sprinkling it with holy water." William Forbes, charter member and longtime deacon of the church, said, "It sounds so ridiculous. It sounds like something out of the Dark Ages."[3]

Some 200 church members were as outraged and heartsick as the Ward family at this demolition of the memorial garden and protested the action at a Sunday evening "family meeting" on Mothers Day, May 12. The Rev. Mr. Jackson held steadfast and presented a slide lecture to explain the "pivotal issue," "the presence of a rose cross, an occult symbol" of Freemasonry in the garden.[4] One wonders if the rose bush in question were part of the original garden, planted nearly two decades ago, a later replacement of an original planting of another plant which was not a rose or, in any case, an aesthetic decision that favored roses over marigolds or other flowers. The choice of plant probably was based on horticultural taste and only coincidentally related to any possible Masonic significance. Undoubtedly, the Rev. Mr. Jackson is confusing the emblem of the Scottish Rite Eighteenth

Degree, Knight Rose Croix, with an emblem from Rosicrucianism, "an intellectual and mystical phase in Germany between the Renaissance and the scientific revolution of the seventeenth century."[5] One of Masonry's well-known scholars, Henry Wilson Coil, notes: "Great confusion has prevailed as to the name Rose Croix and its variations . . . from which Rosicrucianism is presumably derived. This confusion has enabled some writers [and others, like the Rev. Mr. Jackson] to connect Masonry with Rosicrucianism. . . . and has produced a considerable volume of literature principally notable for its imaginative qualities."[6]

True, the rose and cross are central to the Scottish Rite's Eighteenth Degree, but here they maintain the traditional symbolism of western culture, "the cross in Masonry represents a statement of infinity"[7] with allusions in the Degree to suffering, a redeemer, and God's unlimited love. Likewise, "in Masonry, the rose has taken on the meaning of immortality"[8] and, as sometimes in Christian symbology, the blood of Christ or the beauty of "the Rose of Sharon" in the Bible's Song of Solomon, 2: I. Also, Jesus wore a crown of thorns during His passion, thus relating Him to a rose's thorns. The merger of the rose with the cross was inevitable in western civilization and, consequently, it is a symbol shared by Christianity and Freemasonry. The seal and coat of arms adopted by Martin Luther as a publishing trademark, for instance, is a cross rising out of a heart at the center of which is a five-leafed rose.[9]

Thus, in Freemasonry, as in all western culture, the cross and rose have retained their traditional meanings. To see these shared symbols as "occult" in Freemasonry (or Christianity) and, in particular, in the Scottish Rite of Freemasonry is illogical. This absurdity is even more pronounced when a dubious "occult" interpretation of the cross and rose is used to attack Arthur S. Ward who was not a Scottish Rite Mason.

Still, on June 9, 1996, in a formal meeting of the Westwood Hill Baptist Church to consider by vote whether or not to dismiss the Reverend Jess Jackson, a strong majority stood in his defense and he was not dismissed. Why? In recent years, Westwood Hill Baptist Church, like many congregations in the Southern Baptist Convention, has become dominated by newer members and a bolder leadership intent on establishing and defending what it considers fundamental principles of the Baptist faith.

For instance, of the ten people who tore up the Arthur S. Ward garden, only one or two, if any, had ever met Ward, and some had been with the church for two years or less.

Disconnected from the long tradition of toleration within the Baptist faith (Baptists were once a persecuted minority), and probably only tenuously connected to a larger view of religious faith in the world, past and present, these new church members and leaders are likely to embrace ideas and actions which set them apart, in their view, as purer and better and truer to their faith than others.

To attain this exclusionary singleness of character, extreme stances and interpretations of doctrine are embraced, and those who will not toe the new line are sidelined or expelled. When the Rev. Mr. Jackson became pastor of Westwood Hill Baptist Church, for instance, average church attendance was 500. Before the Arthur S. Ward Garden incident, attendance had fallen to about 300. Since the incident, another 140 members of the church have left. Most of the people who left are not Masons. There were very few Masons in the church.[10]

Who, after all, would wish to stay? As news of the garden's destruction spread, a near hysteria, reminiscent of the Salem witch trials of 1791, gripped the congregation. Church members reported nightmarish visions welling up from the garden's soil. Sunday School children, hearing the adults, began stories that bones or bodies were buried in the garden. These reactions following the garden's destruction only seemed to validate the actions of the perpetrators who believed a cloud of evil threatened the church's purity. Clearly, something drastic had to be done to reestablish the church on its primitive principles. Despite the action's macabre aura of resurrected corpses and howling werewolves, the memorial garden was destroyed.

The Reverend Richard D. Marks, a Baptist minister who teaches at Regent University, founded by Pat Robertson, spoke at the May 12, 1996, meeting of Westwood Hill Baptist Church. It was hoped he could help heal the growing divisions within the church. His words form a fitting close to this story:

> I don't think it [the garden with its cross and rose] has any evil import. Evil is in the meaning you attach to something. There are a lot of Masons who are good Christians. . . . To say this whole organization is made

up of thousands of men who are evil, out there practicing as Satanists, I don't believe it.

Don't you believe it, either.

PART 2: STONES OF EVIL

When the *Virginia-Pilot* article concerning the destruction of the Arthur S. Ward Memorial Garden came to the attention of Dr. John W. Boettjer, Managing Editor of the *Scottish Rite Journal*, he researched the news story, wrote the October article, and attempted, unsuccessfully, to locate Brother Ward's widow, Donna Ward-Meekins, before publication. On September 27, Mrs. Ward-Meekins, having been shown the October *Journal* article by a friend, telephoned Dr. Boettjer. The following statement is condensed from that telephone call as well as one to Mrs. Ward-Meekins's friends, John and Betty. It has been reviewed, rewritten, and approved for publication by Donna Ward-Meekins.

> When I became aware that the garden to the memory of my late husband, Arthur, had been viciously and sadistically destroyed, I was in a state of shocked disbelief. The pastor, Rev. Jess Jackson, would only answer my questions with, "It has been done away with."
>
> When I pressed for information about what had become of the garden's benches, bricks, and cobblestones, I got the same answer, "They have been done away with." I asked specifically about the stone with the memorial message, "In Loving Memory of Our Teacher and Friend, ARTHUR S. WARD, 1979," and you guessed it, I got the same answer, "They have been done away with."
>
> I finally got the truth from my friends, Betty and John, who told me the following amazing story. Five members of the church supposedly had made a "prayer walk" of the church grounds and had seen a "vision of evil" in the garden. These people, along with the pastoral staff of the church, and two wives of the staff members, without knowledge of the church membership, entered the garden area on the afternoon of April 23, 1996, and began to dig up and destroy every shrub and tree in the garden and break up every piece of brick and concrete they could find. They removed a cross and burned it and removed every plaque with the name of Arthur Ward on it. They disposed of the plaques apparently in a truckload of brick and stones to the city garbage dump.
>
> One week after the garden was destroyed, word reached Betty and John. They contacted the Reverend Jess Jackson and had a meeting with him on Wednesday May 1, 1996, after the Wednesday night prayer service. John asked the pastor for an explanation and he was told the story about the five

members having discovered "evil in the garden." Rev. Jess Jackson said the garden had been destroyed and that he was "comfortable" with that action.

Before the meeting with the pastor, Betty had observed two cobblestones in the garden area during a brief look at the former garden's site, and she asked the Rev. Jackson's permission to retrieve them. The pastor gave his permission and the next morning John and Betty went to the former garden's site with digging tools and unearthed twelve cobblestones, placed them in the trunk of their car and took them home, placing them in their yard.

The following evening, May 3, Betty and John's daughter returned home from five weeks in St. Louis. Early the next morning, she suffered a cerebral hemorrhage and was taken to the intensive care facility of a local hospital. On Sunday night, May 5, Betty and John received a visit at the hospital from two ladies from the church who had participated in the garden's destruction.

After all the other visitors had left, one of the women informed Betty and John that "We are here by divine appointment." She stated that John's and Betty's daughter's illness was "not physical but spiritual," and was the result of their possession of the stones. The women asked where the stones were and, after learning they were at John's and Betty's residence, asked if they could go and get them.

The same lady said the stones were "too dangerous to be picked up in one vehicle." Six vehicles would be necessary to pick up the stones, she said, because the evil forces in the stones would be increased if the stones were kept together. She said that John and Betty and their daughter would be in great danger as long as they had possession of the stones. The two women did not receive their requested permission to remove the stones and left the hospital soon thereafter.

John immediately called Rev. Jess Jackson expecting to receive spiritual comfort, but got only scriptural references to read, references which appeared to justify the destruction of the garden. After about 45 minutes in prayer in the hospital chapel, John and Betty decided to call another pastor of their acquaintance.

This pastor came to the hospital in the middle of a very powerful and drenching thunderstorm. He heard their story in amazement and anguish since he was well acquainted with the Westwood Hill Church and its pastor. He gave them much encouragement and prayer support and assured them that he did not believe God worked in the manner in which the garden was destroyed and the way the two women visited the hospital.

He said in his opinion God worked through order and unity rather than through confusion and disorder. He agreed that this was a matter that should be brought before the congregation of the church. This pastor ministered lovingly to John and Betty for about three hours that night, ending at about 3:30 the following morning.

Happily, despite the fact that the stones were not surrendered to the women, Betty and John's daughter recovered fully. Later, the stones were brought to my son's home and they are now in his garden. With grim humor, my son Gary said, "Look Mom, they don't even glow in the dark." My family and I continue to feel the pain and live under the shadow of this incident. I grieve that my husband's memory has been tarnished. I was always proud of his Masonic affiliations and when I remarried, I was happy that my second husband, now deceased, was a Mason who served as Master of his Lodge.

From my experience, Masons have been men of high caliber. Incidents such as this should never happen. The destruction of the garden was unconscionable. To assure this never happens again to the widow of any Mason, I have retained a lawyer and have filed suit against the people who took part in this terrible act.

Appendix 3

Please Look a Little Closer[1]

JAMES T. TRESNER II

Here, it seems, we go again. A leaflet focused on Freemasonry has recently been published by the Home Mission Board of the Southern Baptist Convention. It is titled "A Closer Look at *A Bridge to Light*: An Examination of the Religious Teachings of the Scottish Rite." The leaflet, written by William E. Gordon, Jr., purports to be an examination of the book by Rex R. Hutchens, 33°, Grand Cross.

Since 1988, a copy of *A Bridge to Light* has been given to candidates for the Degrees of the Southern Jurisdiction of the Scottish Rite. A second edition of *A Bridge to Light* was prepared in 1995 and is used as the basis of this critique by the Southern Baptist Convention. I'd encourage both Dr. Gordon and the Home Mission Board to look at a little closer.

Among the leadership of the Scottish Rite, there was some debate as to whether or not there should be a response to the leaflet. Finally, it was decided to do so because there are statements in the leaflet which are confusing and should not go uncorrected. Before I discuss some of the specifics of the leaflet, however, there are a few general points to be made.

Within our Fraternity, no one person can speak for Masonry. A Grand Master can speak on organizational matters within his Jurisdiction, just as the Grand Commander can speak on organizational matters within the Southern Jurisdiction of the Scottish Rite. But no one—not a Grand Master, not a Grand Commander, not Albert Pike himself—can speak for Masonry when it comes to the meanings of its teachings. That is some-

236

thing each Mason must seek and find for himself. No one can speak for Freemasonry.

Perhaps the reason some people find that hard to understand is that they themselves are so willing to speak for all of Christianity. They write such things as "All Christians believe. . . ." "Christians would agree. . . ," or "You can't be a Christian and believe. . . ." In the case of "A Closer Look," for example, the author, Dr. Gordon, writes not as an individual, a Southern Baptist, or a representative of the SBC Home Mission Board. Rather, he appears to write for ALL Christians. In doing so, he has asserted as universal Christian belief or universal interpretations of Biblical passages doctrines which are in contradiction to the teachings of several Christian denominations. Perhaps the author of "A Closer Look at *A Bridge to Light*" doesn't consider members of those denominations to be Christians.

A second fact which our critics seem to find hard to understand is that *Morals and Dogma* (and *A Bridge to Light*, which is, in some senses, an explication of *Morals and Dogma*) is not a book of "teachings" nor a statement of what a Mason believes or should believe about religion. *Morals and Dogma* is, essentially, a textbook for a course in philosophy and comparative religion.

The key word there is "comparative." The writers of so many anti-Masonic tracts—"A Closer Look" among them—seem astonished and horrified to find pre-Christian religions included. They appear to think *Morals and Dogma* and *A Bridge to Light* should be limited to Christianity, but that, by definition, is impossible. A textbook on comparative forms of government, for example, which only discussed democracy would not be a textbook on comparative government; it would have to include monarchy, oligarchy, and the many other forms of government people have developed over the centuries.

Thus it is with *Morals and Dogma* and, consequently, with *A Bridge to Light*. Pike believed that you can't understand an idea unless you understand the history of the idea. And so, in *Morals and Dogma*, when he introduces a concept, he also tells you what other philosophers and religious leaders who belonged to the great cultures and religions of the past taught on that same concept.

But never does he say that you, the Scottish Rite Mason of today, have to believe what they taught.

If you want to understand the history of the science of geography, you have to know that people once believed that the earth was flat and square, but no one says you have to believe that today.

And certainly no one says that you aren't smart enough to know the difference.

With those general comments, let us take a look at some of the specifics in "A Closer Look at *A Bridge to Light*," and see why we would ask the author to look closer still.

At the bottom of the first page of Dr. Gordon's leaflet, he writes, "Scottish Rite Freemasonry claims to teach religious truth [pp. vii, 3]." *But that's not what the book says.* The actual passage on page vii says: "The Ancient and Accepted Scottish Rite is above all else an educational institution. Throughout its history it has stood as a beacon on the shores of ignorance. Instruction about the great ideas of morality, philosophy, religion and philanthropy permeates our ritual and our writings, unencumbered by sectarian doctrine. *We have sought, not to teach men the truth, but rather a way to the truth.* Each must find it for himself." I added the italics to make the point of this passage clearer.

We do not claim to teach religious truth, but to teach about the great ideas of religion, along with morality and the other areas mentioned. The passage specifically says *we have tried to teach men how to find truth, but we do not claim to teach religious truth itself.*

It's the same on page three, also cited by the writer of "A Closer Look." Nowhere on that page, or elsewhere, do we claim to teach religious truth. The line on page three reads: "To become a Scottish Rite Mason is to begin the search for philosophical truth in three areas: political, moral and religious." Again, Dr. Rex R. Hutchens, author of *A Bridge to Light*, is simply saying that a Mason searches for truth, not that Freemasonry tells him what the truth should be. I wish the writer of "A Closer Look" had read a little more carefully.

Why do we believe that the growth and development of one's faith is so important? For a thousand years, Christian theologians have emphasized the difference between a "child-like" faith (much to be desired) and a "childish" faith. Only the child-like faith that has grown and developed while retaining its child-like quality can truly be strong.

The great theologian Walter Rauschenbush puts it very well: "The religion of childhood will not satisfy adolescent youth, and the religion of youth ought not to satisfy a mature man or woman. Our soul must build statelier mansions for itself. Religion must continue to answer all our present needs and inspire all our present functions. A person who has failed to adjust his religion to his growing powers and his intellectual horizon, has failed in one of the most important functions of growth, just as if his cranium failed to expand and to give room to his brain. Being *microcephalous* [having an abnormally tiny head] is a misfortune, and nothing to boast of."[2]

There is a subtle twist in Dr. Gordon's next charge, possibly the result of an accidental misreading. He says that "*A Bridge to Light* denies certainty in religious truth claims." He suggests the Scottish Rite teaches that religious truth is "uncertain and relative." He says that *A Bridge to Light* makes that claim on pages 9, 69, 103, and 107. Again, he should have looked a little closer. *A Bridge to Light* does not say there is no certain religious truth. It says *human understanding of religious truth is imperfect*. And it says that since human understanding of religious truth is imperfect, no one should hate someone else just because one person's imperfect understanding is different from another person's imperfect understanding.

This interpretation should not come as a surprise to the writer of "A Closer Look." The Bible relates the same idea in these words: "For now we see through a glass, darkly, but then face to face; now I know in part; but then shall I know even as also I am known" (I Corinthians 13:12).

"A Closer Look" then makes a strange charge: "*A Bridge to Light* teaches that God is a God of love who should not be feared. 'I put my trust in God, is the protest of Masonry against the belief in a cruel, angry, and revengeful God, to be feared and not reverenced by His creatures.'" [The inner quotation is taken by Dr. Gordon from *Morals and Dogma*.] It is rather unusual to be accused of teaching that one should love God, but the writer of "A Closer Look" then lists Biblical quotations to prove that God should be feared.

He is missing the point. Pike and Hutchens were simply trying to correct an error which has crept into thinking because our language has changed. The *Oxford English Dictionary* tells us that, at the time the King James Translation of the Bible was made, a primary meaning of the word "fear" was "to hold in awe and respect." Over time, "fear" has developed the primary meaning it has now—"be terrified of." Pike was simply saying that God is a God of love; you do not need to be terrified of Him. Hold Him in awe and respect certainly, but do not assume that He is a malignant being who is looking for a chance to do you harm.

The next point gets a little abstract and I apologize for dragging the reader through it, but it is important. According to the writer of "A Closer Look," *A Bridge to Light* claims that Christianity accepts the principle of dualism as taught by Zoroaster (page 311). But that's not what *A Bridge to Light* says.

Dualism is a doctrine that says both a good and an evil force exist in the universe. Dualism, *as taught by Zoroaster*, involved two essentially equal gods, one good and one evil, who contested for control of the universe. Dualism, *as it appears in many Christian denominations*, teaches that there are two forces, but that they are not equal. The good force is God, who is omnipotent. The evil force is Satan, who is not omnipotent. Dr. Hutchens is referencing Pike, who observed (as have many Christian theologians) that Zoroaster seems to have originated the idea of dualism, and the idea has found echoes in many Western religions, including Christianity. Dr. Hutchens was not suggesting, as "A Closer Look" implies, that Christianity believes in a good God and an evil God.

Again, I wish the writer had taken a closer look at page 218 of *A Bridge to Light*. He says the Scottish Rite teaches that man cannot have knowledge of God. Had he read more carefully, he would have realized that the book says the Koran teaches that man's limited intellect cannot form a true conception of what God is like. That's hardly a surprising statement. The book also says that when we start describing God, we limit our idea of Him because words are limited. So we should remember that when we try to describe God, there is a danger that we will overlook part of His greatness. Again, that's obviously true. It's just another version of "For now we see through a glass, darkly."

The writer then distorts the references to the Trinity so badly that it is truly offensive. What *A Bridge to Light* actually says is that many religions have conceived of God as triune (three-part) in nature. That is clearly true, as the examples given in *A Bridge to Light* make obvious. But the writer of "A Closer Look" then suggests Masonry teaches that these trinities believed in by ancient religions are the same as the Holy Trinity of Christianity. Nowhere in *Morals and Dogma*, *A Bridge to Light*, or any other Masonic writing of which I am aware is such a claim made! Dr. Gordon's reasoning is the same as saying that because a watch has a face and hands and a human being has a face and hands, a watch and a human being are the same thing!

I would also ask the writer to take a closer look at the concept of a Messiah. He claims that the Scottish Rite teaches that Jesus was not unique. The passage he cites doesn't say that. It says that many religions in the ancient world taught that a Messiah would come. Again, that is provably true. But to say that the Greeks taught that Dionysius was a messiah-figure, or that the Hindus taught that Krishna was a messiah-figure is to make a statement about the teachings of those religions—not to make a statement about Jesus of Nazareth.

The same sort of misunderstanding is responsible for the assertion in "A Closer Look" that the Scottish Rite confuses pagan deities with the one true God. It does not. It describes ancient religions as part of an intellectual study. It tells us what people have believed in the past. It does nothing more.

I really wish that the writer of "A Closer Look" had given more depth to his reading before he wrote, "Scottish Rite uses the occult as a source of religious truth." He cites some instances, including the suggestion that we teach astrology, and then devotes quite a bit of space to showing by Biblical quotations that Christianity disapproves of divination by astrology.

The point he missed is that the Scottish Rite disapproves of it, too. As any Scottish Rite Mason knows, nowhere in the Rite are you taught how to be an astrologer. The Scottish Rite does teach about astrology as divination, however. And what does Pike say about astrology? He refers to it as a "pretended science."[3]

Pike states the study of the heavens was originally a useful means of telling the seasons so that men knew when to plant and when to harvest. This use then expanded to the heavens as a source of inspiration as men and women marveled at the Creator of such perfect order. Finally, astrology deteriorated in the hands of unscrupulous men to nothing more than spurious fortune-telling.[4]

There is more. It really is not worth the space to answer each of the charges. They result from either a misreading or a misunderstanding of the material in *A Bridge to Light*—and, of course, from a starting position that all Christianity must conform to the writer's own denominational doctrines.

It is worthwhile, however, to look at the comments of "A Closer Look" on the Thirty-first degree, because it is clearly a case of misunderstanding the purposes of the Masonic Degrees, and it is possible that a better understanding may help the writer of the leaflet comprehend that there is nothing to cause concern.

He points out that the Degree's initiation ceremony is set in the Egyptian afterlife, and that the candidate is required to swear things in the name of the Egyptian gods. He finds this offensive.

But there are a few things to be remembered and understood.

First of all, the 31° ceremony, like that of all Degrees, is a play. It has a plot and characters like any other play. The candidate is playing the part of a character, like everyone else in the cast. In his case, he is playing the role of an ancient Egyptian who has died and entered into the afterlife as conceived by his people. It is a play just as *Macbeth* is a play, and the actor playing the dead Egyptian is no more engaging in an act of worship to the ancient gods than the actor playing Macbeth is really plotting political assassination.

The 31° is the next-to-last Degree in the basic Degrees of the Scottish Rite. Pike wanted to make the point that the Mason should constantly examine his actions and motives, holding himself to the highest standards of honor and ethics. He wanted a story line which represented the ultimate judgment, when nothing is hidden. He was far too devout a Christian to use a play based on the Last Judgment as seen by Christianity—he would have considered that sacrilege.

But there is another religion, now dead, which contains such a scene, and that is the religion of ancient Egypt. There are no practitioners of that religion left, and so Pike could draw on an old Degree, based on that religion, without fear of giving offense to a member of that faith. He did so, but he also did something more wonderful and subtle, and it is a good example of the way the Rite teaches.

The *Egyptian Book of the Dead* contains a sequence usually called the "negative confession." The soul of the departed asserts that he has never moved the landmarks, he has never cheated in trade, he has never broken the law, etc. Pike uses that, but then tells the character played by the candidate that that is not enough. It is not enough to have avoided evil, one must have done good. It is not enough to have not wronged people, one must have helped them.

Pike is saying that productive living involves being active, helping, making a difference in the world. That's the message. One should no more get upset over the fact that the drama of the 31° is set in ancient Egypt than that the opera *Aïda* is. In both cases, it's just a setting which helps to tell a dramatic and important story.

And there is one more assertion which should be given attention, if only because it is so wrong and so often made. The writer of "A Closer Look" says "*A Bridge to Light* teaches a works salvation." To prove this claim, he says that page 142 "claims that immortality is won by suffering and sorrow." It doesn't. The quotation says that the rose on the cross is a symbol of immortality won by suffering and sorrow. It is, for the Christian, clearly a reference to Christ who won redemption for His followers by His suffering and sorrow—hardly a strange concept.

He says that page 165 "informs the reader that 'a man's actions are a bridge to his own immortality and to the future of mankind.'" But that passage begins, "Will you obey God's law, trust in His goodness, and be patient though the appointed time may seem to draw no nearer during your life, nor your labors and exertions produce any fruit? . . . Each man must act as a bridge builder to the future, being a good example to his children, peers, and brethren. A man's actions are a bridge to his own immortality and to the future of mankind."

Certainly, in most Christian doctrine, a man's actions are a bridge to his own immortality, since it is an action to accept Christ. Many Christian denominations teach that one can, by one's actions, destroy one's hope of salvation even after the person has made a profession of faith.

There are other examples, but the point remains the same. Masonry does not teach a "works salvation." It teaches, over and over again, that it is important to do good in the world because we have a duty to make the lives of others better, not because it is some way of "earning" salvation.

The writer of "A Closer Look" says, in his conclusion, that many of the religious teachings of the Scottish Rite are incompatible with Biblical Christianity. But he has confused "religious teachings" with "teaching about religions." We do not offer religious teachings; we do offer information about religions. The difference between "religious teachings" and "teaching about religions" is like the difference between teaching medicine and teaching about medicine. Any college survey course on social history or economics may well contain a section which teaches about medicine as it relates to the subject matter of the course, but that would hardly make one into a doctor. Again, we would ask Dr. Gordon to please look a little closer, look without preconceptions and prejudices. He will see there is nothing to criticize and even less to fear.

Notes

Chapter 1

1. Robert A. Morey, *The Truth About Masons* (Eugene, Oreg.: Harvest House Publishers, 1993), p. 21.
2. See, for example, Jim Shaw [33rd Degree, past "Worshipful Master" past "Master of all Scottish Rite Bodies"] & Tom C. McKenney, *The Deadly Deception* . . . ; Jack Harris [former "Worshipful Master"], *Freemasonry: The Invisible Cult in Our Midst* . . . ; Claude McClung [Royal Arch Mason 7th Degree], *Why I Left Masonry* (no pub. info given), et al.
3. Robert A. Morey, p. 22.
4. "Freemasonry on Its Own Terms," The John Ankerberg Show, Episode DM-170, 1986.
5. James L. Holly, *The Southern Baptist Convention and Freemasonry*, vol. II (Beaumont, Tex.: Mission and Ministry to Men, 1992), pp. 46–51.
6. Robert A. Morey, p. 21.
7. Of course, conspiracy theorists may already be aware of the following dangerous connections between Freemasonry and golf. For instance, "William St. Clair, the first Grand Master of the Grand Lodge of Scotland, laid the foundation stone of the golf house of the Leith Club, outside Edinburgh in 1767. . . ." St. Clair was "assisted by fourteen 'worthy members of the golfing company,' all Masons." See C. Fred Kleinknecht, "William St. Clair, First Grand Master of Scotland and Master Golfer," in the *Scottish Rite Journal*, Vol. CIII (January 1995), No. 1, pp. 8–13.
8. The Supreme Council 33°, S.J., has published two books to help readers better understand Pike's often dense prose: Rex R. Hutchens and Donald W. Monson, *The Bible in Albert Pike's "Morals and Dogma"* (Washington: The Supreme Council 33°, 1992) and Rex R. Hutchens, *A Glossary to "Morals and Dogma"* (Washington: The Supreme Council, 33°, 1993).
9. Ron Carlson, *Freemasonry and the Masonic Lodge*, preached by the author, audio cassette (Eden Prairie, Minn.: Christian Ministries International, no date), side 2, 34:18. The times listed are measured from the beginning of the audio and may vary slightly depending on the equipment used.
10. Ron Carlson, side 1, 4:41.
11. J. Edward Decker, Jr., *The Question of Freemasonry* (Issaquah, Wash.: Free the Masons Ministries, no date), p. 3.
12. Albert Pike, *Morals and Dogma of the Ancient and Accepted Scottish Rite of Freemasonry*, rev. ed. (Washington: Supreme Council 33°, SJ, 1950), p. iv, emphasis added.
13. Albert Pike, p. 819.
14. See, for example, Josiah Priest, A.M., *Bible Defence of Slavery, and Origin, Fortunes, and History of the Negro Race* (Glasgow, Ky.: Rev. W. S. Brown, M.D., 1849), Rev. Iveson L. Brookes,

A.M., *A Defense of the South . . . in which Slavery is shown to be an Institution from God . . .* (Hamburg, S.C.: Republican Office, 1850), Thornton Stringfellow, D.D., *Scriptural and Statistical Views in Favor of Slavery* (Richmond, Va.: J. W. Randolph, 1856).

15. Henry Wilson Coil et al. *Coil's Masonic Encyclopedia* (New York: Macoy Publishing & Masonic Supply Co., 1961), s.v. "Pike, Albert."

Chapter 2

1. This chapter is largely informed by S. Brent Morris, *The Complete Idiot's Guide to Freemasonry* (New York: Alpha [Penguin Group], 2006), "Religious Concerns About Freemasonry," chapter 16, pp. 201–14, and "Albert Pike: Sovereign Pontiff of Masonic Mythology," chapter 13, pp. 163–78.

2. *Webster's Revised Unabridged Dictionary*. MICRA, Inc.

3. Lolly Zamoisky, *Behind the Façade of the Masonic Temple* (Moscow: Progress Publishers, 1989).

4. Gary H. Kah, *En Route to Global Occupation* (Lafayette, La.: Huntington House Publishers, 1992).

5. Léon de Poncins, *Freemasonry and Judaism: The Secret Powers behind Revolution* (Abbeville, France: F. Paillart, 1929); Adolf Hitler, *Mein Kampf* (England: Secker and Warburg, 1925); "The Covenant of the Islamic Resistance Movement," http://avalon.law.yale.edu/20th_century/hamas.asp (accessed March 6, 2009).

6. William T. Sill, *New World Order: The Ancient Plan of Secret Societies* (Lafayette, La.: Huntington House Publishers, 1990); Jack Harris, *Freemasonry: The Invisible Cult in Our Midst* (Towson, Md.: Jack Harris, 1983); William Schnoebelen, *Masonry: Beyond the Light* (Chino, Calif.: Chick Publications, 1991).

7. Dan Sale, posted March 4, 1997, on www.reptilianagenda.com/research/r020500a.html.

8. "Also men of sutel craft, as fre masons and oþere, semen openly cursed bi þis sentence. For þei conspiren togidere þat no man of here craft schal take lesse on a day þat þei setten, þouȝ he schulde bi good conscience take moche lesse, and þat noon of hem schal make sade trewe werk to lette oþere mennus wynnyng of þe craft, and þat non of hem schal do ouȝt but only hewe stone, þouȝ he myȝt profit his maistir twenti pound bi o daies werk bi leggyng on a wal, wiþouten harm or penyng himself. See hou þis wickid peple conspireþ aȝenst treuþe and charite, and comyn profit of þe lond and ponyschiþ hem þat helpen frely here neiȝeboris." John Wycliffe, "The Grete Sentence of Curs Expouned," in *Select English Works of John Wyclif*, ed. Thomas Arnold (Oxford: Clarendon Press, 1849), vol. 3, pp. 333–34.

9. John Hamill and R. A. Gilbert, *World Freemasonry: An Illustrated History* (Hammersmith, London: Aquarian Press, 1991), p. 172.

10. Wallace McLeod, "The Old Charges," *Heredom*, vol. 14 (2006), pp. 105–44.

11. James Anderson, *The Constitutions of the Free-Masons* (London, 1723).

12. www.papalencyclicals.net (accessed October 7, 2005).

13. Ronny Jenkins, "The Evolution of the Church's Prohibition against Catholic Membership in Freemasonry," *The Jurist*, vol. 56 (1997), pp. 736–37.

14. www.papalencyclicals.net (accessed October 7, 2005).

15. Alain Bernheim et al., "The Confession of Léo Taxil," *Heredom*, vol. 5 (1996), p. 151.

16. Abel Clarin de la Rive, *La Femme et L'Enfant dans la Franc-Maçonnerie Universelle* (Paris & Lyon: Delhomme & Briguet, Editeurs, 1894), pp. 487–89; translated in Lady Queenborough, Edith Starr Miller, *Occult Theocrasy*, 2 vols. (1933; reprint, Hawthorne, Calif.: Christian Book Club of America, 1980), p. 233.

17. Bernheim, pp. 137–68.

18. In Alec Mellor, *Strange Masonic Stories* (Richmond, Va.: Macoy Publishing and Masonic Supply Co., 1982), p. 151.
19. Leon Zeldis, "The Protocols of the Elders of Zion," *Heredom*, vol. 7 (1998), p. 103.
20. http://avalon.law.yale.edu/20th_century/hamas.asp (accessed March 7, 2009).
21. Donald Rumbelow, *Jack the Ripper: The Complete Casebook* (Chicago & New York: Contemporary Books, 1988), pp. 200–13.

Chapter 3

1. A. Bernheim, A.W. Samii, and E. Serejski, trans., "The Confession of Léo Taxil," *Heredom*, vol. 5 (1996), pp. 137–168. A full copy is reprinted in Appendix 1 of this book.
2. R. Limouzin-Lamothe, *New Catholic Encyclopedia*, s.v. "Taxil, Leo."
3. Robert A. Morey, p. 23.
4. Alec Mellor, *Strange Masonic Stories* (Richmond, Va.: Macoy Publishing & Masonic Supply Co., Inc., 1982), p. 151.
5. "I was brought into Palladium Lodge (Resurrection, #13) in Chicago in the late 1970s and received the degree of 'Paladin' in that Lodge in 1981." (William Schnoebelen, *Masonry: Beyond the Light* [Chino, Calif.: Chick Publications, 1991], p. 194.) It is interesting to note that Mr. Schnoebelen has combined two distinct and unrelated ideas in his tale, though both use similar sounding words. *Palladium* refers to a small statue of Pallas Athena which was thought to protect the city of Troy. *Paladin* is a type of European knight descended from Charlemagne's Counts Palatine. The essential point, however, is that no Palladium lodges exist; they are the invention of Léo Taxil.
6. Jack Harris, *Freemasonry: The Invisible Cult in Our Midst* (Towson, Md.: Jack Harris, 1983), pp. 24–25.
7. Harmon R. Taylor, "Mixing Oil with Water," *The Evangelist*, June 1986, pp. 47–49.
8. James L. Holly, *The Southern Baptist Convention and Freemasonry* (Beaumont, Tex.: Mission and Ministry to Men, 1992), p. 19.
9. Martin Short, *Inside the Brotherhood* (New York: Dorset, 1989), pp. 94–95.
10. Taxil confessed his hoax on April 19, 1897, in the hall of the Geographic Society in Paris. A transcript was subsequently published in the Parisian newspaper, *Le Frondeur*, "Twelve Years Under the Banner of the Church," April 25, 1897. A translation was originally published by the Scottish Rite Research Society: Alain Bernheim, A. William Samii, and Eric Serejski, trans., "The Confessions of Léo Taxil," *Heredom*, vol. 5 (1996), pp. 137–168. See Appendix 1.
11. According to Dr. Pugh's webpage, "Her gifts of interpreting prophetic events increased even more after reading the Book of *Revelation* and Hal Lindsey's *Great Late Planet Earth* at age 13." http://www.drjoye.com/ (accessed June 12, 2009).
12. Jack T. Chick, *The Curse of Baphomet* (Chino, Calif: Chick Publications, 1991), p. 10. The general level of Mr. Chick's writing can be inferred by what he has written about Roman Catholicism. "[O]n the whole we feel that Chick Publications does more harm than they do good. Because of its lack of scholarship and, more importantly, Christian sympathy, we can only conclude that Chick Publications promotes what can be called 'Comic-book theology,' something Christians ought to definitely avoid." (Hendrik H. Hanegraaff, "Chick Publications and Roman Catholicism," *CRI Perspective*, CP-0809 [San Juan Capistrano: Christian Research Institute, no date.]).
13. C. Fred Kleinknecht, Washington, D.C., correspondence to Rev. Pat Robertson, Virginia Beach, Va., May 12, 1992, typescript, copy in the Archives of the Supreme Council, 33°, SJ, Washington, D.C.

14. See *Freemasonry and Religion* (Washington, D.C.: Supreme Council, 33°, SJ, 1987) for a collection of essays on Freemasonry by religious leaders, including Rev. Dr. Norman Vincent Peale, Bishop Carl J. Sanders, Rabbi Seymour Atlas, Rev. Dr. W. Kenneth Lyons, Jr., and others.
15. Robert Morey, p. 23.
16. The phrase "Mother Supreme Council" refers to the fact that the Supreme Council for the Southern Jurisdiction of the United States was the first Scottish Rite Supreme Council in the world, formed in 1801. All other Supreme Councils are descended from the "Mother Supreme Council," but are otherwise independent.
17. In 1889, 60 percent of Southern Jurisdiction members were 32° (1,075 out of 1,787), *Transactions of the Supreme Council, 33°, SJ* (Washington, D.C.: Supreme Council, 33°, SJ, 1888), Returns of Subordinate Bodies. In 1998, 99 percent were 32° members (411,692 out of 415,511), *Transactions of the Supreme Council, 33°, SJ* (Washington, D.C.: Supreme Council, 33°, SJ, 1999), p. 364.
18. Quoted in Alec Mellor, *Strange Masonic Stories* (Richmond, Va.: Macoy Publishing & Masonic Supply Co., Inc., 1982), p. 151.

Chapter 4

1. John Ankerberg and John Weldon, rev. ed. *The Secret Teachings of the Masonic Lodge: A Christian Perspective* (Chicago: Moody Press, 1989, 1990, [1993]).
2. "Djwhal Khul" is listed as a "spirit guide" of occultist Alice Bailey on p. 235, and as a Mason on p. 331. In one of their more notable moments of incredulity, Ankerberg and Weldon claim that "Djwhal Khul" is a Mason. They do not state, however, to which lodge this "spirit guide" belongs, if it attends lodge banquets or holds an office; nor how it is able to make annual dues payments.
3. Ankerberg and Weldon (1990), p. 16.
4. Ankerberg and Weldon (1990), pp. 134, 149, 180, 199, 259.
5. ". . . the Masonic ritual[s] are described by Jonathan Blanchard, former president of Wheaton College, who was a former Sovereign Grand Commander and 33d Degree Mason." Ankerberg and Weldon (1990), p. 131.
6. Clyde S. Kilby, *A Minority of One* (Grand Rapids, Mich.: William B. Eerdmans Publishing Co., 1959), p. 168.
7. See the introduction to Arturo de Hoyos, *The Cloud of Prejudice: A Study in Anti-Masonry* (Kila, Mont.: Kessinger Publishing Co., 1992).
8. For a brief historical overview of Cerneauism and its battle with authentic Freemasonry, see Arturo de Hoyos, "The Union of 1867," in *Heredom: The Transactions of the Scottish Rite Research Society*, vol. 4 (1995), pp. 7–46.
9. Jonathan Blanchard, ed., *Scotch Rite Masonry Illustrated*, 2 vols. (Chicago: Ezra A. Cook, 1887–1888; reprint 1979), vol. 1, pp. 124, 145, 303, 358, 419, 436; vol. 2, pp. 137, 242, 340, 388, 445, 462, 464, 470, 472, 475.
10. Henry Wilson Coil et al., *Coil's Masonic Encyclopedia* (New York: Macoy Publishing & Masonic Supply Co., 1961), pp. 612–613; (1996 ed.) pp. 609–610.
11. Herbert Lockyer, ed., *Nelson's Illustrated Bible Dictionary* (Nashville, Tenn.: Thomas Nelson Pub., 1986), p. 767.
12. Robert Jamieson, A. R. Faussett, David Brown, *A Commentary Critical, Experimental, and Practical on the Old and New Testaments*, 3 vols. (Grand Rapids, Mich.: William B. Eerdmans Publishing Company, 1989); Robert Jamieson, A. R. Faussett, David Brown, *Commentary*

Critical and Explanatory on the Whole Bible (Grand Rapids, Mich.: Zondervan, no date), s.v. "Mathew 5."

13. Rev. Dr. Lloyd Workey, *The Philalethes* (April 1987), as quoted in Allen E. Roberts, *Seekers of Truth: The Story of the Philalethes Society 1928–1988* (Highland Springs, Va.: Anchor Communications, 1988), pp. 199–200.

14. *Coil's Masonic Encyclopedia*, (1961 & 1996), s.v. "Penalties."

15. *Monitor of the Lodge* (Waco, Tex.: Grand Lodge of Texas, 1982), p. 69.

16. *Die Aufnahme eines Freimaurer-Lehrling* (Berlin: Grosse Landesloge der Freimaurer von Deutschland, 1969), pp. 18–19.

17. Albert Pike, *Morals and Dogma of the Ancient and Accepted Scottish Rite of Freemasonry*, rev. ed. (Washington, D.C.: Supreme Council 33°, SJ, 1950), p. 329, emphasis added.

18. Ankerberg and Weldon (1990), p. 235.

19. Ankerberg and Weldon (1990), p. 236.

20. Ankerberg and Weldon (1990), p. 236.

21. Ankerberg and Weldon (1990), p. 134.

22. At the time the 1997 edition of this work was prepared, Mr. Duke's article was available on the Internet (http://duke.org). Similar views, including a chapter on "Race, Christianity, and Judaism," are in *David Duke, My Awakening: A Path to Racial Understanding* (Covington, La.: Free Speech Press, 1999).

23. Ankerberg and Weldon (1990), p. 131

24. A. E. Waite, *Brotherhood of the Rosy Cross* (London: Wm. Rider & Son, Ltd., 1924); Christopher McIntosh, *The Rosicrucians* (Wellingborough, UK: Crucible, 1980, 1987).

25. Harold V. B. Voorhis, *A History of Organized Masonic Rosicrucianism* (privately printed, S.R.I.C.F., 1983); Ellic Howe, "Rosicrucians" in *Man, Myth & Magic: An Illustrated Encyclopedia of the Supernatural*, 24 vols. (N.Y.: Marshall Cavendish, 1970), vol. 18, pp. 2, 426–433.

26. *Twenty-fourth Degree. Prince of the Tabernacle.* Tentative edition (Lexington, Mass.: Supreme Council, 33°, 1986).

27. Ellic Howe, *The Magicians of the Golden Dawn* (London: Routledge and Kegan Paul, 1972); R. A. Gilbert, *The Golden Dawn. Twilight of the Magicians* (Wellingborough, UK: The Aquarian Press, 1983).

28. Jan Rachold, Die Illuminaten. *Quellen und Texte zur Aufklärungsideologie des Illuminatenordens (1776–1785)* (Berlin: Akademie Verlag, 1984).

29. In March 2003, we searched abebooks.com and found numerous booksellers listing Jack Harris's anti-Masonic books. For example, E & E Editions, a bookseller in Fort Stockton, Texas, listed a copy of the first edition for $2.50. All the other booksellers carried the title for less than $10.00.

30. Compare Jack Harris, *Freemasonry: The Invisible Cult in Our Midst* (Towson, Md.: Jack Harris, 1983), pp. 24–25, 29 with *Revised Knight Templarism Illustrated* (Chicago: Ezra A. Cook, 1911), pp. 227–28.

31. Ankerberg and Weldon (1990), p. 224; *Ceremonies of Installation and Dedication*, rev. ed. (Washington, D.C.: Supreme Council, 33°, SJ, 1954), p. 44.

32. Ankerberg and Weldon (1990), p. 55.

33. John Hamill, *Ars Quatuor Coronatorum*, vol. 101 (1988), pp. 155–56.

34. Ankerberg and Weldon (1990), pp. 132, 226.

35. Jacques Ellul, *Propaganda: The Formation of Men's Attitudes* (N.Y.: Vintage Books, 1973), p. 49.

36. John Ankerberg and John Weldon, *Protestants and Catholics: Do They Now Agree?* (Chattanooga, Tenn.: ATRI, 1994); John Ankerberg and John Weldon, *Encyclopedia of Cults and New*

Religions: Jehovah's Witnesses, Mormonism, Mind Sciences, Baha'I, Zen, Unitarianism (Eugene, Oreg.: Harvest House Publishers, 1999).

37. Stephen Knight, *The Brotherhood: The Explosive Expose of the Secret World of the Freemasons* (London: Granada/Panther, 1983); published in the United States as *The Brotherhood: The Secret World of the Freemasons* (New York: Stein and Day, 1984).

38. Walton Hannah, *Darkness Visible* (London: Augustine Press, 1952), pp. 34–37.

39. Hubert S. Box, *The Nature of Freemasonry* (London: Augustine Press, 1952).

40. Elsewhere in their text, Ankerberg and Weldon use another form of the word, "Masonry leads men to worship a false god (G.A.O.T.U., Jah-Bul-On)." Ankerberg and Weldon, p. 176

41. Paul Naudon, *La Franc-Maçonnerie chretienne. La tradition operative. L'Arche Royale de Jerusalem. Le Rite Ecossais Rectifie* (Paris: Dervy, 1970); Paul Naudon, *Histoire, Rituels et Tuileur des Haut Grades Maçonniques* (Paris: Dervy, 1993), pp. 315–18.

42. The Hebrew word *giblim* (I Kings 5:18) is translated "stonesquarers" in the authorized version of the Bible but refers to the inhabitants of Gebal, a city in Phoenicia. They were expert craftsmen used in building Solomon's temple.

43. Arturo de Hoyos, "The Mystery of the Royal Arch Word," in *Heredom: The Transactions of the Scottish Rite Research Society*, vol. 2 (1993), pp. 7–34.

44. Albert G. Mackey, *An Encyclopedia of Freemasonry* (Philadelphia: Louis H. Everts, 1905), p. 112, s.v. "Bel."

45. Malcolm C. Duncan, *Duncan's Masonic Ritual and Monitor*, rev. ed. (New York: L. Fitzgerald, 1866), p. 249. It should be observed that Duncan's Ritual (as it is often called) did not represent a correct version of any Masonic ritual in use, but was rather the author's own conglomerated version.

46. David Bernard, *Light on Masonry*, 3d ed. (Utica, N.Y.: William Williams, 1829).

47. William L. Stone, *Letters on Masonry and Anti-Masonry Addressed to the Hon. John. Quincy Adams* (New York: O. Halsted, 1832), pp. 74–75. Additional examples of Bernard's unreliability are cited in *Heredom. The Transactions of the Scottish Rite Research Society*, vol. 4 (1995), p. 23.

48. William Gesenius, *A Hebrew and English Lexicon of the Old Testament* (Oxford University Press, no date), p. 127; Ernest Klein, *A Comprehensive Etymological Dictionary of the Hebrew Language for Readers of English* (New York: Macmillan, 1987), p. 79.

49. James Strong, writing in his *Concise Dictionary of the Words in the Hebrew Language*, says that *Bealiah* (word #1183) is composed of the Hebrew words *ba'al* (word #1167) and *yahh* (word #3050).

50. James Strong, *ibid.* (word #202).

51. Lancelot C. L. Brenton, *The Septuagint with Apocrypha: Greek and English* (reprint ed., Grand Rapids, Mich.: Zondervan, no date), p. 73. If the words are taken from context, it is more proper to refer to *ho On*, "the Being."

52. Jay P. Green, Sr., *The Interlinear Bible. Hebrew-Greek-English* (Peabody, Mass.: Hendrickson, 1976, 1986), p. 951.

53. Edmond Ronayne, *Chapter Masonry* (Chicago: Ezra A. Cook, 1901, 1976), p. 281.

Chapter 5

1. Most of the material on Pastor Carlson is quoted from Arturo de Hoyos, *The Cloud of Prejudice: A Study in Anti-Masonry* (Kila, Mont.: Kessinger Publishing Co., 1992), with the generous permission of the publisher, Bro. Roger Kessinger.

2. According to Dun & Bradstreet's 2001 report, *Christian Ministries International* is run from Pastor Carlson's home in Eden Prairie, Minnesota. It lists one employee and reports his sales volume as $32,000.

3. Ron Carlson, *Freemasonry and the Masonic Lodge*, preached by the author, audio cassette (Eden Prairie, Minn.: Christian Ministries International, no date), side 1, 4:21. The times listed are measured from the beginning of the audio and may vary slightly depending on the equipment used.

4. Ron Carlson, side 2, 17:00.

5. Madsen Pirie, *The Book of the Fallacy: A Training Manual for Intellectual Subversives* (Routledge and Kegan Paul, 1985), pp. 160–61.

6. Ron Carlson, side 1, 11:24.

7. Ron Carlson, side 1, 11:45.

8. Grand Lodge of Texas, *Monitor of the Lodge* (Waco, Tex.: Waco Printing Co., 1982), p. 36.

9. Ron Carlson, side 1, 7:00.

10. Ron Carlson, side 1, 8:03.

11. Albert Pike, *Morals and Dogma*, pp. 744–745. In this instance, Pike translated and extracted a passage from the writings of the French esotericist Eliphas Levi (Alphonse Louis Constant):

> The Bible, with all its allegories, gives to the religious knowledge of the Hebrews only an incomplete and veiled manner. The book which we have mentioned . . . existed certainly before Moses and the prophets, whose doctrine, fundamentally identical with the ancient Egyptians, had also its exotericism and its veils.
>
> The books were written only as memorials of tradition, and in symbols that were unintelligible to the profane. The Pentateuch and the poems of the prophets were, moreover, elementary works, alike in doctrine, ethics and liturgy; the true secret and traditional philosophy was not committed to writing until a later period and under veils even less transparent. Thus arose a second and unknown Bible, or rather one which was not comprehended by the Christians, a storehouse, so they say, of monstrous absurdities . . . but a monument, as we affirm, which comprises all that philosophical and religious genius has ever accomplished or imagined in the sublime order, a treasure encompassed by thorns, a diamond concealed in a rude and opaque stone: our reader will have guessed already that we refer to the Talmud. (Eliphas Levi, *Transcendental Magic* [London: Rider & Company, 1896], p. 18)

If Pastor Carlson is indeed an expert on the occult, why was he unfamiliar with Eliphas Levi as the source of Pike's quote?

12. Ron Carlson, side 2, 3:17.

13. Ron Carlson, side 2, 25:57.

14. Ron Carlson, side 2, 34:18.

15. Ray Baker Harris, *Bibliography of the Writings of Albert Pike* (Washington, D.C.: Supreme Council, 33°, 1957), pp. 89–90.

16. Here are just a few of the places where Pastor Carlson could have borrowed the book in September 1993, according to the Online Computer Library Catalog (OCLC): Auburn University at Montgomery, Alabama; University of Alabama; University of Arkansas; University of Arizona; University of Colorado at Denver; Grinnell College, Iowa; Northwestern College, Iowa; Murray State University, Kentucky; University of New Orleans; University of Minnesota, Duluth; Rust College, Mississippi; University of Nebraska, Kearney; University of Nebraska, Lincoln; Oral Roberts University; University of Central

Oklahoma; Geneva College, Pennsylvania; University of South Carolina; South Dakota School of Mines and Technology; University of the South, Tennessee; Southwestern Baptist Theological Seminary, Fort Worth, Texas; University of Texas at Austin; University of Texas at Permian Basin; University of Texas at El Paso; University of Utah; Liberty University, Lynchburg, Virginia; and West Virginia Wesleyan College.

Chapter 6

1. David S. Janssen, "A Sermon on The Rituals of Freemasonry," compilation of three sermons preached to the State College Christian and Missionary Alliance Church, State College, Pa., Sept. 28, 1997, 28-page typescript, Archives, Supreme Council, 33°, SJ, Washington, D.C.
2. Charles T. McClenachan, *The Book of the Ancient and Accepted Scottish Rite of Freemasonry* (New York: The Masonic Publishing & Manufacturing Co., 1867).
3. While Rev. Janssen found his copy of McClenachan in the Rare Books Room, Pattee Library, Pennsylvania State University (Janssen, p. 9), the book is common and easily available to interested readers. In April 1998, the Online Computer Library Catalog (OCLC) showed fourteen copies of various editions of McClenachan's book available for interlibrary loan: Brown University, Buffalo & Erie County Public Library, Carthage College, Cleveland Public Library, Indiana University, Kent State University, Minnesota Historical Society, New York Public Library, Toledo-Lucas County Public Library, University of Alabama, University of California, Berkeley, University of Delaware, University of South Florida, University of Utah. A search of the Internet (www.bibliofind.com and www.interloc.com) on April 8, 1998, found several copies of the book for sale: the 1914 edition from Book Quest, Centralia, Wash., for $65.50, the 1867 edition from Arney Spondler, Mechanicsburg, Pa., for $35.00, and the 1901 edition from Booklook, Warwick, N.Y., for $75.00.
4. http://www.ovrlnd.com/Masonry/freemasonry.html.
5. Janssen, p. 10.
6. For a detailed history of Scottish Rite monitors, see Arturo de Hoyos, *Scottish Rite Ritual Monitor and Guide* (Washington, D.C.: Supreme Council, 33°, 2007).
7. Alain Bernheim, "Questions About Albany," *Heredom*, vol. 4 (1995), pp. 139–187.
8. [Thomas Smith Webb], *The Freemason's Monitor, or Illustrations of Masonry: in Two Parts* (Albany, N.Y.: Spencer and Webb, 1797). A facsimile edition was published by the Masonic Book Club, Bloomington, Ill., in 1996.
9. Herbert T. Leyland, *Thomas Smith Webb: Freemason, Musician, Entrepreneur* (Dayton, Ohio: The Otterbein Press, 1965), pp. 429–451; Colin Dyer, *William Preston and His Work* (Shepperton, England: Lewis Masonic, 1987), pp. 126, 154.
10. Kent Walgren, "A Bibliography of Pre-1826 American Scottish Rite Imprints (non-Louisiana)," *Heredom*, vol. 3 (1994), pp. 63–93.
11. See Michael R. Poll, "The Question of Joseph Cerneau: A Brief Examination," *Heredom*, vol. 4 (1995), pp. 47–61, and Samuel H. Baynard, Jr., *History of the Supreme Council, 33°*, 2 vols. (Boston: Supreme Council, 33°, NMJ, 1938).
12. Arturo de Hoyos, "The Union of 1867," *Heredom*, vol. 4 (1995), pp. 7–45.
13. See, for example, William Preston Vaughn, *The Anti-Masonic Party in the United States 1826–1843* (Lexington, Ky.: University Press of Kentucky, 1983).
14. *Sublime Freemasonry*, 2 Parts, (Albany, N.Y.: L.G. Hoffman, ca. 1842); Walgren, p. 109.
15. Henry C. Atwood, *The Master Workman* (New York: Macoy, 1850).
16. Robert Macoy, *The True Masonic Guide* (New York: Clark, Austin & Co., 1852).

17. Jeremy L. Cross, *The Supplement to the Templar's Chart: Containing the Following Thirty Ineffable Degrees with Their Emblems and Illustrations* . . . (New York: 1852).

18. Enoch T. Carson, *Monitor of the Ancient and Accepted Rite* . . . (Cincinnati, Ohio: Applegate & Co., 1858).

19. Enoch T. Carson, *The Freemason's Monitor: by Thomas Smith Webb to Which is Added, A Monitor of the Ancient and Accepted Rite, Thirty-three Degrees, Including Those Generally Known as the Ineffable Degrees* (Cincinnati, Ohio: Applegate & Co., 1863).

20. Will C. Cunningham, *Manual of the Ancient and Accepted Scottish Rite, Arranged to Correspond with the Ritual of the Supreme Council of the 33rd Degree for the Northern Masonic Jurisdiction of the United States: Together with the Revised Constitutions of the Order* (Philadelphia: Moss & Co., 1864).

21. *Transactions of the Supreme Council (Mother Council of the World) of the 33° of the Southern Jurisdiction of the United States of America.* Sessions of 1952 and 1953 (Washington, D.C., 1953), p. 196.

22. Baynard, vol. I, pp. 343–344.

23. Irving E. Partridge, Jr., *The Rituals of the Supreme Council, 33°, for the Northern Masonic Jurisdiction U.S.A.* (1976), pp. 23, 58–60.

24. In 1857, Albert Pike completed his first revision of the rituals from the 4° to 32° and had one hundred copies printed. Albert Mackey described the untitled volume as Pike's "*Magnum Opus,*" and this name stuck. Despite the improvement over existing rituals, the Supreme Council did not adopt the revision. Large parts of the *Magnum Opus*, including entire degrees, have never been used.

25. Pike's first ritual to be officially adopted was *The Inner Sanctuary. Part First. The Book of the Lodge of Perfection* (Latomopolis [New York]: A.M. 5621 [1861]).

26. Godfrey Higgins, *Anacalypsis, an Attempt to Draw Aside the Veil of the Saitic Isis*, 2 vols. (London: Longman, Rees, Ormes, Brown, Green, and Longman, 1836).

27. *Transactions of the Supreme Council of the 33d Degree, for the Southern Jurisdiction of the United States. Orient of Washington, May 1876* (New York: J. J. Little & Co., Printers, 10 to 20 Astor Place, 1877), p. 39.

28. Albert Pike, *Liturgy of the Ancient and Accepted Scottish Rite of Freemasonry for the Southern Jurisdiction of the United States, Part III* (New York: Robert Macoy, 1878), p. 167.

29. *Reprint of the Proceedings of the Supreme Council, 338, A∴ and A∴ Scottish Rite, N.M.J. Volume II, Part I. 1860 to 1866* (Portland, [Maine], Stephen Berry, printer, 1881), pp. 187–188.

30. The 1941 report of the Supreme Council's Committee on Rituals and Ritualistic Matter provided a brief chronology of the ritual revisions from 1867 onward. See *1941 Abstract of Proceedings of the Supreme Council, 33°, AASR, NMJ, USA* (Boston, Mass.: Supreme Council, 33°, NMJ, 1941), pp. 111–113. See also "Chronological Development of the Rituals of the Northern Masonic Jurisdiction since the Union of 1867" in Partridge, p. 38.

31. For example, the 1997 Report of the Committee on Rituals and Ritualistic Matter of the Northern Masonic Jurisdiction showed a willingness of the Supreme Council to consider degree settings from the Biblical past to the immediate present:

> Your committee is now directing its major emphasis toward a goal of ensuring that our degrees continue to present lessons which address the relevant issues in our rapidly changing times and society. As the initial step toward that end, we are evaluating the lessons of the existing 29 degrees. We have postponed action on the two potential degree themes (i.e. "David and Goliath" and "The Third Bomb"), which were authorized by the 1997 Supreme Council, until we can evaluate where and how they

might best fit into the future degree theme/lesson structure. (*1997 Abstract of Proceedings of the Supreme Council, 33°, AASR, NMJ, USA* [Lexington, Mass.: Supreme Council, 33°, NMJ, 1997], p. 261)

32. The 1986 Report of the Committee on Rituals and Ritualistic Matter recommended "That the Supreme Council adopt the new proposed 24° (American Indian) as the Tentative 24° Ritual of 1986." *1986 Abstract of Proceedings of the Supreme Council* ([Lexington, Massachusetts: Supreme Council, 33°, 1986), p. 23. The ritual was then printed and distributed as Twenty-fourth Degree, Prince of the Tabernacle (Lexington, Mass.: Supreme Council, 33°, 1986) [Tentative Ritual].

33. *Twentieth Degree. Master Ad Vitam* (Boston, Mass.: Supreme Council, 33°, 1951).

34. The 1988 Report of the Committee on Rituals and Ritualistic Matter recommended "That the proposed 23°, Chief of the Tabernacle, telling the story of The Four Chaplains, be adopted as the Tentative 23° Ritual, 1988." *1988 Abstract of Proceedings of the Supreme Council* ([Lexington, Mass.: Supreme Council, 33°, 1988), p. 251. The ritual was then printed and distributed as Twenty-third Degree, Chief of the Tabernacle (Lexington, Mass.: Supreme Council, 33°, 1988) [Tentative Ritual].

35. Montague Summers, trans., Heinrich Kramer and James Sprenger, *The Malleus Maleficarum* (Escondido, Calif.: The Book Tree, 2000).

36. As part of a study on documenting the American South, the University of North Carolina at Chapel Hill Libraries has a Web page on "The Church in the Southern Black Community" (http://docsouth.unc.edu/church/). In June 2003, the site included online editions of two of Pastor Stringfellow's pro-slavery works: *A Brief Examination of Scripture Testimony on the Institution of Slavery, in an Essay, First Published in the Religious Herald, and Republished by Request: With Remarks on a Letter of Elder Galusha, of New York, to Dr. R. Fuller, of South Carolina* (Washington, D.C.: Printed at the Congressional Globe Office, 1850) and *Scriptural and Statistical Views in Favor of Slavery* (Richmond, Va.: J. W. Randolph, 1856).

37. "Thus saith the LORD, Learn not the way of the heathen, and be not dismayed at the signs of heaven; for the heathen are dismayed at them. For the customs of the people are vain: for one cutteth a tree out of the forest, the work of the hands of the workman, with the ax. They deck it with silver and with gold; they fasten it with nails and with hammers, that it move not." (Jeremiah 10:2–4)

38. See Clement A. Miles, *Christmas in Ritual and Tradition, Christian and Pagan* (T. Fisher Unwin, 1912).

39. Jack Finegan, *Myth & Mystery: An Introduction to the Pagan Religions of the Biblical World* (Grand Rapids, Mich.: Baker Book House, 1989), pp. 209–212.

40. Arturo de Hoyos, *Scottish Rite Ritual Monitor and Guide* (Washington, D.C.: Supreme Council, 33°) (2007 ed.), pp. 105–06.

41. McClenachan, pp. 432–433.

42. Partridge, p. 38.

43. McClenachan, p. 365.

44. McClenachan, p. 358.

45. McClenachan, p. 358.

46. Partridge, p. 38.

47. McClenachan, p. 413.

48. McClenachan, p. 346.

49. The passage appeared in the first official ritual of the Supreme Council, 33°, S.J., *The Inner Sanctuary* ([*Heredom*]: A∴M∴ 5627 [1867]), part iv, p. 115, and was imported by the Northern Masonic Jurisdiction into *The Secret Directory*, book 4, p. 125.

50. Albert Pike to Brenton D. Babcock, Jan. 25, 1887, in Albert G. Mackey, *An Encyclopedia of Freemasonry*, ed. rev. and enl. by Robert I. Clegg with suppl. vol. by H. L. Haywood, 3 vols. (Chicago: Masonic History Co., 1946), vol. 2, pp. 775–776.

51. Albert G. Mackey, *A Manual of the Lodge* (New York: Clark & Maynard, Publishers, No. 5 Barclay Street, 1866), p. 30.

52. Partridge, p. 38.

53. Bruce M. Metzger and Michael D. Coogan, eds., *The Oxford Companion to the Bible* (Oxford: Oxford University Press, 1993), pp. 268–269.

54. Alexander Heidel, *The Gilgamesh Epic and Old Testament Parallels*, 2d ed. (Chicago: University of Chicago Press, 1949).

55. Jeremy L. Cross, *The True Masonic Chart or Hieroglyphic Monitor*, 3rd ed. (New Haven, Conn: The Author, 1824), p. 16.

56. McClenachan, p. 43.

57. Gershom Scholem, *Kabbalah* (Keter Publishing House Jerusalem Ltd., 1974; reprint, New York: Dorset Press, 1987), pp. 196–201.

58. Partridge, p. 38.

59. McClenachan, p. 93.

60. William L. Fox, *Lodge of the Double-Headed Eagle* (Fayetteville, Ark.: The University of Arkansas Press, 1997), p. 492.

61. W. J. Chetwode Crawley, "Two Corner Stones Laid in the Olden Time," *Ars Quatuor Coronatorum*, vol. 24 (1911), pp. 21–26.

62. S. Brent Morris, *Masonic Philanthropies*, 2nd ed. (Washington, D.C., and Lexington, Mass.: The Supreme Councils, 33°, SJ & NMJ, 1997), p. 18.

Chapter 7

1. This is similar to the tactic used by Mr. Tom McKenney in defending the charge that there are no records that Rev. James D. Shaw received the 33rd Degree: "What reason have we to believe that a system based on lies and deception, with that much time, hasn't 'lost' or altered the records? . . ." Tom McKenney, 22 Feb. 1995, "Position Paper: James D. Shaw and the 33rd Degree." See chapter 9, "T. N. Sampson: Defending the Deception."

2. Jack Finegan, *Myth & Mystery: An Introduction to the Pagan Religions of the Biblical World* (Grand Rapids, Mich.: Baker Book House, 1989), pp. 233–35.

Chapter 8

1. S. Brent Morris, Washington, D.C., letter to *Charisma & Christian Life*, Lake Mary, Fla., Jan. 14, 1998, typescript in the possession of the author.

2. Albert Pike, *Morals and Dogma of the Ancient and Accepted Scottish Rite of Freemasonry*, rev. ed. (Washington, D.C.: Supreme Council 33°, SJ, 1950), p. iv.

3. Phillip R. Johnson, *A Wolf in Sheep's Clothing: How Charles Finney's Theology Ravaged the Evangelical Movement*, http://www.gty.org/~phil/articles/finney.htm.

4. Charles E. Hambrick-Stowe, *Charles G. Finney and the Spirit of American Evangelicalism* (Grand Rapids, Mich.: William B. Eerdmans Publishing Co., 1996).

5. "Statement on Freemasonry and Religion" (Silver Spring, Md.: Masonic Information Center, 1993).

6. S. Brent Morris, *Masonic Philanthropies: A Tradition of Caring* (Washington, D.C.: Supreme Council, 33°, 1997).

7. Thomas Paine, *An Essay on the Origin of Free Masonry* (London: R. Carlisle, 1826).

8. Steven Bullock, *Revolutionary Brotherhood* (Chapel Hill, N.C.: University of North Carolina Press, 1996); David Stevenson, *The Origins of Freemasonry: Scotland's Century, 1590–1710* (Cambridge: Cambridge Univ. Press, 1988); John Hamill, *The History of English Freemasonry* (Addlestone, Surrey: Lewis Masonic, 1994).

9. Henry W. Coil et al., *Coil's Masonic Encyclopedia*, rev. ed. (Richmond, Va.: Macoy Publishing and Masonic Supply Co., 1997), p. 219.

10. Harry Carr, "The Transition from Operative to Speculative Masonry" (1957 Prestonian Lecture), *The Collected Prestonian Lectures, 1925–1960*, ed. Harry Carr (London: Quatuor Coronati Lodge, 1967).

11. S. Brent Morris, "The Eye in the Pyramid," *Short Talk Bulletin*, vol. 73, no. 9, Sept. 1995.

12. William R. Denslow, *10,000 Famous Freemasons*, 4 vols. (Missouri: Missouri Lodge of Research, 1957, 1958, 1959, 1960).

13. S. Brent Morris, *Cornerstones of Freedom* (Washington, D.C.: Supreme Council, 33°, SJ, 1993), pp. 44–45.

14. Arturo de Hoyos and S. Brent Morris, *Is It True What They Say About Freemasonry?* 2nd ed. (Silver Spring, Md.: Masonic Information Center, 1997), pp. 80–82.

15. Jewel P. Lightfoot, *Lightfoot's Manual of the Lodge* (Ft. Worth, Tex.: Grand Lodge of Texas, 1934), pp. 45, 26.

16. Wallace McLeod, "The Great Architect of the Universe," *The Grand Design* (Highland Springs, Va.: Anchor Communications, 1991), p. 108.

Chapter 9

1. Tom C. McKenney, "Position Paper: James D. Shaw and the 33rd Degree" (Marion, Ky.: Tom C. McKenney, Feb. 22, 1995). The full Position Paper is reproduced in chapter 9 of this book, "T. N. Sampson: Defending the Deception."

2. Tom C. McKenney, Ocean Springs, Miss., 31 Oct. 1996, letter to S. Brent Morris, Columbia, Md.

3. Rollin O. Simpson, Grand Secretary, F.&A.M., Indianapolis, Ind., letter to S. Brent Morris, Columbia, Md., June 10, 1993. Typescript in the possession of the author.

4. Irwin Kirby, Scottish Rite General Secretary, Miami, Florida, letter to John W. Boettjer, Editor, *Scottish Rite Journal*, Washington, D.C., Oct. 8, 1992, Archives, Supreme Council, 33°, SJ, Washington.

5. Jim Shaw and Tom McKenney, *The Deadly Deception* (Layfayette, La.: Huntington House, 1988), p. 90.

6. Tom C. McKenney, "Position Paper: James D. Shaw and the 33rd Degree."

7. James D. Shaw, introduction to *The Masonic Report* by C. F. McQuaig (Norcross, Ga.: Answer Books and Tapes, 1976).

8. Henry W. Coil et al., *Coil's Masonic Encyclopedia* (New York: Macoy Masonic Publishing and Masonic Supply Co., Inc., 1961, 1996), s.v. "Penalties, Masonic." *Coil's Masonic Encyclopedia* is an excellent general references on Freemasonry. It is not official in any way, but it does provide a good overview of most Masonic topics. It occasionally interjects opinion and commentary, but on the whole is a good source of conservative, factual history.

9. Jim Shaw and Tom McKenney, *The Deadly Deception* (Lafayette, La.: Huntington House, 1988), p. 83.

10. Grand Lodge of Florida, F.&A.M., *Digest of the Masonic Law of Florida* F&AM (Tallahassee, Fla.: Rose Printing Co., 1954), p. 157.

11. Grand Lodge of Florida, F.&A.M., *Digest of the Masonic Law of Florida* F&AM (Jacksonville, Fla.: Grand Lodge F.&A.M., 1976), p. 245.

12. William G. Wolf, Gr. Secretary, Jacksonville, Fla., letter to S. Brent Morris, Columbia, Md., Nov. 18, 1992, in the possession of the author.
13. *Statutes of the Supreme Council* ([Washington]: [Supreme Council, SJ], October 1953), p. 60. The prohibition remains in the 2001 *Statutes*, renumbered as Art. XV, §25, though the Supreme Council now allows variances on a case-by-case basis.
14. Shaw and McKenney, cover.
15. Shaw and McKenney, p. 151
16. Shaw and McKenney, pp. 84–85.
17. Shaw and McKenney, p. 85.

Chapter 10

1. The addendum to this book, "Please Look a Little Closer," addresses some of the misunderstandings and misrepresentations of *A Bridge to Light*.
2. The article by Norman Williams Crabbe actually appeared in the summer 1993 *Royal Arch Mason Magazine*. See [Letter 6].
3. "Dear Dr. Morris: Your charge that the cover of *The Deadly Deception* evinces four 'deliberate' and 'verifiable lies' is very serious. You asked in your letter whether we have evidence to refute your case against Reverend Shaw. The answer is yes. You paint a very injurious picture of both Tom McKenney and Jim Shaw. And, we are consulting with everyone concerned to determine our best course of action." Mark Anthony, Editor-in-Chief, Huntington House Publishers, Lafayette, La., letter to S. Brent Morris, Washington, D.C., May 31, 1994. Typescript in the possession of the author.
    This is the last communication from Huntington House Publishers. Dr. Morris wrote to them again on June 11, 1994, July 29, 1994, and April 18, 1995, the latter by certified mail, signed return receipt received. Each time he offered to correct any error of fact and asked if they could provide the following information:

    • What year and in what lodge did Reverend Shaw serve as Master?
    • What years and where did he serve as Master of all Scottish Rite bodies?
    • What year did Reverend Shaw receive the Thirty-third Degree?

    Huntington House Publishers never answered Dr. Morris after May 31, 1994.
4. Cowan: One who works as a mason without having served a regular apprenticeship. [Scot.] Note: Among Freemasons, it is a cant term for pretender, interloper. *Webster's Revised Unabridged Dictionary* © 1996, 1998 MICRA, Inc.
5. See [Letter 12] for Mr. Kleinknecht's response to Mr. Sampson.
6. Since this correspondence, the Supreme Council, 33°, S.J. has allowed variances from its alcohol policy on a case-by-case basis. The Grand Lodge of Florida has not changed its regulations.
7. This article has been correctly typeset and appears as chapter 2 of this book, "Enchanter!: A Virtual Anti-Mason."
8. The correct title of the article is "The Dawning [not Damning!] of Spiritual Masonry" from *The Philalethes*, April 1994. It is preceded by this editor's note, "In the interest of presenting various viewpoints, we present Brother Crabbe's thoughts on 'Spiritual' Masonry."
9. Chapter 6 of this book, "Rev. James Dayton Shaw: *The Deadly Deception*," lists every elected officer of Allapattah Lodge (1°–3°) from 1952 to 1967, the years of Rev. Shaw's membership, and every Venerable Master of Miami Lodge of Perfection (4°–14°) from 1917 to 1967.

10. Mr. McKenney described Rev. Shaw's 33rd Degree "medal" as having a "purple ribbon." The Statutes of the Supreme Council (1969), Art. XIII, Sec. 5, specify that the authentic Southern Jurisdiction 33rd Degree jewel is "suspended by a white ribbon." Wherever he obtained it, Rev. Shaw's jewel was not issued by the Supreme Council for the Southern Jurisdiction.

Chapter 11

1. S. Brent Morris, *Masonic Philanthropies: A Tradition of Caring*, 2d ed. (Lexington, Mass. & Washington, D.C.: The Supreme Councils 33°, 1997), p. 18.

Appendix 1

1. In French: *arrières-loges*, literally back-lodges, in the sense they are in the back, behind the scenes, but secretly running everything.
2. The French stereotype those born in Marseilles as makers of pranks.
3. Literally, *The Hobby-Horse, Journal for Fools*.
4. *La Fronde* was a seditious party during the minority of Louis XIV. It gave birth to the word *Frondeur*, designating generally speaking all those who criticize the authorities and the government without restraint or deference.
5. In French: *Conseiller prudhommal.*
6. This alludes to one of the *Fables de La Fontaine*, well known to French children, about a cat who covered himself with flour in hopes that mice would be fooled and come close enough to be caught.
7. Two murderers whose exactions and execution at the guillotine were famous in the time of Taxil.
8. Pope Léo XIII.
9. A famous French politician.
10. One of the strongholds of Catholicism in Switzerland.
11. *Actor* rather than author is probably meant here.
12. Jean Eugene Robert-Houdin, a famous French magician. The Hungarian emigrant Erich Weiss named himself Houdini in homage to Robert-Houdin.
13. Residence of the president of the French Republic.
14. Dr. Battle.
15. Part of Paris where many students live.
16. A Parisian daily newspaper.
17. Both sentences are based on a joke almost impossible to render in English. "Monter un bateau" is the French equivalent of "to pull one's leg." Taxil combines it with the tugboat of his youth, which grows into a squadron, and then a whole navy. Meaning that the prank becomes more and more enormous.
18. A religious ceremony which lasts three days.
19. This is an allusion to a legend from the fifteenth century that the birth house of the Virgin Mary in Nazareth was brought to Ancona in Italy by angels.
20. J. G. Findel, author of *History of Freemasonry*, 1861.
21. In addition to the obvious imagery of a stone disturbing frogs, French priests are sometimes called "frogs of the holy water basin."
22. An *oubliette* is a secret dungeon where people were thrown, forgotten, and died. Taxil plays on the double meaning of *oublier*, to forget, and *oubliette*, a secret dungeon.

Appendix 2

1. "Garden of Evil?" and "Stones of Evil" were originally published in *The Scottish Rite Journal* (Oct. and Dec. 1996, respectively) and are reproduced with the permission of their author, Dr. John W. Boettjer, Managing Editor, *The Scottish Rite Journal*.
2. *Virginia-Pilot*, June 16, 1996, p. A10.
3. *Virginia-Pilot*.
4. *Virginia-Pilot*.
5. Rex Hutchens, *A Glossary to "Morals and Dogma"* (Washington, D.C.: Supreme Council 33°, 1993), p. 385.
6. *Coil's Masonic Encyclopedia* (1961 ed.) p. 187; (1996 ed.), p. 192.
7. Rex Hutchens, *A Bridge to Light* (Washington, D.C.: Supreme Council 33°, 1988), p. 149.
8. Hutchens, *A Bridge to Light*, p. 148.
9. Hutchens, *A Bridge to Light*, pp. 148–149. CIS [Center for Interfaith Studies] *Masonic Report*, vol. 2, no. 3 (July 1996), p. 2.
10. *CIS Masonic Report*, p. 137.

Appendix 3

1. "Please Look a Little Closer" was published in *The Scottish Rite Journal* (Nov. 1996) and is reproduced here with the permission of the author, Dr. James T. Tresner II, Director Masonic Leadership Institute.
2. Walter Rauschenbush, "The Social Principles of Jesus" in *The World Treasury of Modern Religious Thought* (New York: Little, Brown & Co., 1990), pp. 588–589.
3. Albert Pike, *Morals and Dogma*, p. 463.
4. Albert Pike, *Morals and Dogma*, pp. 444–463, passim.

Works Cited

Allgemeines Handbuch der Freimaurerei. 3d ed. 2 vols. Leipzig: Max Hesse's Verlag, 1901, s.v. "Taxil, Leo."

Amini, Muhammad Safwat al-Saqqa and Sa'di Abu Habib. *Freemasonry.* New York: Muslim World League, 1982.

Ankerberg, John and John Weldon. *The Secret Teachings of the Masonic Lodge: A Christian Perspective.* Chicago: Moody Press, 1989, 1990, [1993].

Anonymous. *Freemasonry Antichrist Upon Us.* 3rd ed. Boring, Oreg.: CPA Books, n.d.

Bernard, David. *Light on Masonry.* Utica, N. Y.: William Williams, 1829.

Blanchard, Jonathan, ed. *Scotch Rite Masonry Illustrated.* 2 vols. Chicago: Ezra A. Cook, 1887–88; reprint 1979.

Box, Hubert S. *The Nature of Freemasonry.* London: Augustine Press, 1952.

Brenton, Lancelot C. L. *The Septuagint with Apocrypha: Greek and English.* Grand Rapids, Mich.: Zondervan, reprint, no date.

Burns, Cathy. *Hidden Secrets of Masonry.* Mt. Carmel, Penn.: Sharing, 1990.

Carlson, Ron. *Freemasonry and the Masonic Lodge.* Audio cassette. Eden Prairie, Minn.: Christian Ministries International, no date.

Ceremonies of Installation and Dedication. rev. ed. Washington, D.C.: Supreme Council, 33°, SJ, 1954.

Chick, Jack T. *The Curse of Baphomet.* Chino, Calif.: Chick Publications, 1991, 1993.

Coil, Henry W., et al. *Coil's Masonic Encyclopedia.* New York: Macoy Publishing & Masonic Supply Co., 1961. S.v. "Pike, Albert," "Penalties, Masonic," and "Taxil, Leo."

Decker, J. Edward, Jr., and Dave Hunt. *The God Makers.* Eugene, Oreg.: Harvest House, 1984.

Decker, J. Edward, Jr. *The Question of Freemasonry.* Issaquah, Wash.: Free the Masons Ministries, no date.

de Hoyos, Art. *The Cloud of Prejudice: A Study in Anti-Masonry.* Kila, Mont.: Kessinger Publishing Co., 1993.

—————. "The Mystery of the Royal Arch Word," *Heredom, Transactions of the Scottish Rite Research Society,* vol. 2 (1993), pp. 7–34.

—————, trans. *The Reception of an Apprentice Freemason According to the Swedish Rite Ritual of the Grand National Lodge of Freemasons of Germany.* McAllen, Tex.: 1995. Note: this is a translation of Die Aufnahme eines Freimaurer-Lehrling. Berlin: Grosse Landesloge der Freimaurer von Deutschland, 1969.

—————. "The Union of 1867," *Heredom, Transactions of the Scottish Rite Research Society,* vol. 4 (1995), pp. 7–45.

[de la Rive, Abel Clarin.] *La Femme at L'Enfant dans la Franc-Maçonnerie Universelle.* Paris and Lyons: Dalhomme and Briguet, 1894.

[Delaunay, François H. Stanislaus.] *Thuileur des Trente-trois Degres de L'Ecossisme dit Rit Ancien, dit Accepté.* Paris: Delaunay, Libraire, Palais-Royal, 1813, 1821.

Diestel, Ernst. "La Diablerie de Leo Taxil." *Le Symbolisme,* nos. 77 & 78, Sept. & Oct. 1924, pp. 212–223, 245–249.

Duncan, Malcolm C. *Duncan's Masonic Ritual and Monitor,* rev. ed. New York: L. Fitzgerald, 1866.

Ellul, Jacques. *Propaganda: The Formation of Men's Attitudes.* New York: Vintage Books, 1973.

Farina, S. *Il Libro Completo dei Rituali Massonici Rito Scozzese Antico ed Accettato.* Rome: 1946.

"Freemasonry on Its Own Terms." *The John Ankerberg Show.* Episode DM-170. Chattanooga, Tenn.: John Ankerberg Evangelistic Association, 1986.

Gaudart de Soulages, Michel, and Hubert Lamant. *Dictionnaire des Francs Maçons Français.* Paris: Editions Albatros, 1980. S.v. "Taxil."

Gerber, Hildebrand. [H. Gruber, S.J.]. *Leo Taxil's Palladismus-Roman.* 3 vols. Berlin: Verlag der Germania, 1897.

Gesenius, William. *A Hebrew and English Lexicon of the Old Testament.* Oxford: Oxford University Press.

Gilbert, Robert A. *The Golden Dawn: Twilight of the Magicians.* Wellingborough, UK: Aquarian Press, 1983.

Grand Lodge of Florida, F&AM. *Digest of the Masonic Law of Florida F&AM.* Tallahassee, Fla.: Rose Printing Co., 1954.

———. *Digest of the Masonic Law of Florida F.&A.M.* Jacksonville, Fla.: Grand Lodge F.&A.M., 1976.

Grand Lodge of Texas. *Monitor of the Lodge.* Waco, Tex.: Waco Printing Co., 1982.

Great Soviet Encyclopedia, 3rd ed. S.v. "Taxil, Leo."

Green, Jay P., Sr., *The Interlinear Bible: Hebrew-Greek-English.* Peabody, Mass.: Hendrickson, 1976, 1986.

Griffin, Des. *Fourth Reich of the Rich.* Clackamas, Oreg.: Emissary Pub., 1976.

Haffner, Christopher. *Workman Unashamed.* Shepperton, England: Lewis Masonic, 1989.

Hamill, John. "The Sins of Our Masonic Fathers . . . ," *Ars Quatuor Coronatorum*, vol. 101 (1988), pp. 133–159.

Hanegraaff, Hendrik H. "Chick Publications and Roman Catholicism," *CRI Perspective*, CP-0809. San Juan Capistrano, Calif.: Christian Research Institute, no date.

Harris, Jack. *Freemasonry: The Invisible Cult in Our Midst.* Towson, Md.: Jack Harris, 1983.

Harris, Ray Baker. *Bibliography of the Writings of Albert Pike.* Washington, D.C.: Supreme Council, 33°, SJ, 1957.

Hastings, James, ed. *Encyclopedia of Religion and Ethics.* S.v. "Satanism," by E. Sidney Hartland.

Holly, James L. *The Southern Baptist Convention and Freemasonry.* Vol. II. Beaumont, Tex.: Mission and Ministry to Men, 1992.

Howe, Ellic. *The Magicians of the Golden Dawn.* London: Routledge and Kegan Paul, 1972.

———. "Rosicrucians" in *Man, Myth, & Magic. An Illustrated Encyclopedia of the Supernatural.* 24 vols. New York: Marshall Cavendish, 1970. vol. 18, pp. 2,426–2,433.

Hutchens, Rex R. *A Bridge to Light.* Washington, D.C.: Supreme Council 33°, 1988.

———. *A Glossary to "Morals and Dogma."* Washington, D.C.: Supreme Council 33°, 1993.

Jachin and Boaz. London: 1762; reprint, Bloomington, Ill.: The Masonic Book Club, 1981.

Jarrige, Michel. "La Franc-Maçonnerie Demasquée: D'Apres un fonds inedit de la Bibliotheque National." *Politica Hermetica,* no. 4, 1990, pp. 38–53.

Kah, Gary H. *En Route to Global Occupation.* Lafayette, La.: Huntington House Publishers, 1992.

Kilby, Clyde S. *A Minority of One.* Grand Rapids, Mich.: William B. Eerdmans Publishing Co., 1959.

Kirban, Salem. *Satan's Angels Exposed.* Huntingdon Valley, Penn.: Salem Kirban, 1980.

Works Cited

Klein, Ernest. *A Comprehensive Etymological Dictionary of the Hebrew Language for Readers of English*. New York: Macmillan, 1987.

Laurant, Jean-Pierre. "Le Dossier Leo Taxil du fonds Jean Baylot de la Bibliotheque National." *Politica Hermetica*, no. 4, 1990, pp. 55–67.

Lennhoff, Eugen and Oskar Posner. *Internationales Freimauerlexikon*. Munich: Amalthea Verlag, 1932 ed. S.v. "Taxil, Leo."

MacDougall, Curtis D. *Hoaxes*. New York: MacMillan Co., 1949; reprint New York: Dover Publications, Inc., 1958.

MacKenzie, Norman. *Secret Societies*. London: George Redway, 1897.

Mackey, Albert G. *An Encyclopedia of Freemasonry*. Philadelphia: Louis H. Everts, 1905.

———. *A Manual of the Lodge*. New York: Clark & Maynard, 1870.

Marrs, Texe. *Dark Secrets of the New Age*. Westchester, Ill.: Crossway Books, 1987.

McIntosh, Christopher. *Eliphas Levi and the French Occult Revival*. New York: Samuel Weiser, Inc., 1974.

———. *The Rosicrucians*. Wellingborough, UK: Crucible, 1980, 1987.

Mellor, Alec. *Dictionnaire de la Franc-Maçonnerie et des Franc-Maçons*. Paris: Editions Pierre Belfond, 1975. S.v. "Taxil Gabriel-Antoine (Jogand-Pagès dit Léo)," "Anti-Maçonnerie: Le XIXe siecle."

———. *Our Separated Brethren, the Freemasons*. Translated by B. R. Feinson. London: G. G. Harrap & Co., 1961.

———. *Strange Masonic Stories*. Richmond, Va.: Macoy Publishing & Masonic Supply Co., Inc., 1982.

Miller, Edith Starr, Lady Queensborough. *Occult Theocrasy*. Hawthorne, Calif.: The Christian Book Blub of America, 1980.

Monitor of the Lodge. Waco, Tex.: Grand Lodge of Texas, 1982.

Morey, Robert A. *The Truth About Masons*. Eugene, Oreg.: Harvest House Publishers,1993.

Morgan, William. *Illustrations of Masonry by One of the Fraternity*. Batavia, N.Y.: Printed for the author, 1826.

Morris, S. Brent. "Albert Pike and Lucifer: The Lie That Will Not Die." *The Short Talk Bulletin*, vol. 71, no. 6, Jun. 1993.

————. *Masonic Philanthropies: A Tradition of Caring*. Lexington, Mass. & Washington, D.C.: The Supreme Councils, 33°, 1991.

Mullins, Eustace. *The Curse of Canaan*. Staunton, Va.: Revelation Books, 1986.

Naudon, Paul. *Histoire, Rituels et Tuileur des Haut Grades Maçonniques*. Paris: Dervy, 1993.

————. *La Franc-Maçonnerie chretienne. La tradition operative. L'Arche Royale de Jerusalem. Le Rite Ecossais Rectifié*. Paris: Dervy, 1970.

New Catholic Encyclopedia. S.v. "Taxil, Leo," by R. Limouzin-Lamothe.

Pike, Albert. *Liturgy of the Ancient and Accepted Scottish Rite of Freemasonry, for the Southern Jurisdiction of the United States*. Part IV. Charleston, S.C.: 1878; reprinted, n.p. 1944.

————. *Morals and Dogma of the Ancient and Accepted Scottish Rite of Freemasonry*, rev. ed. Washington, D.C.: Supreme Council 33°, SJ, 1950.

Prichard, Samuel. *Masonry Dissected*. London: 1730; reprint, Bloomington, Ill.: The Masonic Book Club, 1977.

Rachold, Jan. *Die Illuminaten. Quellen und Texte zur Auflärungsideologie des Illuminatenordens (1776–1785)*. Berlin: Akademie Verlag, 1984.

Robertson, Pat. *The New World Order*. Waco, Tex.: Word Publishing, 1991.

Ronayne, Edmond. *Chapter Masonry*. Chicago: Ezra A. Cook, 1901, 1976.

Rudwin, Maximilian. *The Devil in Legend and Literature*. Chicago: Open Court Publishing Co., 1931.

Works Cited

Schnoebelen, William. *Masonry: Beyond the Light*. Chino, Calif.: Chick Publications, 1991.

Shaw, James D. Introduction to *The Masonic Report* by C. F. McQuaig. Norcross, Ga.: Answer Books and Tapes, 1976.

———— and Tom McKenney. *The Deadly Deception*. Lafayette, La.: Huntington House, 1988.

Short, Martin. *Inside the Brotherhood*. New York: Dorset Press, 1990.

Steiner, Rudolf. *The Temple Legend*. Trans. John M. Wood. London: Rudolf Steiner Press, 1985.

Stone, William L. *Letters on Masonry and Anti-Masonry Addressed to the Hon. John Quincy Adams*. New York: O. Halsted, 1832.

Strong, James. "Concise Dictionary of the Words in the Hebrew Language" in Spiros Zodhiates, ed., *The Hebrew/Greek Key Study Bible, King James Version*. Rev. ed. AMG Publishers, 1991.

Supreme Council, 33°, SJ. *Statutes of the Supreme Council (Mother Council of the World) of the Thirty-Third Degree, Ancient & Accepted Scottish Rite of Freemasonry, Southern Jurisdiction, United States of America*. [Washington, D.C.]: [Supreme Council, SJ], Oct. 1953.

Tanner, Jerald and Sandra. *The Lucifer-God Doctrine*. Salt Lake City, Ut.: Utah Lighthouse Ministry, 1988.

Taylor, Harmon R. "Mixing Oil with Water," *The Evangelist*. Jun. 1986, pp. 47–49.

"Taxil-Schwindel, Der." *Freimaurer: Solange die Welt besteht*. Catalog of a special exhibition of the History Museum of Vienna, Sept. 18, 1992–Jan. 10, 1993, pp. 268–370.

Three Distinct Knocks. London: 1760; reprint, Bloomington, Ill.: The Masonic Book Club, 1981.

Twenty-fourth Degree. Prince of the Tabernacle. Tentative edition. Lexington, Mass.: Supreme Council, 33°, NMJ, 1986.

Voorhis, Harold Van Buren. *A History of Organized Masonic Rosicrucianism.* Privately printed: Societas Rosicruciana in Civitibus Foederatis, 1983.

Vuillaume, Manuel. *Maçonnique ou Tuileur des Divers Rites de Trente-trois Degres de L'Ecossisme di Rit Ancien, Maçonnerie Practiqués en France.* 1830. Paris: Dervy-Livres, 1975, reprint.

Waite, Arthur E. *Brotherhood of the Rosy Cross.* London: Will. Rider & Son, Ltd., 1924.

———. *Devil Worship in France or the Question of Lucifer.* London: George Redway, 1896.

———. *A New Encyclopedia of Freemasonry.* New & rev. ed. New York: Weathervane Books, 1970.

Waiters, Wesley P. "A Curious Case of Fraud," *The Quarterly Journal,* vol. 9, no. 4 (Oct.-Dec. 1989), pp. 4, 7.

Weber, Eugen. *Satan Franc-Maçon: La mystification de Léo Taxil.* Mesnilsur-l'Estrée, France: Collection Archives Julliard, 1964.

Wright, Gordon. *Notable or Notorious?* Cambridge, Mass.: Harvard University Press, 1991.

About the Authors

Authors Arturo de Hoyos and S. Brent Morris are considered America's foremost Masonic scholars, and have collaborated on a number of projects, including *Freemasonry in Context* (Lexington Books, 2008) and *Committed to the Flames: The History and Rituals of a Secret Masonic Rite* (London: Lewis Masonic, 2008).

Arturo de Hoyos, 33°, is the Grand Archivist and Grand Historian for the Supreme Council, 33°, Southern Jurisdiction, USA. He is America's leading authority on the Scottish Rite's early history and rituals, and most other Masonic organizations. He is the author, coauthor, translator, and editor of over twenty-five books and many articles on Freemasonry and is a board member of the Scottish Rite Research Society.

S. Brent Morris, 33°, is Managing Editor of *The Scottish Rite Journal* of the Supreme Council, 33°, Southern Jurisdiction, USA, and is the only U.S. Past Master of Quatuor Coronati Lodge No. 2076 of London, the premier organization of Masonic research. He is author and editor of over twenty-five volumes on Freemasonry and one book on mathematics. He is a board member of the Scottish Rite Research Society and is the founding editor of *Heredom*, its transactions. In addition to writing, Brent has taught at Duke, Johns Hopkins, and George Washington universities. He is retired after twenty-five years as a mathematician with the federal government.